Velázquez
Spanish and English
Glossary
for the
Social Studies
Classroom

Spanish – English/English – Spanish

Velázquez
Spanish and English
Glossary
for the
Social Studies
Classroom

Spanish - English/English – Spanish

Velázquez Press: 9682 Telstar Ave. Ste 110
El Monte, CA 91731 USA

Visit www.VelazquezPress.com or www.AskVelazquez.com

ISBN 10: 1-59495-014-8
ISBN 13: 978-1-59495-014-8

Fourth Edition

23 22 21 20 19 18   4 5 6 7

Library of Congress Number: 2010008123

Velazquez Spanish and English glossary for the social studies
classroom / created in cooperation with the editors of
Velazquez Press. p. cm.

  ISBN 978-1-59495-014-8

1. Social sciences--Dictionaries--Spanish. 2. Spanish language--
Dictionaries--English. 3. English language--Dictionaries--Spanish.
I. Velázquez Press.
H49.S7V45 2010
300.3--dc22

List of Contributors

Lexicon researched and compiled by
Arthur C and editors at Velázquez Press

Thanks to Sandra Strikovsky for her review of
Spanish-English terms

Thanks to Gary Baltazar, Jr. for the cover
Design

Preface

Limited English speakers in United States schools are faced with a double hurdle. They not only must learn a second language in an ESL setting, but also must keep up with their peers in terms of content. In the case of abstract thought, such as social studies, a student may enter an ESL program with already well-formed concepts in his or her native language. The student and the teacher must bridge this gap, especially if this student is to succeed in the current American educational system.

The Velázquez Spanish and English Glossary for the Social Studies Classroom is a newly compiled work that presents a breadth of vocabulary that all bilingual students and teachers will find to be an indispensable supplementary resource. These new bilingual glossaries are convenient and relevant to classroom study and examinations because they offer a comprehensive array of lexical terms and translations. Here, the ESL student and social studies teacher will find not only technical terminology presented in English and Spanish, but also entries for the type of discourse most commonly used to discuss social studies.

These glossaries fill a specific niche in elementary, middle and high school ESL and bilingual education by aspiring to the following objectives. First, these glossaries are a resource used by limited English speaking students in the classroom to aid them in the comprehension of social studies terms and in their own expression of the language of social studies. Second, they are designed to be used by these same students during standardized social studies exams. Third, schools and districts provide this resource to parents as a means to increase parent involvement. Parents use the glossaries to support student homework assignments. Finally, *the Velázquez Spanish and English Glossary for the Social Studies Classroom* can be used as a handy bibliographic reference for bilingual social studies teachers who must overcome questions of translation equivalents of specific terminology. Look no further than *the Velázquez Spanish and English Glossary for the Social Studies Classroom* for all student, teacher and administrative social studies needs!

Velázquez Press

Prefacio

Los estudiantes que asisten a escuelas norteamericanas y que hablan un inglés limitado tienen que confrontar principalmente dos obstáculos: no sólo deben aprender el inglés como una segunda lengua sino que también deben permanecer a la par de sus compañeros de clase en las demás materias. En los casos de asignaturas de pensamiento abstracto, como lo son las ciencias sociales, un estudiante puede ingresar a cualquier programa bilingüe con ciertos conceptos bien formados en su primera lengua. El estudiante y el maestro deben trabajar para hacer más pequeña esta diferencia lingüística, sobre todo si el estudiante pretende tener logros importantes dentro del sistema educativo estadounidense.

El glosario bilingüe de términos de ciencias sociales es para el uso en salones de clase. *El Velázquez Spanish and English Glossary for the Social Studies Classroom* es una compilación moderna que presenta un vocabulario amplio, indispensable como recurso suplementario para todo estudiante y maestro bilingüe. Este nuevo glosario bilingüe resulta muy conveniente y relevante para su uso tanto en salones de clase como en exámenes estandarizados, debido a su gran abanico comprensible de términos y traducciones. En este libro, el estudiante de inglés como segunda lengua y su maestro de ciencias sociales no sólo encontrarán terminología técnica presentada en inglés y español sino también distintas palabras sobre el tipo de discurso que se emplea comúnmente al hablar sobre las ciencias sociales.

Este glosario cubre una necesidad especial de las escuelas primarias, secundarias y preparatorias que cuentan con educación bilingüe y aspira a los siguientes objetivos. Primero, es un recurso que los estudiantes con inglés limitado usarán en su salón de clase para ayudarles a comprender términos de las ciencias sociales, abstracciones y a expresarse en el lenguaje técnico correctamente. Segundo, está diseñado para que estos mismos estudiantes puedan utilizarlo durante los exámenes estandarizados de ciencias sociales. Tercero, escuelas y distritos lo proveen a padres como herramienta para incrementar su participación en la educación de estudiantes. Los padres lo utilizan para traducir y entender vocabulario en inglés ayudar al estudiante con su tarea. Por último, los maestros bilingües de ciencias sociales que quieran aclarar dudas sobre traducciones de terminología específica tendrán a la mano como recurso bibliográfico el *Velázquez Spanish and English Glossary for the Social Studies Classroom*. ¡No busque más! El *Velázquez Spanish and English Glossary for the Social Studies Classroom* resolverá toda duda técnica como estudiante, maestro o administrador bilingüe.

Velázquez Press

User's Guide

This dictionary is unique in that its word-to-word translation format meets requirements for school standardized testing. Disallowed are pronunciation keys, parts of speech, and guide words.

This dictionary includes bold face entry words in alphabetical order. Homonyms that are different parts of speech are denoted with superscript. Commas are used to list synonymous translations. Related terms are indented beneath the main entry word in bold face to facilitate searchability.

Bold face entry word

Homonym with different part of speech

account[1], computar
    to account for, explicar

Entry word translation(s)

Guía del usuario

Este diccionario es único ya que su formato de presentar las traducciones palabra por palabra cumple los requisitos para exámenes escolares estandarizados. No están permitidas la pronunciación fonética, las categorías gramaticales ni las palabras para guiar la traducción.

Este diccionario incluye vocablos en orden alfabético que están en negrita. Los homónimos que tienen diferentes categorías gramaticales están indicados con un superíndice. Las comas se usan para sentar los equivalentes sinónimos en una lista. Las palabras asociadas están dentellados de bajo de la entrada principal y están en negrita para facilitar la búsqueda.

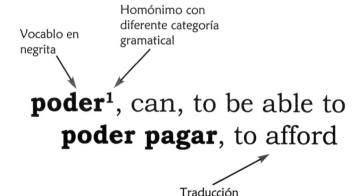

Vocablo en negrita

Homónimo con diferente categoría gramatical

poder[1], can, to be able to
poder pagar, to afford

Traducción del vocablo

Section I
Español – Inglés

A

a. de C. (antes de Cristo), B.C., Before Christ
A.D. (Anno Domini), A.D.
a. JC, a. de J.C. (antes de Jesucristo), B.C., Before Christ
abajo, down
abanico aluvial, alluvial fan
abastecedor, supplier
abastecimiento de agua, water supply
abastecimiento de alimentos, food supply
abdicación, abdication
abdicar, abdicate
abolengo, ancestry
abolición, abolishment, abolition
abolición de la segregación, desegregation
abolicionismo, abolitionism
abolicionista, abolitionist
abolir, abolish
abolir la segregación, desegregate
aborigen, aboriginal
aborto, abortion
aborto selectivo de niñas, female infanticide
abreviación, abbreviation
abreviar, abbreviate
abreviatura, abbreviation
absolución, acquittal
absolutismo, absolutism
absolutismo imperial, imperial absolutism, royal absolutism
absolutismo ruso, Russian absolutism
absoluto, absolute
absolver, acquit
Abstraccionismo, Abstractionism
aburguesamiento, gentrification
abuso, abuse
abuso de poder, abuse of power
aC, B.C., Before Christ
academia privada de blancos, private white academy
acantilados, cliffs
acaparamiento, hoarding
acaparar el mercado, corner the market
aceptable, adequate
accesibilidad, accessibility
acceso, access
accidente geográfico, landform relief, landform
accidente geográfico básico, basic landform
accidente nuclear de Chérnobil, Chernobyl nuclear accident
accidentes geográficos, key landforms
acción[1], action
acción afirmativa, affirmative action
acción de capital, capital stock
Acción de gracias, Thanksgiving
acción directa no violenta, nonviolent

direct action
acción estatal,
state action
acción política,
political action
acciones sociales,
social actions
acciones², stock
accionista,
share-holder,
stockholder
acero, steel
acidificación de suelo,
soil acidification
aclaración, clarification
aclarar, clarify
acontecimiento, event
**acontecimiento
mundial importante,**
major world event
**acontecimiento sig-
nificativo,**
significant event
**acontecimientos in-
ternacionales,**
international events
**acontecimientos
mundiales,**
world events
**acontecimientos
nacionales,**
national events
acordar, agree
acoso sexual,
sexual harassment
acreedor, creditor
acrópolis, acropolis
acta, act, brief
**Acta de estableci-
miento,** Act of
Settlement
acta de información,
bill of information

**Acta de Norteaméri-
ca británica,** British
North America Act
Acta de Supremacía,
Act of Supremacy
actitud antiinmigrante,
anti-immigrant
attitude
actitud natural,
natural attitude
actitude, attitude
actitudes sociales,
social attitudes
actividad económica,
economic activity
**actividad económica
principal,** primary
economic activity
**actividad econó-
mica secundaria,**
secondary economic
activity
**actividad económi-
ca terciaria,** tertiary
economic activity
actividad sísmica,
seismic activity
actividades recreativas,
leisure activity
activismo judicial,
judicial activism
activos, assets
actual, current
actualmente, currently
acueducto, aqueduct
acuerdo, accommodation,
agreement
acuerdo bilateral,
bilateral agreement
acuerdo comercial,
trade agreement
acuerdo de licencia,
licensing

acuerdo de no impor-tación, nonimportation agreement
acuerdo ejecutivo, executive agreement
acuerdo entre la defensa y la parte acusadora, plea bargain
Acuerdo General de Aranceles y Comercio (GATT), Geneva Accords
acuerdo multilateral, multilateral agreement
acuerdo vinculante, binding agreement
Acuerdos de Camp David, Camp David Accords
Acuerdos de Ginebra, Geneva Accords
Acuerdos de Helsinki, Helsinki Accords
Acuerdos de Múnich, Munich Agreement
Acuerdos de Paz de París, Paris Peace Accords
acuerdos internacionales de libre comercio, International Free-Trade Agreements
acuífero, aquifer
acuífero de Ogallala, Ogallala Aquifer
aculturación, acculturation
aculturar, acculturate
acumulación de capital, capital accumulation
acumulación de sal, salt accumulation
acuñar dinero, coining money
acupuntura, acupuncture
acusación, impeachment, indictment
acusación y juicio del presidente, presidential impeachment and trial
acusado, accused, defendant
acusar, impeach, indict
adaptación, adaptation
adaptación humana, human adaptation
adaptar, adapt, accommodate
adecuado, adequate
adivinos, soothsayers
adjudicación, allotment
adjudicar, allot
administración, administration
administración científica, scientific management
Administración de Alimentos y Fármacos, Food and Drug Administration
Administración de Aviación Federal, Federal Aviation Administration (FAA)
Administración de Electrificación Rural, Rural Electrification Administration
Administración de Obras Públicas, Public Works Administration

3

Administración de Seguridad Social, Social Security Administration

Administración de Trabajos Civiles, Civil Works Administration

administración fiscal, fiscal management

administración indirecta, indirect rule

Administración Nacional de Aeronáutica y del Espacio (NASA), National Aeronautics and Space Administration

Administración para el Progreso del Empleo, Works Progress Administration

Administración para la recuperación nacional, National Recovery Administration

adobe, adobe

adoctrinamiento, indoctrination

adoctrinar, indoctrinate

adquisición de mercado abierto, open market purchase

adquisición territorial, territorial acquisition

adulto, adult

advertencia Miranda, Miranda rule

aeroespacial, aerospace

aerofotografía, aerial photograph

aeropuerto, airport

afán de lucro, profit motive

Afganistán, Afghanistan

afijo, affix

AFL-CIO (Federación Estadounidense del Trabajo y Congreso de Organizaciones Industriales), AFL-CIO (American Federation of Labor and Congress of Industrial Organizations)

afluencia, influx

afluente, tributary

África, Africa

África Central, Central Africa

África colonial, colonial Africa

África del Norte, North Africa

África del Sur, Southern Africa

África Occidental, West Africa

África Oriental, East Africa

África Subsahariana, sub-Saharan Africa

afroamericano, African American

agave, sisal

agencia, agency

Agencia Central de Inteligencia, Central Intelligence Agency (CIA)

agencias ejecutivas independientes, independent executive agencies

agenda pública,
public agenda
agente de erosión,
erosion agent
agente del orden,
law enforcers
agitadores, agitators
agolpamiento de gente,
squash
ágora, agora
agrario, agrarian, tort
agravio, grievance
agregado, aggregate
agresión, aggression
   agresión fascista,
   fascist aggression
   agresión militar,
   military aggression
agresivo, belligerent
agricola, agricultural
agricultor arrendatario,
tenant farmer
**agricultor por contrato
de medianería,**
tenant farmer
agricultura, agriculture
   **agricultura comer-
   cial,** commercial agriculture, commercial
   farming
   **agricultura de planta-
   ción,** plantation
   agriculture
   **agricultura de sub-
   sistencia,** subsistence
   agriculture
   **agricultura de tala
   y quema,** slash-and-
   burn farming
   **agricultura de terra-
   zas,** terrace farming
   **agricultura extensi-
   va,** extensive farming

   agricultura intensiva,
   intensive farming
   **agricultura
   itinerante,**
   shifting agriculture
   **agricultura orien-
   tada al mercado,**
   market-oriented agri-
   culture
   agricultura seca,
   dry farming
   **agricultura sedenta-
   ria,** sedentary agri-
   culture
agrimensor, surveyor
agroindustria,
agribusiness
agua, water
   agua corriente,
   running water
   agua local,
   local water
   agua subterránea,
   groundwater
   aguas arriba,
   head water
aguacero, cloudburst
aguas arriba, head water
águila, eagle
agujero de ozono,
ozone depletion
Agustín de Iturbide,
Agustin de Iturbide
ahora, now
ahorrar, save
   ahorrar dinero,
   storing money
ahorros, savings
aire acondicionado,
air conditioning
aislamiento geográfico,
geographic isolation
aislacionismo, isolationism

aislacionista, isolationist
aislar, isolate
Ajenatón (Amenhotep IV), Akhenaton (Amenhotep IV)
Akenatón (Amenhotep IV), Akhenaton (Amenhotep IV)
Álamo, Alamo
albergar, accommodate
albergue, shelter
alcalde, mayor
alcances, scope
aldea, village
aldea tradicional, traditional village
Alejandro, Alexander
Alejandro de Macedonia, Alexander of Macedon
Alemania, Germany
   Alemania Occidental, West Germany
   Alemania Oriental, East Germany
   Alemania posterior a la reunificación, post-reunification Germany
alemán, German
alfabetismo, literacy
alfabetización, literacy
alfabeto, alphabet
   alfabeto braille, Braille alphabet
alfarería, pottery
Alfredo el Grande, Alfred the Great
álgebra, algebra
algodón, cotton
algonquino, Algonquian
alguacil, bailiff
aliado, ally
alianza, alliance
   alianza de familias, family alliance
   alianza económica, economic alliance
   alianza interregional, transregional alliance
   Alianza para el progreso, Alliance for Progress
   alianza política, political alliance
aliarse, ally
alienación, alienation
alijo, cache
alimento, food
   alimento básico, staple crop
   alimentos excedentes, surplus food
alineación, alignment
alineados, aligned
alistamiento, conscription
alivio, relief
allanamiento de morada, search and seizure
alma, soul
almacenamiento, storage
   almacenamiento de alimentos, food storage
   almacenamiento de residuos nucleares, nuclear-waste storage
almanaque, almanac
alojar, accommodate
alopatría, geographic isolation
Alpes, Alps
alquiler, rent
alquimia, alchemy
alta burguesía, gentry
Alta Edad Media, Early Middle Ages
alternativas, alternatives

altiplanicie, high plains
altiplano, altiplano
altitud, altitude
Alto Renacimiento,
    High Renaissance
alto veld, high veld
altruismo, altruism
altura, elevation
aluvión, flood
amalgama de culturas,
    melting pot
amazona, Amazon
ambientales, environmental degradation
ambientalismo,
    environmentalism
ambiente, environment
    ambiente físico,
    physical environment
    ambiente humano,
    human environment
    ambiente natural,
    natural environment
    ambiente sustentable, sustainable environment
ámbito privado,
    private domain
América, America
    América colonial,
    colonial America
    América del Norte,
    North America
    América Latina,
    Latin America
americano de origen asiático,
    Asian American
americanización,
    Americanization
las Américas, the Americas
americentrista,
    Americentric

amerindio,
    American Indian,
    Amerindian
Amiano Marcelino, Ammianus Marcellinus
amicus curiae,
    amicus curiae
amigo, friend
    amigo de la corte,
    amicus curiae
amish, Amish
amnistía, amnesty
Amnistía Internacional,
    Amnesty International
amo de esclavos,
    slave holder
amor cortés,
    courtly love
amortiguamiento,
    buffering
amotinado, mutinous
ampliación de las redes,
    net widening
Ámsterdam, Amsterdam
análisis, analysis
    análisis costo-beneficio,
    cost-benefit analysis
    análisis crítico de textos,
    critical text analysis
    análisis de clases,
    class analysis
    análisis de contenido, content analysis
    análisis histórico,
    historical analysis
    análisis intercultural,
    cross-cultural analysis
    análisis marginal,
    marginal analysis
    análisis multivariado,
    multivariate analysis

análisis textual,
textual analysis
analizar, analyze
analogías históricas,
historical analogies
anarquía, anarchy
anarquista, anarchist
ancestral, ancestral
ancestro, ancestor
anciano, elder
anexar, annex
anexión, annexation
anexión de Filipinas,
Philippine annexation
anexionar, Annex
anglosajón, Anglo-Saxon
animal de trabajo,
work animal
animal domesticado,
domesticated animal
animismo, animism
Antártica, Antarctica
antecedentes,
background cause
antepasado, ancestor
**antepasados nativos
americanos,**
Native American
ancestors
anterioridad,
precedence
antibiótico, antibiotics
anticipo, preview
anticlericalismo,
anticlericalism
anticonstitucional,
unconstitutional
antifederalista,
Anti-Federalist
Antigua Grecia,
ancient Greece
Antigua Roma,
ancient Rome

antigüedad grecolatina,
Greco-Roman anti-
quity
antiguo, ancient, former
antiguo amo,
former master
antiguo esclavo,
former slave
**Antiguo régimen
francés,**
Old Regime France
Antiguo Testamento,
Old Testament
**antiguos inmigran-
tes,** old immigrants
Antillas Francesas,
French West Indies
Antillas Neerlandesas,
Dutch West Indies
antisemita, anti-Semitist
antisemitismo,
anti-Semitism
antiterrorismo,
anti-terrorism
antracita, anthracite
antropología, anthropology
antropologia cultural,
cultural anthropology
antropología física,
physical anthropology
antropología forense,
forensic anthropology
antropología social,
social anthropology
antropólogo,
anthropologist
antropólogo físico,
physical anthropolo-
gist
antropólogo forense,
forensic anthropologist
anual, annual
anualmente, annually

anular, nullify
    anular el veto,
    veto override
anunciar, advertise
anuncio, advertisement
año, year
    año fiscal,
    fiscal year
    año lunar,
    lunar year
    Año Nuevo,
    New Years Day
    Año nuevo chino,
    Chinese New Year
    año solar, solar year
Años Locos,
    Roaring Twenties
apaciguamiento,
    appeasement
apaciguar, appease
apagar incendios,
    firefighting
Apalachia, Appalachia
aparato electrodoméstico,
    household appliance
aparcería, sharecropping
aparcero, sharecropper
apartheid, apartheid
(de) apelación, appellate
apelar, appeal
    apelar a la emoción,
    appeal to emotion
    apelar a la ignorancia, appeal to ignorance
apéndice, appendix
aplacar, appease
aplazamiento,
    deferment of loan
aplicación de las leyes,
    law enforcement
apologistas, apologists
aportación, input

aportación por hora,
    input per hour
aportación por máquina,
    input per machine
aportación por trabajador,
    input per worker
aportación por unidad de tierra,
    input per unit of land
apoyo, support
aprender, learn
aprendiz, apprentice
aprendizaje,
    apprenticeship
aprendizaje clásico,
    classical learning
aprobar (una ley),
    pass a law
árabe, Arabic
    árabe musulmán,
    Arab Muslim
    árabe palestino,
    Arab Palestinian
Arabia Saudita,
    Saudi Arabia
arado de hierro en tres piezas, three piece iron
arancel, tariff
    arancel proteccionista, protective tariff
    aranceles altos,
    high tariffs
    aranceles de ventaja comparativa,
    comparative advantage tariffs
arbitraje, arbitration
arbitrar, arbitrate
árbol de hoja ancha,
    broadleaf tree

árbol genealógico, family tree
archipiélago, archipelago
  archipiélago de Filipinas, Philippine archipelago
  archipiélago de Indonesia, Indonesian archipelago
arco y flecha, bow and arrow
área, area
  áreas agricolas, agricultural area
  área de recreo, recreation area
  área estadística metropolitana, metropolitan statistical area
  áreas geográficas, geographic areas
  área metropolitana, metropolitan area
  área rural, rural area
  área suburbana, suburban area
  área urbana de periferia, edge city
arena de rutilo, rutile sand
Argelia, Algeria
argumentación, argumentation
argumentado, reasoned
argumentar, argue
argumento, argument, plot
  argumento de la tesis, thesis statement
  argumento evangélico, evangelical argument

árido, arid
aristocracia, aristocracy
aristócrata, aristocrat
Aristóteles, Aristotle
arma, arms, weapon
  armas nucleares, nuclear weapons
  arma química, chemical warfare
Armada Invencible, Spanish Armada
armada, armada
armamento, weaponry
armisticio, armistice
arpón, harpoon
arqueología, archaeology
arqueólogo, archaeologist
arquitecto, architect
arquitectura, architecture
  arquitectura y arte griego clásico, classical Greek art and architecture
arraigado (costumbre), established
arrecife, reef, skerry
  arrecife de coral, coral reef
arreglo espacial, spatial arrangement
arrendatario, tenant
arriba, up
arroyo, arroyo, creek
arrozales, paddies
  arrozales en terrazas, terraced rice fields
arsenal, arsenal
  Arsenal de Democracia, Arsenal of Democracy
arte, art, craft
  arte barroco, baroque art

arte contemporáneo, contemporary art
arte del amor cortés, art of courtly love
arte etíope, Ethiopian art
arte étnico, ethnic art
arte gótico, gothic art
arte griego, Greek art
arte helenístico, Hellenistic art
arte medieval, medieval art
arte moderno, modern art
arte occidental, Western art
arte pop, pop art
el arte por el arte, art for art's sake
arte posmoderno, postmodern art
arte religioso cristiano, Christian religious art
arte renacentista, Renaissance art
artefacto, artifact
arterias de transporte, transportation arteries
artesanía, arts and crafts
artesano, artisan, craftsmen
Ártico, Arctic
artículo, article, commodity
artículo importado, import

artículos de El Federalista, Federalist Papers
Artículos de la Confederación, Articles of Confederation
artículos manufacturados, manufactured goods
artículos perecederos, nondurable goods
artillería, artillery
artista, artist
arzobispos, archbishops
asamblea, assembly, powwow
Asamblea de expertos, Assembly of Experts
Asamblea General, General Assembly
Asamblea Nacional, National Assembly
asamblea partidista, caucus
ascendencia, descent, ancestry
asegurar, insure
asentamiento, settlement
asentamiento español, Spanish settlement
asentamiento inglés, English settlement
asentarse, settle
asesinar, assassinate
asesinato, assassination
asesinato de Kennedy, Kennedy assassination
Asia, Asia
Asia Central, Central Asia, Inner

Asia
Asia del Este, East Asia
Asia Meridional, South Asia
Asia Occidental, West Asia
asiático americano, Asian-American
asignación, allocation
asignación de poder, allocation of power
asignación de recursos, resource allocation
asignar, allot, allocate
asilo, home, asylum
asilo de ancianos, senior citizen home
asimilación, assimilation
asimilar, assimilate
Asiria, Assyria
asistente del gobernador, lieutenant governor
asistencia escolar, school attendance
asistencia pública, public welfare
asistencia social, social agency, social welfare
asociación, association, society, league, partnership
asociación arqueológica, archaeological association
Asociación Nacional de Educación, National Education Association
Asociación Nacional para el Avance de la Gente de Color (NAACP), National Association for the Advancement of Colored People (NAACP)
Asociación Nacional del Fusil, National Rifle Association (NRA),
Asociación Nacional por el Sufragio de la Mujer, National Woman Suffrage Association
asociación sin fines de lucro, not-for-profit
Asoka, Ashoka
aspectos económicos del consumo, consumer economics
aspectos geográficos de los acontecimientos mundiales, geographic aspects of world events
aspectos invisibles de la cultura, invisible aspects of culture
astrolabio, astrolabe
astronauta, astronaut
astronomía, astronomy
astrónomo, astronomer
asueto (día de fiesta) bancario, bank holiday
asumir, assume
asunción, assumption
asunto, question
asunto de normativa, policy issue
asuntos básicos, bread-and-butter issues
asuntos civiles, civic affairs

asuntos contemporáneos, contemporary issues
asuntos exteriores, foreign affairs
asuntos nacionales, national issues
asuntos políticos, political issues, political affairs
atacar, attack
ataque preventivo, preemptive strike
ateísmo, atheism
Atenas, Athens
ateo, atheist
atlas, atlas
atmósfera, atmosphere
atonismo, atonism
auge, boom
Augusto, Augustus
aula, classroom
aumentar, escalate
aumento de la población, population increase
ausencia de reglas y leyes, absence of rules and laws
austeridad, austerity
Australia, Australia
Australia Oriental, eastern Australia
Austria, Austria
auto de avocación, writ of certiorari
auto de ejecución, writ of mandamus
autobiografía, autobiography
autocracia, autocracy
autócrata, autocrat
autocrático, autocratic
autodeterminación, self-determination
autodeterminación nacional, national self-rule
autodisciplina, self-discipline
autoempleo, self-employment
autogobierno, self government
autogobierno local, home rule
automatización, automation
autonomía, autonomy, self-governance, self-rule
autonomía nacional, national autonomy
autonomía personal, personal autonomy
autonomía política, political autonomy
autonomía relativa, relative autonomy
autónomo, autonomous
autopista, autobahn
autopista de cuota, turnpike
autopista de peaje, turnpike
autopistas interestatales, interstate highways
autoprotección, self-protection
autor, author
autoridad, authority
autoridad central, central authority
autoridad del Congreso, Congressional authority

Autoridad del Valle del Tennessee, Tennessee Valley Authority Act
autoridad policial, police authority
autoridades administrativas independientes, quangos
autoridades de primera línea, first line of authorities
Autoridades federales de vivienda, Federal Housing Authorities
autoritario, authoritative
autoritarismo, authoritarianism
autorizar, authorize
autosuficiencia, self-sufficiency
avance de la medicina, medical advance
avaricia de tierras europea, European land hunger
avena, oats
aventurero político, carpetbaggers
aviación, aviation
ayatola, ayatollah
ayatolá, ayatollah
ayer, yesterday
Ayuda a Familias con Niños Dependientes (AFDC), Aid to Families with Dependent Children
ayuda económica, economic aid
ayuda extranjera, foreign aid

ayuda gubernamental, government aid
ayuda humanitaria, humanitarian aid
ayuda social, relief
ayuntamiento, city council, township
azaque, zakah
azteca, Aztec
azúcar de Jamaica, Jamaican sugar

B

Babilonia, Babylon
Bagdad, Baghdad
bahía, bay
Bahía de Cochinos, Bay of Pigs
bajío, lowland
balada, ballad
balance, balance
balanza comercial, balance of trade, trade balance
balanza de pagos, balance of payments
Balcanes, Balkans
balcanización, Balkanization
banca, banking
banca comercial, commercial banking
banca riesgosa, wildcat bank
bancarrota, bankruptcy
banco, bank
banco central, national bank

banco central independiente, independent central bank
Banco Mundial, World Bank
bandera, flag
Bandera Llena de Estrellas, Star-Spangled Banner
bandera nacional, national flag
bandido, outlaw
bantú, Bantu
bar clandestino, speakeasies
bárbaro, barbarian
barcaza, barge
barco, ship
barco de vapor, steamboat, steamship
barlovento, windward
barón, baron
barrera arancelaria, trade barrier
barrera de hielo, ice shelf
barreras naturales, natural barriers
barriada, slum
barrio, quarter
barrio bajo, slum
Barrio chino, Chinatown
base de datos, database
base de recursos, resource base
base económica, economic base
base legal, legal basis
bases de poder, bases of power
batalla, battle

Batalla de Buena Vista, Battle of Buena Vista
Batalla de Hastings, Battle of Hastings
Batalla de Inglaterra, Battle for Britain
Batalla de las Ardenas, Battle of the Bulge
Batalla de Normandía, Normandy Invasion
Batalla de Nueva Orleans, Battle of New Orleans
Batalla de Poitiers, Battle of Tours
Batalla de Quebec, Battle of Quebec
Batalla de Tippecanoe, Battle of Tippecanoe
Batalla de Tours, Battle of Tours
batallas de Bull Run, bull run
Baviera, Bavaria
bayou, bayou
bazar, bazaar
bebidas alcohólicas, spirits
Bélgica, Belgium
beligerante, belligerent
beneficio, benefit, profit
beneficio de oportunidad, opportunity benefit
beneficio económico, economic profit
beneficio público, public benefit
beneficio total,

total benefit
Benín, Benin
Berlín, Berlin
Bután, Bhután
Biblia, Bible
bíblico, biblical
bibliografía,
    bibliography
biblioteca, library
    **Biblioteca del Con-
    greso,** Library of
    Congress
bicameral, bicameral
bicicarril, bicycle lane
bicultural, bicultural
biculturalismo,
    biculturalism
bien[1], good
    bien común,
    common good
    bien de capital,
    capital equpiment
    bien público,
    public good
bienes[2], goods
    bienes de capital,
    capital goods
    bienes de consumo,
    consumer goods
    **bienes de consumo
    no esenciales,**
    non-essential consu-
    mer goods
    bienes de lujo,
    luxury goods
    bienes duraderos,
    durable goods
    bienes económicos,
    economic goods
    bienes intermedios,
    intermediate goods
    **bienes manufactu-
    rados,** manufactured

goods
    bienes muebles,
    chattel
    bienes no durables,
    nondurable goods
    bienes privados,
    private goods
    bienes sustitutivos,
    substitute goods
    bienes sustitutos,
    substitute goods
bienestar, welfare
    bienestar general,
    general welfare
    bienestar público,
    public well-being,
    public welfare
    bienestar social,
    social welfare
bilateral, bilateral
bilateralismo, bilateralism
bilingüe, bilingual
bilingüismo, bilingualism
billetes (verdes),
    greenbacks
billetes de banco,
    greenbacks
biodiversidad, biodiversity
biografía, biography
    biografías históricas,
    historical biographies
biográfico, biographical
biología, biology
bioma, biome
biomagnificación, biologi-
    cal magnification
biopsicología,
    biopsychology
biosfera, biosphere
    biosfera-atmósfera,
    atmosphere biosphere
bipartidismo, bipartisan-
    ship, two-party system

bipartidista, bipartisan
Bizancio, Byzantium
blitzkrieg, blitzkrieg
bloque de poder,
   power bloc
bloque soviético,
   Soviet bloc
bloqueo, blockade
   bloqueo de Berlín,
   Berlin blockade
   bloqueo en el papel,
   paper blockade
bóer, Boer
boicotear, boycott
boicot, boycott
   **Boicot de los Autobu-
   ses en Montgomery,**
   Montgomery Bus
   Boycott
bolchevique, Bolshevik
boleta electoral, ballot
bolígrafo, pen
bolsa de valores,
   stock exchange
bolsa de Nueva York,
   New York stock
   exchange
bomba atómica,
   atomic bomb
bono, bond
   bono de guerra,
   war bond
   **bono de privatiza-
   ción,** privatization
   voucher
   bono escolar,
   school voucher
boom, boom
Bosnia-Hercegovina,
   Bosnia and
   Herzegovina
bosque, woodland, forest
   bosque de latitud me-

dia, midlaltitude forest
bosque nacional,
   national forest
bosque prístino,
   old-growth forest
bosque virgen,
   old-growth forest
Bosques orientales,
   Eastern woodlands
botánica, botany
Botsuana, Botswana
boya, buoy
boyardos, boyars
braceros contratados,
   contract labor
brahmanismo,
   Brahmanism
Brasil, Brazil
brecha de género,
   gender gap
brecha de los ingresos,
   income gap
británico(a), British
**Brown contra la Junta
   Educativa de Tope-
   ka,** Brown v. Board of
   Education
Brujas, Bruges
brújula,
   compass, magnetic
   compass
bucle de realimentación,
   feedback loop
Buda, Buddha
budismo, Buddhism
buen carácter,
   good character
buen salvaje,
   noble savage
buena fe objetiva,
   objective good faith
buena ley, good law
buena norma, good rule

buque clíper,
    clipper ship
buque corsario,
    privateer
burbuja económica,
    economic bubble
burgos, burgs
burgués, burgess
burgueses, burghers
burguesía, bourgeoisie
    burguesía urbana,
    urban bourgeoisie
burocracia, bureaucracy
    burocracia estatal,
    state bureaucracy
burócrata, bureaucrat
Bushido, Bushido
búsqueda de rentas,
    rent-seeking

caballería, cavalry
    caballería de Magyar,
    Magyar cavalry
caballero, knight
    **Caballeros del
    Trabajo,**
    Knights of Labor
caballerosidad, chivalry
cabaña de sudación,
    sweat lodge
La Cabaña del Tío Tom,
    Uncle Tom's Cabin
cabecilla, chieftain
cabeza de línea, railhead
cabezas redondas,
    roundhead
cabildear, lobby
cabildeo, lobbying

cabildero, lobbyist
cable, cable
cabo, cape
cacería de brujas,
    witch hunt
Cachemira, Kashmir
cacique, chieftain, sachem
cadena alimenticia,
    food chain
cadena trófica, food chain
caduco, deciduous
El Cairo, Cairo
caída, bust
cala, creek
colapso, bust
calamidad, calamity
calendario, calendar
    calendario maya,
    Mayan calendar
    **calendario maya de
    cuenta larga,**
    Mayan "Long Count"
    calendar
    calendario semilunar,
    semilunar calendar
**calentamiento atmos-
    férico,** atmospheric
    warming
calentamiento global,
    global warming
calidad de la información,
    information quality
**calidad de las aguas sub-
    terráneas,**
    groundwater quality
calidad de vida,
    quality of life
califa árabe, Arab Caliph
califato, caliphate
caligrafía, calligraphy
calle peatonal,
    auto-free zone
calumnia, slander

calzada

calzada, causeway
cámara de ahumado, smokehouse
Cámara de comercio, Chamber of Commerce
Cámara de los Burgueses, House of Burgesses
Cámara de los Burgueses de Virginia, Virginia House of Burgesses
Cámara de los Comunes, House of Commons
Cámara de los Lores, House of Lords
Cámara de Representantes, House of Representatives
camarilla política, caucus
cambio, change, shift
   cambio ambiental, environmental change
   cambio cultural, cultural change
   cambio de divisas, currency exchange
   cambio demográfico, demographic shift
   cambio en la curva de demanda, shift in demand curve
   cambio en la curva de oferta, shift in supply curve
   cambio en la demanda, change in demand
   cambio en la oferta, change in supply
   cambio inducido por los humanos, human-induced change
   cambio regional, regional change
   cambio social, social change
   cambios climáticos, climate changes
Camboya, Cambodia
camello, camel
camino, road
   Camino de Birmania, Burma Pass
   camino de sirga, towpath
   camino del inca, Incan highway
Camisas Rojas, Red Shirts
   Camisas Rojas de Garibaldi, Garibaldi's nationalist redshirts
campaña, campaign
   campaña crítica, hammering campaign
   Campaña de la Libertad, Liberty Bell
   Campaña de las cien flores, Hundred Flowers Movement
   campaña de la bases, grass roots campaign
   campaña militar, military campaign
   campaña presidencial de 1960, 1960 presidential campaign
   campaña propagandística, propaganda campaign **campañas de bonos de guerra,** bond drives
campesinado, peasantry
   campesinado ruso, Russian peasantry
campesino, peasant

campo petrolero, oil field

campo de concentración,
concentration camp

**campos de concentración
para japoneses,**
Japanese internment

**campos de concentración
para japoneses en
EE.UU.,** internment of
Japanese Americans

caña de azúcar,
sugar cane

Canadá, Canada

canal, canal, channel

Canal de Erie,
Erie Canal

Canal de Panamá,
Panama Canal

Canal de Suez,
Suez Canal

canal navegable,
waterway

cáñamo, hemp

Canberra, Canberra

canciller, chancellor

canción regional,
regional song

candidato, candidate

candidato político,
political candidate

**candidato por el
Partido Demócrata,**
Democratic nominee

cañón[1], cannon

cañón[2], canyon

cantera, quarry

cantidad, quantity

cantón, Canton

Guangzhou o Cantón,
Guangzhou (Canton)

capa de ozono,
ozone layer

capacidad, capacity,

qualification

**capacidad de per-
sistencia,**
carrying capacity

capacidad de carga,
carrying capacity

capacitación, training

capataz, overseer

capital, capital

capital económico,
economic capital

capital extranjero,
foreign capital

capital físico,
physical capital

capital humano,
human capital

capital nacional,
national capital

capitalismo,
capitalism

**capitalismo de
bienestar,**
welfare capitalism

**capitalismo de
estado,** state capita-
lism

capitanes de la industria,
captains of industry

capitanías, captaincies

Capitolio, Capitol Hill

capitolio estatal,
state capitol

capítulo, chapter

captores, captors

**captura de Constantino-
pla,** capture of Con-
stantinople

carabela, caravel

carabela portuguesa,
Portuguese caravel

característica distintiva,
defining characteristic

características culturales

características culturales, cultural traits, cultural characteristics

características de la comunidad, community characteristics

características distintivas, distinctive characteristics

características físicas, physical characteristics

características geográficas, geographic features, geographic characteristics

características humanas, human characteristics

características humanas de un lugar, human characteristics of a place

características políticas, political characteristics

caravana, caravan, mobile home
    caravana de camellos, camel caravan

carbón, coal

carga del hombre blanco, White Man's Burden

La carga del hombre blanco de Rudyard Kipling, Rudyard Kipling's "White Man's Burden"

cargo público, political office, public office, elected office

Caribe, Caribbean

caricatura política, political cartoon

Carlomagno, Charlemagne

Carlos II de Inglaterra, Charles II (King of England)

Carolina del Sur, South Carolina

carrera, career, race
    carrera armamentista, arms race
    carrera espacial, space race
    carrera hacia la luna, moon race
    carrera por la tierra, land run

carreta Conestoga, Conestoga Wagon

carreta con toldo, covered wagon

carretera, highway, road
    carretera de cuota, toll road
    carretera de peaje, toll road

carro (de guerra), chariot

carromato, covered wagon

carta, charter

carta, chart, letter, bill
    carta al editor, letter to the editor
    Carta de Derechos de los Veteranos, GI Bill
    Carta de Derechos de los Veteranos respecto a la educación superior, GI Bill on higher education
    carta de derechos del estado, state bill of rights
    Carta de Juramento de 1868,

Charter Oath of 1868
**Carta de las Nacio-
nes Unidas,** United
Nations Charter
Carta del Atlántico,
Atlantic Charter
Carta Magna,
Magna Carta
Carta de derechos,
Bill of Rights
carta personal,
personal letter
Cartago, Carthage
cartas coloniales,
colonial charters
cartel, cartel
cartel de drogas,
drug cartel
cartela, Cartouche
cartismo,
Chartist movement
cartografía, cartography
cartógrafo, cartographer
cartograma, cartogram
cartón político,
political cartoon
cartucho, Cartouche
Casa Blanca, White House
casa comunal, longhouse
casa de ayuda,
Settlement House
casa de beneficencia,
almshouse
casa de oración,
house of worship
casba, casbah
cascada, waterfall
cascadas, the Cascades
casero negligente,
slumlord
caso, case
caso Alger Hiss,
Alger Hiss case

caso ante la Corte,
court case
caso civil, civil case
**caso de diversidad de
ciudadanía,** diversity
of citizenship suit
**caso Dred Scott con-
tra Sandford,**
Dred Scott v. Sandford
**caso Engel contra
Vitale,** Engel v. Vitale
**caso Estados Unidos
contra Nixon,**
U.S. vs. Nixon
**caso Gibbons
contra Ogden,**
Gibbons v. Ogden
**caso Mapp contra
Ohio,** Mapp v. Ohio
**caso Marbury con-
tra Madison,**
Marbury v. Madison
**caso McCulloch con-
tra Maryland,** McCu-
lloch v. Maryland
**caso Miranda con-
tra Arizona,**
Miranda v. Arizona
**caso Plessy contra
Ferguson,**
Plessy v. Ferguson
**caso que sien-
ta precedente,**
landmark case
**caso Reynolds con-
tra Sims,**
Reynolds v. Sims
**caso Roe contra
Wade,** Roe v. Wade
**caso Schenck contra
los Estados Unidos,**
Schenck v. United
States

caso Tinker contra el Distrito escolar independiente de Des Moines, Tinker v. Des Moines

caso Universidad de California contra Bakke, Regents of the University of California v. Bakke

Caso Zenger, the Zenger Case

casos de los mataderos, Slaughterhouse Cases

casta, caste

castigo, retribution, punishment, penalty

    castigo cruel e inusual, cruel and unusual punishment

castillo, castle, chateaux

catacumbas, catacombs

Catalina la Grande, Catherine the Great

catarata, cataract

catedral gótica, Gothic cathedral

categoría, category

católico romano, Roman Catholic

Catorce puntos de Wilson, Wilson's Fourteen Points

caudillo, warlord

cuadriga, covered wagon

causa, cause

    causa común, common cause

    causa inmediata, immediate cause

    causa probable, probable cause

    causa y efecto, cause and effect

causalidad, causality

cavalier, Cavalier

cazador, hunter

    cazador de monopolios, trustbuster

    cazador-recolector, hunter-gatherer

ceder, cede

Ceilán, Ceylon

celdas de presión atmosférica, atmospheric pressure cells

celebración, celebration

celebrar, celebrate

censo, census

censura, censorship

censurar, censor

centralismo democrático, democratic centralism

centro, center, middle

    centro comercial, commercial center, shopping center

    centro de comunicación, communication hub

    centro de la ciudad, city center, downtown

    centro de la Península Ibérica, Central Iberia

    centro de reubicación, relocation center

    centro industrial, industrial center

    centro metropolitano importante, major metropolitan center

    centro turístico, tourist center

    centro urbano,

urban center
centros bipolares del poder, bipolar centers of power
Centroamérica, Central America
cerámica, pottery
cerámica de arcilla, clay pottery
cerca, near
cerdos, hogs
cereales, grains
ceremonia, ceremony
ceremonia del té japonesa, Japanese tea ceremony
cerro, hill
certificado de depósito, certificate of deposit
César Chávez, Cesar Chavez
cesión, cession
Cesión Mexicana, Mexican Cession
chamán, shaman
chaparrón, cloudburst
charlas informales, fireside chats
charlas junto al fuego, fireside chats
Cherokee, Cherokee
Chiang Kai-shek o Jiang Jieshi, Jiang Jieshi
chicas de fábrica, factory girls
chiismo, Shi'ism
chiita, Shi'ite
Chile, Chile
China, China
China de Tang, Tang China
China moderna, modern China

China posterior a Mao, post-Mao China
chino(a), Chinese
chovinismo, chauvinism
Cicerón, Cicero
ciclo, cycle
ciclo de energía, cycling of energy
ciclo de vida, life cycle
ciclo de violencia, cycle of abuse
ciclo del agua, water cycle
ciclo del carbono, carbon cycle
ciclo del nitrógeno, nitrogen cycle
ciclo del oxígeno, oxygen cycle
ciclo dinástico, dynastic cycle
ciclo económico, business cycle
ciclo estacional de vida, seasonal pattern of life
ciclo hidrológico, hydrologic cycle
ciclo químico, chemical cycle
ciclón, cyclone
ciclopista, bicycle lane
ciclovía, bicycle lane
ciénaga, bog, swamp
ciencias naturales, natural sciences
ciencias políticas, political science
ciencias sociales, social sciences
cieno, silt
científico, scientific

cierre patronal, lockout
cigoñal, shadoof
cima de montaña,
    mountain peak
Cimientos del cielo azteca, Aztec Foundation
    of Heaven
Cincinato, Cincinnatus
Cinco Naciones,
    Five Nations
Cinco pilares del islam,
    Five Pillars of Islam
Cinco relaciones sociales,
    Five Relationships
Cinco Tribus Civilizadas,
    Five Civilized Tribes
Cinturón de Fuego del
    Pacífico, Ring of Fire
cinturón del cobre,
    copper belt
Cinturón del Sol,
    Sunbelt
cinturón industrial,
    Rust Belt
circo, circus
circulación,
    circulation
    circulación atmosférica, air-mass circulation
    circulación atmosférica mundial,
        world atmospheric
        circulation
    circulación del dinero, circulation of
        money
    circulación monetaria, circulation of
        money
    circulación oceánica,
        ocean circulation
círculo polar antártico,

    Antarctic Circle
círculo polar ártico,
    Arctic Circle
círculo social,
    social group
circunnavegar,
    circumnavigate
circunscripción,
    precinct, constituency
Ciro I, Cyrus I
cita, citation
citación, citation
citar, cite
ciudad, city, town
    ciudad con rápido
        desarrollo, boomtown
    ciudad monoindustrial, single-industry
        city
    ciudad planificada,
        planned city
    ciudad portuaria,
        port city
    ciudad principal,
        primary city
    ciudad santa,
        holy city
    ciudad satélite,
        satellite city
    ciudad textil en Nueva Inglaterra, New
        England mill town
ciudadanía,
    citizenry, citizenship
    ciudadanía estadounidense, American
        citizenship, United
        States citizenship
    ciudadanía informada, informed citizenry
    ciudadanía por
        nacimiento,
        citizenship by birth

ciudadano, citizen
   ciudadano inhabilitado, disabled citizen
   ciudadano naturalizado, naturalized citizen
ciudadela, citadel
ciudades gemelas, twin cities
ciudad-estado, city-state
   ciudad-estado del norte de Italia, northern Italian city-state
   ciudad-estado electrónica, electronic city-state
   ciudad-estado griega, Greek city-state
   ciudad-estado maya, Mayan city-state
cívico(a), civic
civil¹, civil
civil², civilian
   civiles armados, minutemen
civilización, civilization
   Civilización africana, African civilization
   civilización agraria, agrarian civlization
   civilización antigua, ancient civilization
   civilización cambiante, shifting civilization
   civilización china, Chinese civilization
   civilización clásica, classical civilization
   civilización de Huang He (Río Amarillo), Huang He (Yellow River) civilization
   civilización egipcia, Egyptian civilization
   civilización global, global civilization
   civilización grecocristiana, Greek Christian civilization
   civilización griega, Greek civilization
   civilización inca, Incan civilization
   civilización judía, Jewish civilization
   civilización maya, Mayan civilization
   civilización mesoamérica, Mesoamerica civilization
   civilización mesopotámica, Mesopotamia civilization
   civilización moche, Moche civilization
   civilización mochica, Moche civilization
   civilización olmeca, Olmec civilization
   civilización preeuropea en América, pre-European life in Americas
   civilización romana, Roman civilization
   civilización teotihuacana, Teotihuacan civilization
   civilizaciones de los valles fluviales, river valley civilizations
   Civilizaciones Precolombinas, Pre-Columbian civilizations
civilizado, civilized

civismo, civic-mindedness
clan, clan
clase, class
    clase burguesa,
    bourgeois class
    clase caballeresca,
    knightly class
    clase comerciante
    holandesa,
    Dutch merchant class
    clase de los samu-
    ráis, Samurai class
    clase deudora,
    debtor class
    clase dirigente,
    ruling class
    (la) clase intelectual,
    intelligentsia
    clase marginada,
    underclass
    clase media,
    middle class
    clase social,
    social class
    clase trabajadora,
    working-class
clásico, classical
clasificar, classify
cláusula, clause, rider
    cláusula de comer-
    cio, commerce clause
    cláusula de debido
    proceso,
    due process clause
    cláusula de entera
    fe y crédito,
    full faith and credit
    clause
    cláusula de estable-
    cimiento del Estado
    laico, establishment
    clause
    cláusula de garantía,

    guarantee clause
    cláusula de la nación
    más favorecida,
    Most Favored Nation
    Agreements
    cláusula de libre
    ejercicio,
    free exercise clause
    cláusula de privi-
    legios e inmunida-
    des, privileges and
    immunities clause
    Cláusula de supre-
    macía, highest law of
    the land, supremacy
    clause
    cláusula de suprema-
    cía federal,
    federal supremacy
    clause
    cláusula del abuelo,
    grandfather clause
    cláusula del bienes-
    tar general,
    general welfare clause
    cláusula flexible,
    necessary and proper
    clause, elastic clause
    cláusula necesaria y
    apropriada,
    necessary and proper
    clause
    cláusula sobre pro-
    tección igualitaria,
    equal protection
    clause
clausura, cloture
clave, key
claves contextuales,
    context clues
clero, clergy
    clero católico,
    Catholic clergy

clero protestante, Protestant clergy
clientelismo[1], clientelism
clientelismo político, political machine
clientelismo[2], logrolling, pork-barrel
clima, climate
clima árido, arid climate
clima continental, continental climate
clima continental húmedo, humid continental climate
clima frío, cold climate
clima oceánico, marine climate
clima subártico, sub-Arctic environment
clima tropical húmedo, humid tropical climate
climático, climatic
climograma, climate graph (climograph)
clínica de asistencia médica, health care facility
Clístenes, Cleisthenes
Clodoveo, Clovis
clorofluorocarbonos, chlorofluorocarbons
coacción, coercion
coactivo, coercive
coalición, coalition
coalición de la voluntad, coalition of the willing
coalición de Roosevelt, Roosevelt

coalition
cobertura forestal, forest cover
cobertura médica, medical coverage
código, code
código civil, civil code
código de caballería, code of chivalry
Código de Hammurabi, code of Hammurabi
codigo de vestimenta, dress code
código de zona geográfica, geocode
código escrito, written code
código legal, law code, legal code
código napoleónico, code Napoleon, Napoleonic Code
códigos de esclavitud, slave codes
códigos negros, black codes
coetáneo, peer
coexistente, concurrent
coexistencia pacífica, peaceful coexistence
cognición, cognition
cohesión, cohesion, cohesiveness
coincidencia de grupos, group overlap
colaboradores de juramento, oath helpers
colapso de la bolsa, stock market crash
colapso político, political collapse
colectivismo, collectivism

colectivización,
collectivization
**colectivización
forzada,** forced collec-
tivization
colectivo, corporate
colegio electoral,
electoral college
colegio sin internado,
day school
colina, hill
Colón, Columbus
colonia, colony
colonia británica,
British colony
colonia de carta,
charter colony
**colonia de Nueva
Inglaterra,**
New England colony
**colonia de plan-
tación,** plantation
colony
Colonia de Plymouth,
Plymouth colony
colonia del Sur,
lower South colony
**colonia en Massa-
chusetts,** colony in
Massachusetts
colonia española,
Spanish colony
colonia francesa,
French colony
**colonia india
occidental,**
West Indian colony
colonia inglesa,
English colony
colonia propietaria,
proprietary, proprie-
tary colony
colonia real,

royal colony
colonias centrales,
Middle Colonies
**colonias del Atlánti-
co central,**
Mid-Atlantic colony
colonias holandesas,
Dutch colonies
colonial, colonial
colonialismo, colonialism
colonialismo europeo
European colonialism
colonización, colonization,
settlement
**colonización euro-
pea,** European coloni-
zation
**colonización fran-
cesa,** French coloni-
zation, French settle-
ment
**colonización francesa
de Indochina,**
French colonization of
Indochina
**colonización holan-
desa o neerlandesa,**
Dutch colonization
colonizador, colonist, frontiersman, settler
colonizar, colonize
**colono del Pacífico asiá-
tico,** Asian Pacific
settler
colono europeo,
European settler
color primario,
primary color
color secundario,
secondary color
columna griega,
Greek column
colusión, collusion

comandante, commander
comandante en jefe,
commander in chief
combate de hombre a
hombre, man-to-man
combat
combinar, combine
combustible, fuel
combustible fósil,
fossil fuel
comedia griega,
Greek comedy
comedor de beneficencia,
soup kitchen
comentario,
observation
comentario social,
social commentary
comercialización,
commercialization,
merchandising
comercialización
directa, direct trading
comerciante, merchant
comercio,
commerce, trade
comercio de diaman-
tes, diamond trade
comercio de escla-
vos, slave trade
comercio de larga
distancia,
long-distance trade
comercio de las espe-
cias, spice trade
comercio de pieles,
fur trade
comercio del café,
coffee trade
comercio directo,
direct trade
comercio electróni-
co, online commerce

comercio exterior,
foreign trade, overseas
trade
comercio global,
global trade
comercio interesta-
tal, interstate
commerce
comercio interior,
internal trade
comercio interna-
cional, international
trade
comercio justo,
fair trade
comercio trasatlán-
tico de esclavos,
trans-Atlantic slave
trade
comercio triangular,
triangle trade
comida, food
comienzo, beginning
comisión, commission
Comisión de Comer-
cio Interestatal,
Interstate Commerce
Commission
comisión de investi-
gación civil,
civilian review board
comisión de servicio
público, public service
commission
Comisión de Valores
y Cambios,
Securities and Ex-
change Commission
(SEC)
Comisión Federal de
Comercio, Federal
Trade Commission
(FTC)

Comisión Federal de Comunicaciones, Federal Communications Commission (FCC)

Comisión para la Igualdad de Oportunidades de Empleo, Equal Employment Opportunities Commission (EEOC)

comisión reguladora, regulatory commission

comité, committee

comité de acción política, political action committee (PAC)

Comité de Actividades Antiestadounidenses, House of Un-American Activities Committee (HUAC)

comité de conferencia, conference committee

Comité de correspondencia, Committee of Correspondence

Comité de Organizaciones Industriales (CIO), Committee for Industrial Organizations (CIO)

Comité de Reglas de la Casa de Representantes, House Rules Committee

comité del Congreso, Congressional committee

comité especial, select committee

comité mixto, joint committee

Comité No Violento Coordinador de Estudiantes, Student Nonviolent Coordinating Committee (SNCC)

comité permanente, standing committee

Comité Político Nacional de Mujeres, National Women's Political Caucus

Comités de Correspondencia, Committees of Correspondence

comodidades, facilities

comodoro, commodore

compacto, compact

compañía, business firm, company

Compañía Británica de las Indias Orientales, British East India Company

compañía de exportación, exporting firm

compañía de té, tea company

Compañía Francesa de las Indias Orientales, French East India company

compañía Standard Oil, Standard Oil Company

comparar, compare

comparar el pasado, comparing the past

comparar y contrastar, compare and contrast

comparativo, comparative

comparecencia,
arraignment
compartir la riqueza,
share the wealth
compendio estadístico,
statistical abstract
compensación justa,
just compensation
competencia, competition
competencia compartida, concurrent
jurisdiction
competencia extranjera, foreign competition
competencia monopolística, monopolistic competition
competencia no relacionada con los precios, nonprice
competition
competencia promovida por el gobierno,
government fostered
competition
competencia pura,
pure competition
complejidad, complexity
complejo industrial militar, military industrial
complex
complementariamente,
complementarily
complot, plot
comportamiento,
behavior
comportamiento aceptable,
acceptable behavior
comportamiento competitivo,
competitive behavior

comportamiento de grupos,
group behavior
comportamiento genéticamente determinado, genetically
determined behavior
comportamiento humano,
human behavior
comportamiento instintivo,
instinctive behavior
comportamiento político,
political behavior
comportarse, behave
composición étnica,
ethnic composition
compra de la Luisiana,
Louisiana Purchase
compra en descubierto,
buying on margin
comprador, buyer
comprar, buy
comprar a plazos,
installment buying
compras apalancadas,
leveraged buy-outs
comprender, comprehend
comprensión, understanding, comprehension
comprensión cultural, cultural understanding
comprobación de ingresos, means test
compromiso[1], pledge,
commitment
compromiso[2], compromise
Compromiso de 1850, Compromise
of 1850

Compromiso de Atlanta, Atlanta Compromise
Compromiso de Connecticut, Connecticut Compromise
Compromiso de los tres quintos, Three-Fifths Compromise
computadora, computer
común, common
comuna, commune
comunas del pueblo, people's communes
comunicación, communication
comunicación global, global communication
comunidad, community
comunidad afroamericana, African American community
comunidad agraria, agrarian community
comunidad biótica, biotic community
comunidad china, Chinese community
comunidad colonial, colonial community
comunidad cristiana, Christian community
comunidad de alianza, covenant community
Comunidad de Estados Independientes, Commonwealth of Independent States
comunidad de homínidos, hominid community
comunidad de huertas, truck-farming community
comunidad de naciones, commonwealth
Comunidad Económica de Estados de África Occidental, Economic Community of West African States (ECOWAS)
Comunidad Económica Europea, European Economic Community
Comunidad Europea, European Community
comunidad extranjera, migrant community
comunidad global, global community
comunidad humana, human community
comunidad local, local community
comunidad musulmana española, Spanish Muslim society
comunidad pesquera, fishing community
comunidad planificada, planned community
comunidad urbana, urban community
comunidad utópica, utopian community
comunidad vegetal, plant community
comunismo, Communism
comunismo primitivo, primitive commu-

nism

comunitario, communitarian

conceder, grant

conceder el derecho al voto, enfranchise

concentración, rally, concentration

concentración de la población, population concentration

concentración de servicios, concentration of services

concepto, concept

concepto alemán de Kultur, German concept of Kultur

concepto indio de la monarquía ideal, Indian concept of ideal kingship

conceptos económicos, economic concepts

concesión del derecho al voto, enfranchisement

concesiones de tierras, land grants

conciencia de clase, class consciousness

concubina, concubine

concurrente, concurrent

condado, county, shire

Conde de Dalhousie, Lord Dalhousie

condensación, condensation

condes, jarls

condición, condition, proviso, status

condición de estado, statehood

condición de individuo, individual status

condición necesaria, necessary condition

condición previa de servidumbre, previous condition of servitude

condición social, social status

condición socioeconómica, socioeconomic status

condición suficiente, sufficient condition

condición Wilmot, Wilmot Proviso

condiciones ambientales, environmental conditions

condiciones de trabajo, working conditions

condicionalidad, conditionality

condicionamiento clásico, classical conditioning

condicionamiento operante, operant conditioning

conducta de los ciudadanos, conduct of citizens

conducta social, social behavior

conductismo, behaviorism

conestoga, Conestoga

conexiones políticas y económicas, economic and political connections

confederación, confederation

**confederación inau-
gurada,** inaugurated
confederation
**Confederación iro-
quesa,** Iroquois
Confederacy
confederado, confederate
Conferencia de Helsinki,
Helsinki Accord
**Conferencia de Líderes
Cristianos del Sur,**
Southern Christian
Leadership Conference
**Conferencia de Paz de Pa-
rís,** Peace of Paris
Conferencia de San Remo,
Conference at San
Remo
Conferencia de Yalta,
Yalta Conference
**Conferencia Internacional
sobre la Población
y el Desarrollo en
El Cairo en 1994,**
International Confe-
rence on Population
and Development
confiable, reliable
confiscar, confiscate
conflicto, conflict
    **conflicto árabe-israe-
lí,** Arab-Israeli crisis
    **conflicto de lealta-
des,** divided loyalties
    conflicto étnico,
ethnic conflict
    conflicto fronterizo,
border conflict
    **conflicto genera-
cional,** generational
conflict
    conflicto ideológico,
ideological conflict

    conflicto inevitable,
unavoidable conflict
    **conflicto interna-
cional,** international
conflict
    **conflicto palestino-
israelí,**
Israeli-Palestinian
conflict
    conflictos laborales,
labor conflicts
conformidad, conformity
confucianismo,
Confucianism
Confucio, Confucius
confusión política,
political turmoil
conglomerado,
conglomerate
Congo, Congo
congregacionalistas,
Congregationalists
congregarse, assemble
congregado, assembled
Congreso,
    Congress, powwow
    (del) Congreso,
Congressional
    **Congreso Continen-
tal,** Continental
Congress
    **Congreso de Recons-
trucción Radical,**
Radical Reconstruc-
tion Congress
    Congreso de Viena,
Congress of Vienna
    **Congreso de Organi-
zaciones Industriales
(COI),** Congressional
Industrial Organiza-
tion (CIO)
    Congreso Nacional

Africano, African National Congress

Congreso sobre la Ley de Estampillas, Stamp Act Congress

congresos continentales, continental congresses

conífero, coniferous

conjunto de datos, data set

conjura, plot

conmutar, commute

connivencia, collusion

conocimiento, knowledge

    conocimientos previos, background knowledge

conquista, conquest

    conquista europea, European conquest

    conquista imperial, imperial conquest

    conquista mongola, Mongol conquest

conquistado, conquered

consecuencias, consequences

    consecuencias a corto y largo plazo, short-term and long-term consequences

    consecuencias ambientales, environmental consequences

    consecuenciaa del comportamiento, behavior consequence

    consecuencias globales, global consequences

consejo, council

    consejo de administración, board of directors

    Consejo de Ciudadanos Blancos, White Citizen Council

    Consejo de Discernimiento, Expediency Council

    Consejo de Guardianes, Guardian Council

    consejo de guerra, court-martial

    consejo escolar, school board

    Consejo Mundial de Iglesias, World Council of Churches

    Consejo Nacional de Seguridad, National Security Council

    consejo tribal, tribal council

    consejo y consentimiento, advice and consent

    consejos de administración vinculados, interlocking directorate

    consenso popular, popular consent

consentimiento, consent

    consentimiento de los gobernados, consent of the governed

conservación, conservation, preservation

    conservación de recursos, conservation of resources

conservacionista, conservationist

conservador, conservative

conservadurismo,
conservatism
conservar, conserve
consideración,
consideration
**consideraciones
éticas,** ethical consi-
derations
**considerar los derechos
e intereses de otros,**
consider the rights
and interests of others
consigna, motto
consolidacion vertical,
vertical merger
consolidado, established
consorcios, pools
conspiración, conspiracy
Constantino, Constantine
Constantinopla,
Constantinople
constitución, constitution
**Constitución
británica,** British
constitution
**Constitución de
EE.UU.,** U.S.
Constitution
**Constitución de los
Estados Unidos,**
United States Consti-
tution
**constitución del
estado de Massachu-
setts,** Massachusetts
state constitution
constitución estatal,
state constitution
**Constitución Mac-
Arthur,** MacArthur
Constitution
**constitución no
escrita,** unwritten

constitution
constitucional,
Constitutional
**constitucionalidad de las
leyes,** constitutionali-
ty of laws
constitucionalismo,
constitutionalism
construcción, construction
**construcción
cultural,** cultural
construction
**construcción de
acero,** steel
construction
**construcción de
ferrocarriles,**
railroad construction
**construcción de
la nación,**
nation building
**construcción megalí-
tica,** megalithic stone
building
**construcción social
de la realidad,**
social construction
of reality
construccionismo amplio,
broad constructionism
**construccionismo
estricto,** strict
constructionism
**construccionismo estricto
de la Constitución,**
strict interpretation of
Constitution
construccionismo social,
social constructionism
**constructor de montícu-
los,** mound builder
**constructor de un impe-
rio,** empire-builder

cónsul, consul
consulado, consulate
consumidor, consumer
consumismo,
    consumerism
consumo, consumption
    **consumo comparti-
    do,** shared con-
    sumption
    consumo de energía,
    energy consumption
    consumo de masas,
    mass consumption
    **consumo de petró-
    leo,** petroleum con-
    sumption
    consumo ostentoso,
    conspicuous
    consumption
consunción, consumption
contabilidad, accounting
contacto cultural,
    cultural contact
contacto entre culturas,
    cross-cultural contact
contaminación, pollution
    **contaminación
    atmosférica,**
    air pollution
    **contaminación
    de los océanos,**
    ocean pollution
    **contaminación del
    agua,** water pollution
contemporáneo,
    contemporary
contención, containment
contenido, content
contexto, context
    contexto histórico,
    historical context
contextual, contextual
contiguo, contiguous

continental, continental
continentalismo,
    continentalism
continente,
    continent, mainland
    **continente america-
    no,** the Americas
    **continente euroasiá-
    tico africano,**
    Afro-Eurasia
continuidad, continuity
    continuidad cultural,
    cultural continuity
    **continuidad histó-
    rica,** historical
    continuity
contorno, contour
contraargumento,
    counterargument
contrabando,
    smuggling, contraband
**contracorriente migra-
toria,** migration
    counterstream
contracultura,
    counterculture
contrainterrogación,
    cross-examination
contrapartida,
    trade-off
contrapeso, balance
contrarreforma,
    Counter Reformation,
    Catholic Reformation
contras, contras
contraste, contrast
contrato, contract
    **contrato con pro-
    mesa de no afiliarse
    a ningún sindicato,**
    yellow dog contract
    contrato social,
    social contract

contrato social tácito, tacit social contract

contrato vinculante, binding contract

contribución, contribution

contribuciones culturales, cultural contributions

contribuciones sobre ingresos federales, federal income tax

control, control

control armado, armed control

control centralizado, centralized control

control civil de los militares, civilian control of the military

control de alquileres, rent control

control de armas, gun control

control de calidad, quality control

control de los salarios, wage controls

control de precios, price control

control humano sobre la naturaleza, human control over nature

control judicial, judicial review

controles y contrapesos, checks and balances

controversia, controversy

convención, convention

Convención constitu-cional, Constitutional Convention

Convención de Filadelfia, Philadelphia Convention

Convención de Poughkeepsie, Poughkeepsie Convention

convención de ratificación, ratifying convention

Convención de Seneca Falls, Seneca Falls Convention

convención nacional, national convention

convención social, social convention

convenio, covenant

Convenio de Mayflower, Mayflower Compact

convenio ejecutivo, executive agreement

convento, convent

convergencia cultural, cultural convergence

convergencia de roles, role convergence

conversión, conversion

convertir, convert

convertirse, convert

cooperación, cooperation

cooperar, cooperate

cooperativa, cooperative

cooptación, co-optation

coordinador de la bancada mayoritaria, majority whip

coordinador de la bancada minoritaria, minority whip

Copérnico,
Copernicus
coraje, courage
Corán, Qur'an/Koran
cordillera, mountain range
  cordillera costera,
  coastal range
**CORE (Congreso de la
  Igualdad Racial),**
  Congress of Racial
  Equality (CORE)
Corea, Korea
  Corea del Norte,
  North Korea
  Corea del Sur,
  South Korea
corolario, corollary
  corolario Roosevelt,
  Roosevelt Corollary
corporación, corporation
  **corporación de la
  Corona,**
  crown corporation
  **Corporación Federal
  de Seguro de Depó-
  sitos,** Federal Deposit
  Insurance Corporation
  (FDIC)
  **corporación multi-
  lateral,** multinational
  corporation
  **corporación transna-
  cional,** transnational
  corporation
  corporativismo,
  corporatism
  **corporativismo esta-
  tal,** state corporatism
corral, stockyard
corredor de los bosques,
  coureur de bois
corredor de transporte,
  transportation corridor

corredor metropolitano,
  metropolitan corridor
correlación, correlation
correo a caballo,
  pony express
corriente, stream
  corriente del Golfo,
  gulf stream
  corriente marina,
  ocean current
  corriente migratoria,
  migration stream
  **corrimiento de tie-
  rras,** soil creep
corrupción, corruption,
  graft
  corrupción política,
  political corruption
corte, court
  corte de Heian,
  court of Heian
  Corte de Warren,
  Warren Court
  Corte Internacional,
  World Court
  **Corte Internacional
  de Justicia,**
  International Court of
  Justice
  corte marcial,
  court-martial
  corte noble,
  royal court
  corte penal,
  criminal court, penal
  court
  corte real, royal court
  Corte Suprema,
  Supreme Court
  **Corte Suprema de los
  Estados Unidos,** U.S.
  Supreme Court
cortesía, chivalry, civility

cortesía senatorial,
senatorial courtesy
corteza, crust
Cortina de Hierro,
Iron Curtain
cosecha, harvest, crop
cosmopolita, cosmopolitan
cosmos, cosmos
costa, coast
Costa de Oro,
Gold Coast
**Costa Este (de los
EE.UU.),**
East Coast
Costa oeste,
West Coast
costo, cost
**costo de oportuni-
dad,** opportunity cost
costo de producción,
cost of production,
production cost
costo de transacción,
transaction cost
costo de transporte,
transportation cost
costo humano,
human cost
costo marginal,
marginal cost
costo real,
real cost
costo total,
total cost
costo-distancia,
cost-distance
costumbre,
custom, practice
cota, contour line
Creciente Fértil,
Fertile Crescent
crecimiento, growth
crecimiento de la

población china,
China's population
growth
**crecimiento de la
población mundial,**
world population
growth
**crecimiento de la
población natural,**
natural population
increase
**crecimiento demo-
gráfico,**
population growth
**crecimiento econó-
mico,**
economic growth
**crecimiento expo-
nencial,** exponential
growth
crecimiento urbano,
urban growth
credibilidad, credibility
crédito,
credit, lending, loan
crédito al consumo,
consumer credit
**crédito por compra
adelantada de
cosecha,**
crop lien system
creencia, belief
creencia ética,
ethical belief
**creencia fundamen-
tal,** fundamental belief
creencia religiosa,
religious belief
creencias budistas,
Buddhist beliefs
creencias cristianas,
Christian beliefs
creencias islámicas,

Islamic beliefs
creer, believe
creíble, credible
cremación, cremation
cresta, ridge
Creta, Crete
    Creta minoica,
    Minoan Crete
cría de ganado,
    stock breeding
criadero, hatchery
crimen, crime
    crimen capital,
    capital crime
    crimen corporativo,
    corporate crime
    crimen de guerra,
    war crime
    crimen organizado,
    organized crime
    crimen con pena
    de muerte,
    capital crime
    crimen sin víctimas,
    victimless crime
    crímenes contra la
    humanidad, crimes
    against humanity
criminal de carrera,
    career criminal
criminología, criminology
    criminología clásica,
    classical criminology
criollo, Creole
crisis, crisis, depression
    (economic)
    crisis de la deuda
    externa, international
    debt crisis
    crisis de legitimidad,
    legitimation crisis
    Crisis de los misiles
    en Cuba,

Cuban Missile Crisis
Crisis de los rehenes
en Irán, Iranian hos-
tage crisis
Crisis del Golfo Pérsi-
co, Persian Gulf Crisis
crisis energética,
energy crisis
crisis fiscal,
fiscal crisis
crisis árabe-israelí,
Arab-Israeli crisis
crisis petrolera,
oil crisis
crisol cultural,
    culture hearth
crisol de culturas,
    melting pot
Cristiandad, Christendom
cristianismo, Christianity
    cristianismo
    católico, Catholic
    Christianity
    cristianismo
    ortodoxo, Orthodox
    Christianity
    cristianismo orto-
    doxo griego, Greek
    Orthodox Christianity
    cristianismo pro-
    testante, Protestant
    Christianity
cristiano, Christian
    cristianos coptos,
    Coptic Christians
Cristóbal Colón,
    Christopher Columbus
criterio amplio,
    open-mindedness
criterio guiado,
    guided discretion
criterio no guiado,
    unguided discretion

Cro-Magnon, Cro-Magnon
Cromañón, Cro-Magnon
crónica rusa,
Russian Chronicle
cronología, chronology
croquis, sketch maps
Cruz Roja Internacional,
International Red
Cross
Cruzadas, Crusades
Cruzadas europeas,
European Crusades
cruzado, crusader
cuadrante, quadrant
cuadrícula, grid
**cuadrícula alfanumé-
rica,** alpha
numeric grid
cuadrícula de letras,
letter grid
cuadrícula de mapa,
map grid
**cuadrícula de
números,**
number grid
cuadriculado, map grid
cuadro, cadre
cuáquero, Quaker
cuarta parte, quarter
cuasi experimento,
quasi-experiment
Cuatro modernizaciones,
Four Modernizations
Cuatro nobles verdades,
Four Noble Truths
**Cuatro principios cardi-
nales,** Four Cardinal
Principles
Cuba, Cuba
cubierta, forest cover
cubismo, Cubism
cubista, Cubist
cuello blanco, white-collar

cuenca, basin
cuenca de agua,
water basin
Cuenca de Polvo,
Dust Bowl
Cuenca del Atlántico,
Atlantic basin
Cuenca del Caribe,
Caribbean Basin
Cuenca del Pacífico,
Pacific Rim
cuenca hidrográfica,
drainage basin
Cuenca y cordillera,
Basin and Range
cuenta corriente,
checking account
cuenta de ahorros,
savings account
cuenta de cheques,
checking account
cuento increíble, tall tale
cuentos jataka,
Jataka tales
**Cuerpo Civil de Conserva-
ción,** Civilian Conser-
vation Corps
cuerpo de agua,
body of water
**Cuerpo de libertades de
Massachusetts,**
Massachusetts Body of
Liberties
Cuerpo de paz,
Peace Corps
cuerpo político,
body politic
cuestión,
issue, question
cuestión política,
political question
**cuestiones económi-
cas,** economic issues

culpa, fault
   culpa del sobreviviente, survivor's guilt
cultivo, crop
   cultivo comercial, cash crop
   cultivo de maíz, maize cultivation
   cultivo de plantas, plant cultivation
   cultivo doméstico, domestic crop
   cultivo intensivo, intensive cultivation
   cultivos comerciales de trabajo intensivo, labor-intensive cash crops
culto, cult
   culto a la domesticidad, cult of domesticity
   culto a los antepasados, ancestor worship
cultura, culture
   cultura aria, Aryan culture
   cultura chimú, Chimu society
   cultura coreana, Korean culture
   cultura de clase media, middle-class culture
   cultura de consumo, consumer culture
   cultura de Kush, Kush culture
   cultura de la India, Indian culture
   cultura de masas, mass culture
   cultura de vaqueros, cowboy culture
   cultura del escándalo, culture of shock
   cultura del miedo, culture of fear
   cultura dominante de EE.UU., mainstream America
   cultura guerrera, warrior culture
   cultura hawaiana, Hawaiian culture
   cultura helenística, Hellenist culture
   cultura hindú-budista, Buddhist-Hindu culture
   cultura madre, culture hearth
   cultura misisipiense, Mississippian culture
   cultura occidental, Western culture
   cultura policial, police culture
   cultura política, political culture
   cultura popular, popular culture
   cultura Tiahuanaco, Tiahuanaco society
   culturas indígenas, indigenous cultures
cultural, cultural
cumbre diplomática entre Reagan y Gorbachov, Reagan-Gorbachev summit diplomacy
cumplir, observe
cuneiforme, cuneiform
cuota, fee, quota, toll
cupón de privatización, privatization voucher

Cura Miguel Hidalgo,
Father Miguel Hidalgo
**cursos alternativos de
acción,** alternative
courses of action
curva de campana,
bell curve
curva de demanda,
demand curve
curva de la oferta,
supply curve
curva de nivel,
contour line
**curva de posibilidades de
producción,**
production possibili-
ties curve
curva económica,
economic curve
curva normal, bell curve

D

dadaísmo, Dadaism
daimio, daimyo
Damasco, Damascus
danza, dance
Darío el Grande,
Darius the Great
Darío I, Darius I
darwinismo social,
Social Darwinism
datación de los restos,
incremental dating
datos, data
datos básicos,
primary data
datos del censo,
census data
datos económicos,
economic data
de facto, de facto
de mucho, uno,
out of many, one
debate, debate
debatible, moot
debatir, discuss, argue
deber, duty
debido proceso,
due process
**debido proceso sustanti-
vo,** substantive due
process
debilidades,
weaknesses
década, decade
decisión, decision
decisión colectiva,
collective decision
**decisión de Dred Sco-
tt,** Dred Scott decision
decisión histórica,
landmark decision
**decisiones clave
o cruciales,** key or
pivotal decisions
**decisiones econó-
micas,** economic
decisions
declaración,
declaration, statement
Declaración Balfour,
Balfour Declaration
**Declaración de dere-
chos,** Bill of Rights
**Declaración de Dere-
chos de Canadá,**
Canadian Bill of
Rights
**Declaración de De-
rechos de Virginia,**
Virginia Declaration of
Rights

Declaración de derechos inglesa, English Bill of Rights

Declaración de Independencia, Declaration of Independence

Declaración de los Derechos de la Mujer y de la Ciudadana, Declaration of the Rights of Women

Declaración de los Derechos del Hombre y del Ciudadano, Declaration of the Rights of Man

Declaración de sentimientos, Declaration of Sentiments

Declaración francesa de los Derechos del Hombre y del Ciudadano, French Declaration of the Rights of Man

Declaración Universal de Derechos Humanos, Universal Declaration of Human Rights

declinar, decline

decreto, act

decreto de consentimiento unánime, unanimous consent decree

decretos ministeriales, orders in council

deducción de impuestos, tax deduction

deducción de negocio, business deduction

deducir, infer

defensa militar, military defense

defensa nacional, national defense

Defensa "Star Wars", Star Wars

defensa verbal, oral argument

defensor de los derechos humanos, ombudsman

déficit, deficit

déficit comercial, trade deficit, trade imbalance

déficit federal, federal deficit

déficit presupuestario, budget deficit

definido operacionalmente, operationally defined

deflación, deflation

deforestación, clearing of forest, deforestation

degradación de los suelos tropicales, tropical soil degradation

degradación de zonas urbanas, urban decay

degradación del suelo, land degradation

deísmo, deism

deísta, deist

(del) Congreso, Congressional

(del) norte, northern

(del) Sur, southern

delegación, delegation

delegados, delegates

delincuencia juvenil, juvenile delinquency

delito capital,
capital offense
**delito con pena de
muerte,** capital
offense
delito convencional,
conventional crime
delito de cuello blanco,
occupational crime,
white-collar crime
delito grave, felony
delito menor,
misdemeanor
delitos graves,
high crimes
delta, delta
   delta del Nilo,
   Nile Delta
   delta fluvial,
   river delta
demagógico, demagogic
demagogo, demagogue
demanda, demand
   demanda agregada,
   aggregate demand
demandante, plaintiff
democracia, democracy
   democracia ateniense, Athenian
   demo-cracy
   democracia constitucional, constitutional
   democracy
   democracia constitucional estadounidense, American constitutional democracy
   democracia contemporánea, contemporary democracy
   democracia directa,
   direct democracy
   democracia griega,

Greek democracy
   democracia indirecta, indirect democracy
   democracia jacksoniana, Jacksonian
   Democracy
   democracia jeffersoniana, Jeffersonian
   democracy
   democracia liberal,
   liberal democracy
   democracia parlamentaria,
   parliamentary democracy
   democracia representativa, representative
   democracy
   democracia social,
   social democracy
   democracia socialista, socialist democracy
demócrata, Democrat
democrático, democratic
democratización,
democratization
   democratización social, social democratization
demografía, demographics,
demography
demostración en círculo,
circular reasoning,
circular thinking
denominación,
denomination
   **denominación
cristiana,** Christian
denomination
densidad, density
   densidad de población, density of
population, population

density
densidad fisiológica de población, physiological population density
densidad vegetal, plant population
Departamento de Agricultura, Department of Agriculture
Departamento de Asuntos de los Veteranos, Department of Veteran's Affairs
Departamento de Comercio, Department of Commerce
Departamento de Defensa, Department of Defense
Departamento de Educación, Department of Education
Departamento de Energía, Department of Energy
Departamento de Estado, Department of State
Departamento de Justicia, Department of Justice
Departamento de Salud y Servicios Humanos, Department of Health and Human Services
Departamento de Trabajo, Department of Labor
Departamento de Vivienda y Desarrollo Urbano, Department of Housing and Urban Development
Departamento del Interior, Department of the Interior

Departamento del Tesoro, Department of the Treasury
departamentos del poder ejecutivo, executive departments
dependencia económica, economic dependency
dependencias, facilities
dependiente, dependent
deporte de espectáculo, spectator sport
deporte profesional, professional sport
deposición, deposition
depreciar, depreciate
depresión, depression
derecha política, right wing
derecho, right, law
derecho a adquirir una propiedad, right to acquire a property
derecho a afiliarse a un partido político, right to join a political party
derecho a afiliarse a una asociación política, right to join a professional association
derecho a celebrar un contrato lícito, right to enter into a lawful contract
derecho a criticar al gobierno, right to criticize the government

derecho a disponer de una propiedad, right to dispose of a property
derecho a elegir trabajo, right to choose one's work
derecho a establecer un negocio, right to establish a business
derecho a la asistencia de un abogado, right to counsel
derecho a la educación pública, right to public education
derecho a la información, right to know
derecho a la jurisdicción, right to due process of law
derecho a la privacidad, right to privacy
derecho a la propiedad, right to property
derecho a la protección igualitaria ante la ley, right to equal protection of the law
derecho a la vida, right to life
derecho a la vida, la libertad y la búsqueda de la felicidad, right to life, liberty, and the pursuit of happiness
derecho a ocupar un cargo público, right to hold office
derecho a patentar, right to patent
derecho a sindicalizarse, right to join a labor union
derecho a trabajar, right to work
derecho a un juicio justo, right to a fair trial
derecho a votar, right to vote
derecho al voto, sufragio, franchise
derecho anglosajón, English Common Law
derecho canónico, canon laws
derecho civil, civil law
derecho constitucional, constitutional law
derecho consuetudinario, common law
derecho contra la autoincriminación, right against self-incrimination
derecho de apelación, right of appeal
derecho de extraterritorialidad, right of extraterritoriality
derecho de petición, freedom of petition
derecho de reunión, freedom of assembly
derecho divino, divine right
derecho divino de los reyes, divine right of kings
derecho económico, economic law
derecho escrito,

statute law, statutory law
derecho inherente al autogobierno, inherent right to self-government
derecho internacional, international law
derecho legal, legal right
derecho militar, military law
derecho natural, natural law
derecho penal, criminal law
derecho privado, private law
derecho procesal, procedural law
derecho público, public law
derecho religioso, religious right
derechos civiles, civil rights
derechos de aguas, water rights
derechos de autor, copyright, right to copyright
derechos de grupo, group entitlements
derechos de las minorías, minority rights
derechos de las mujeres, women's rights
derechos de las personas con discapacidad, rights of the disabled
derechos de los acu-

sados, rights of the accused
derechos de los estados, states' rights
derechos de los homosexuales, gay rights
derechos de los ingleses, rights of Englishmen
derechos de propiedad, property rights
derechos de reproducción, copyright
derechos de voto, voting rights
derechos del consumidor, consumer's rights
derechos económicos, entitlements, economic rights
derechos enumerados, enumerated rights
derechos especiales, special rights
derechos estudiantiles, student rights
derechos fundamentales, fundamental rights, unenumerated rights
derechos humanos, human rights
derechos inalienables, inalienable rights
derechos individuales, individual rights
derechos inviolables, inviolable rights
derechos marítimos, maritime rights

derechos Miranda, Miranda rights

derechos naturales, natural rights

derechos políticos, political rights

derechos positivos, positive rights

derechos sociales, social rights

deriva continental, continental drift

derivación, derivation

derogar, nullify

derrocamiento, overthrow

desacato al tribunal, contempt of court

desacuerdo, disagreement

desalación, desalinization

desalineación partidista, party dealignment

desalinización, desalinization

desarrollar, develop

desarrollismo, developmentalism

desarrollo, development

(en) desarrollo, developing

desarrollo comunitario, community development

desarrollo cultural, cultural development

desarrollo de carreteras, road development

desarrollo de vivienda, housing development

desarrollo dependiente, dependent development

desarrollo económico, economic development

desarrollo humano, human development

desarrollo industrial, industrial development

desarrollo político, political development

desarrollo sostenible, sustainable development

desarrollo sustentable, sustainable development

desarrollo urbano, urban development

desarrollos críticos, critical developments

desastre natural, natural disaster

descendiente, descendant

descendiente patrilineal, patrilineal descent

descentralización, decentralization

descentralizar, decentralize

descolonización, decolonization

descomposición a distancia, distance decay

descontento civil, civil unrest

describir, describe

descripción, description

descriptivo, descriptive

descubrimiento, discovery

descubrimiento astronómico, astronomical discovery

descubrimiento

científico, scientific breakthrough

descubrimiento de diamantes, discovery of diamonds

descubrimiento de oro, discovery of gold

descubrimiento inevitable, inevitable discovery

descuento, rebate

desecación de lagos, lake desiccation

desembocadura de un río, mouth of a river

desempleo, unemployment

desempleo cíclico, cyclical unemployment

desempleo coyuntural, cyclical unemployment

desempleo estacional, seasonal unemployment

desempleo estructural, structural unemployment

desempleo friccional, frictional unemployment

desempleo normal, normal unemployment

desempleo tecnológico, technological unemployment

deseos, wants

deseos humanos, human wants

deseos ilimitados, unlimited wants

desertar, desert

desertificación, desertification

desertización, desertification

desfiladero de Cumberland, Cumberland Gap

desgaste, weathering

deshumanización, objectification

deshumanizar, objectify

desierto, desert

desierto del Sahara, Sahara desert

designado, appointed

designar, appoint

desigual, unequal

desigualdad, inequality

desigualdad de condiciones, inequality of condition

desigualdad de oportunidades, inequality of opportunity

desigualdad social, social inequality

desintegración de la Unión Soviética, breakup of Soviet Union

desmotadora de algodón, cotton gin

desmovilización, demobilization

desnutrición, malnutrition

desobediencia civil, civil disobedience

despepitadora de algodón, cotton gin

despilfarrador, spender

desplazamiento, displacement

despoblación, underpopulation

déspota, despot

déspota ilustrado, Enlightened Despot

despotismo, despotism

despotismo democrático, democratic despotism

desregularización, deregulation

destino manifiesto, manifest destiny

destitución, recall

destreza de supervivencia diaria, daily survival skill

destrucción de hábitat, habitat destruction

detalles de apoyo, supporting details

détente, détente

determinantes de la oferta y la demanda, determinants of supply and demand

determinismo, determinism

determinismo ambiental, environmental determinism

determinismo económico, economic determinism

deuda, debt

deuda estatal, state debt

deuda externa, foreign debt

deuda piramidal, pyramid debt

deuda pública, national debt, public debt

deuda sin fundamentos, unfunded liability

deudas de guerra, war debts

deudor, debtor

dharma, dharma

día, day

Día D, D-Day

Día de la Bandera, Flag Day

Día de la Independencia, Independence Day

Día de la Independencia de los Estados Unidos, Fourth of July

Día de la Raza, Columbus Day

Día de las Elecciones, Election Day

Día de los Caídos, Memorial Day

Día de los Veteranos, Veterans Day

Día de Martin Luther King Jr., Martin Luther King Jr. Day

Día del Presidente, Presidents Day

Día del Trabajo en EE.UU., Labor Day

día festivo, holiday

día festivo estadounidense, American holiday

diagrama, diagram, bar graph, chart

diagrama de flujo, flowchart

diagrama en sección, cutaway diagram

diagrama transversal, cross-section diagram

dialecto, dialect

diálogo, dialogue
diario, journal
diáspora, diaspora
   diáspora judía,
   Jewish diaspora
dibujos animados,
  cartoons
dictador, dictator
dictadura, dictatorship
dictamen consultivo,
  advisory opinion
dictamen divergente,
  dissenting opinion
Diez mandamientos,
  Ten Commandments
diezmo, tithe
difamación, libel, slander
   difamación sediciosa,
   seditious libel
diferencias constitucio-
  nales, constitutional
  differences
diferencias culturales,
  cultural differences
diferencias económicas,
  economic differences
diferentes, different
difusión cultural,
  cultural diffusion
difusión de humo del
  tabaco, diffusion of
  tobacco smoking
dilema ético,
  ethical dilemma
diligencia, stagecoach
Dinamarca, Denmark
dinámica de la población,
  population dynamics
dinastía, dynasty
   dinastía Chou (Zhou),
   Chou dynasty
   dinastía Han,
   Han dynasty

   dinastía Ming,
   Ming Dynasty
   dinastía Omeya,
   Umayyad Dynasty
   dinastía Shang,
   Shang Dynasty
   dinastía Song,
   Song Dynasty
   dinastía Sui,
   Sui dynasty
   dinastía Yuan,
   Yuan Dynasty
   dinastía Zagüe,
   Zagwe Dynasty
   dinastía Zhou,
   Zhou Dynasty
dinástico, dynastic
dinero, money
   dinero en efectivo,
   cash
   dinero metálico,
   hard money
diócesis, diocese
diosas, goddesses
dioses, gods
   dioses védicos,
   Vedic gods
diplomacia, diplomacy
   diplomacia atómica,
   atomic diplomacy
   diplomacia de lanza-
   dera, Shuttle
   Diplomacy
   diplomacia de mano
   dura, big stick diplomacy
   diplomacia del dólar,
   dollar diplomacy
   diplomacia en tiem-
   pos de guerra,
   wartime diplomacy
   diplomacia itineran-
   te, Shuttle Diplomacy

diplomático[1], diplomat,
diplomático[2], diplomatic
dique, dike, dyke,
 levee, dam
 dique de mar,
 sea wall
dirección, direction
 (en) la dirección del
 viento, downwind
directiva de gobierno,
 government directive
directo, direct
discípulo, disciple
discriminación,
 discrimination
 discriminación basa-
 da en las creencias,
 discrimination based
 on religious belief
 discriminación basa-
 da en discapacidad,
 discrimination based
 on disability
 discriminación ba-
 sada en el género,
 discrimination based
 on gender
 discriminación
 basada en el origen
 étnico,
 discrimination based
 on ethnicity
 discriminación
 basada en la edad,
 discrimination based
 on age
 discriminación basa-
 da en la religión o las
 creencias,
 discrimination based
 on religious belief
 discriminación inver-
 sa, reverse discrimination
discriminación
lingüística,
 discrimination based
 on language
discriminación posi-
tiva, affirmative action
discriminación ra-
cial, racial discrimination
discriminación
religiosa,
 religious discrimina-
tion
discurso, speech
 discurso "hierro y
 sangre" de Bismarck,
 Bismarck's "Blood and
 Iron" speech
 Discurso "La ciu-
 dad en la colina" de
 Kennedy, "City Upon
 a Hill" speech
 Discurso "Yo tengo
 un sueño", I Have a
 Dream speech
 Discurso de despe-
 dida de Washington,
 Washington's Farewell
 Address
 Discurso de Gettys-
 burg, Gettysburg
 Address
 discurso de inves-
 tidura, inaugural
 address
 Discurso de la Cruz
 de oro,
 Cross of Gold speech
 Discurso de las cua-
 tro libertades,
 Four Freedoms speech
 discurso de Lincoln

sobre "la casa dividi-
da", Lincoln's "House
Divided" speech
discurso de odio,
hate speech
**discurso de toma de
posesión,**
inaugural address
**"Discurso del mé-
todo" de Descartes,**
Descartes' "Discourse
on Method"
discurso simbólico,
symbolic speech
discusión,
discussion, argumen-
tation, argument
discutir, discuss, argue
diseminar, disseminate
diseño naval, ship design
diseño urbano,
urban design
disensión, dissent
disgustar, dislike
disidente, dissenter
disidente religioso,
religious dissenter
disminución, diminishing
**disminución de pre-
cios,** price decrease
disparidad, disparity
**disparidad econó-
mica,** economic
disparity
**disparidades entre
los ideales y la reali-
dad estadounidenses,**
disparities in Ameri-
can ideals and realities
**disparo que se escuchó en
todo el mundo,** shot
heard round the world
dispersado, dispersed

dispersión, dispersion
disponibilidad, availability
**disponibilidad de
agua,** water availa-
bility
disposición, provision
disposición cívica,
civic disposition
disputa, dispute
disputa económica,
economic dispute
disputa fronteriza,
boundary dispute
disputa por África,
Scramble for Africa
distancia, distance
**distancia ocupa-
cional,** occupational
distance
distensión, détente
distorsión, distortion
distribución,
distribution, allocation
**distribución anticipa-
da,** front-loading
**distribución de
bienes y servicios,**
distribution of goods
and services
**distribución de la
población,**
population distribu-
tion
**distribución de los
ecosistemas,**
distribution of ecosys-
tems
**distribución de los
ingresos,** revenue
sharing
**distribución de
poder,** distribution of
power

distribución de recursos, distribution of resources

distribución del ingreso, income distribution

distribución espacial, spatial distribution

distribución funcional del ingreso, functional distribution of income

distribución justa de la riqueza, fair distribution of wealth

distribución personal del ingreso, personal distribution of income

distribución normal, bell curve, normal curve

distribuidor, distributor

distribuir, allocate

distrito, district, ward

distrito de censo, census district

distrito de planeación regional, regional planning district

distrito de tribunal de circuito, circuit court district

distrito electoral, congressional district, constituency, voting ward

distrito escolar, school district

distrito industrial, industrial district

distrito legislativo, legislative district, legislative districting

disturbio urbano, urban riot

disturbios contra el reclutamiento militar en Nueva York, New York City draft riots

disturbios raciales, race riots

disuasión, deterrence

diversidad, diversity

diversidad cultural, cultural diversity

diversidad de género, gender diversity

diversidad de la población, population diversity

diversidad en la cultura estadounidense, diversity in American life

diversidad étnica, ethnic diversity

diversidad lingüística, linguistic diversity

diversidad racial, racial diversity

diversificación, diversification

diversificar, diversify

diverso, diverse

divergencia cultural, cultural divergence

dividendo, dividend

dividendo en acciones, stock dividends

dividir, divide

dividir y vencerás, divide and rule

divinidad, divinity

divinidades griegas, Greek gods and

goddesses
divino, divine
divisa, foreign currency,
currency
divisa estándar,
standard currency
división, division
división continental,
continental divide
**división (de la su-
perficie terrestre),**
division (of Earth's
surface)
**división de Alemania
y Berlín,** division of
Germany and Berlin
**división de impues-
tos,** tax division
división de poderes,
separation of powers
división de zonas,
zoning
**división del subconti-
nente,** division of the
subcontinent
división del trabajo,
division of labor
**división sexual del
trabajo,** sexual divi-
sion of labor
divisoria continental,
continental divide
divorcio, divorce
Djenné, Jenne
Djenné-Djeno, Jenne-jeno
doble moral,
double standard
Doce Tablas, Twelve Tables
doctrina, doctrine
**doctrina de la anu-
lación,** nullification
doctrine
doctrina de la incor-

poración, incorpora-
tion doctrine
doctrina económica,
economic doctrine
Doctrina Eisenhower,
Eisenhower Doctrine
Doctrina Monroe,
Monroe Doctrine
Doctrina Truman,
Truman Doctrine
doctrinal, doctrinal
documentación,
documentation
documental, documentary
documento, document
documento anexo,
enclosure
documento histórico,
historical document
**documentos
primarios,** primary
documents
dogo (dux), doge
dólar, dollar
domesticación,
domestication
**domesticación ani-
mal,** animal domesti-
cation
**domesticación de
plantas alimenticias,**
food plant domestica-
tion
domesticado,
domesticated
doméstico, domestic
dominación, domination
**dominación soviéti-
ca,** Soviet domination
**dominación tempo-
ral,** temporary domi-
nance
dominar, dominate

domingo (cristianos), sabbath

Domingo Sangriento, Bloody Sunday

dominio, dominion

dominio colonial, colonial rule

Dominio de Nueva Inglaterra, dominion of New England

dominio económico, economic dominance

donación, endowment

donación caritativa, charitable giving

donaciones globales, block grants

Dos tratados sobre el gobierno civil, Two Treatises on Government

dosel, canopy

dotación, endowment

dotado, endowed

dotar, endow

dote, dowry, bride price

dragar, dredge

drama, drama

dramatización, dramatization

dramatizar, dramatize

dudoso, moot

duna, dune

dunas de arena, sand dunes

duque, duke, jarl

E Pluribus Unum, E Pluribus Unum

EC (Era Común), C.E.

ecología, ecology

ecología cultural, cultural ecology

ecología de población, population ecology

ecología urbana, urban ecology

ecológico, ecological

economía, economics, economy

economía agrícola, agricultural economy

economía capitalista, capitalist economy

economía capitalista emergente, emerging capitalist economy

economía de colapso político, political collapse economy

economía de consumo de masas, mass consumer economy

economía de cultivos comerciales, cash crop economy

economía de goteo, trickle down economics

economía de la Cuenca del Pacífico,

Pacific Rim economy
economía de la información, information economics, information economy
economía de mercado, market economy
economía de mercado libre, free market economy
economía de mercado socialista, socialist market economy
economía de oferta, supply-side economics
economía de planificación, command economy
economía de producción de bienes, goods producing economy
economía de servicios, service economy
economía de subsistencia, subsistence economy
economía del trueque, barter economy
economía dirigida o planificada, command economic system
economía doméstica, domestic economy
economía global, global economy
economía industrial, industrial economy
economía informal, informal economy
economía institucional, institutional economics

economía internacional, international economy
economía keynesiana, Keynesian economics
economía minera, mining economy
economía mixta, mixed economy
economía moral, moral economy
economía mundial, world economy
economía nacional, national economy
economía oculta, hidden economy
economía primitiva, primitive economy
economía subterránea, underground economy, hidden economy
economía tradicional, traditional economy
economías de extracción, extractive economies
económico, economic
economista, economist
ecosistema, ecosystem
ecosistema costero, coastal ecosystem
ecosistema de lago, lake ecosystem
ecosistema de los Grandes Lagos, Great Lakes ecosystem
ecosistema marino, ocean ecosystem
ecuador, equator

edad, age
    Edad de Bronce, Bronze Age
    Edad de Hielo, Ice Age
    Edad de la Razón, Age of Reason
    Edad de Oro, Golden Age
    Edad Media, Middle Ages
    edad nuclear, nuclear age
    Edad Preindustrial, Preindustrial Age
edición, edition
    edición pirata, bootlegging
edificio, building
    edificios municipales, civic centers
editor, publisher
editorial, editorial, publishing house
educación, education
    educación bilingüe, bilingual education
    educación cívica, civics
    educación obligatoria, compulsory education
    educación pública, public education
    educación secundaria, secondary education
efecto, effect
    efecto colateral, side effect
    efecto de amplificación, bandwagon
    efecto de arrastre, bandwagon
    efecto Dust Bowl de las Grandes Llanuras, Great Plains Dust Bowl
    efecto invernadero, greenhouse effect
    efecto secundario, side effect
    efectos externos, externalities
efectos comerciales, commercial paper
eficacia, efficacy
    eficacia civil, civic efficacy
    eficacia política, political efficacy
Egipto, Egypt
(el) ego, ego
eje, axis
ejecución de hipoteca, foreclosure
ejecutivo, executive
ejemplo, lead
Ejército confederado, Confederate Army
 Ejército Continental, Continental Army
Ejército de la Unión, Union Army
ejército de reserva, reserve army
Ejército Republicano Irlandés, Irish Republican Army (IRA)
Ejército Rojo, Red Army
elaboración, elaboration
elaborar, elaborate
elasticidad, elasticity
elección, election
    elección de revocación, recall election

elección directa, direct election
elección directa de los senadores, direct election of senators
elección económica, economic choice
elección estatal, state election
elección general, general election
elección indirecta, indirect election
elección individual, individual choice
elección local, local election
elección preliminar comprensiva, blanket primary
elección presiden-cial, presidential election
elección primaria, primary election
elección primaria abierta, open primary
elección primaria cerrada, closed primary
elección primaria directa, direct primary
elecciones parlamen-tarias, congressional election
elecciones primarias, primaries
elecciones primaras para los blancos, white primaries
electo, elect

elector, constituent
electorado, electorate
electoral, electoral
electricidad, electricity
elegir, elect
elementos de mapa, map elements
elevación, elevation
élite, elite
élite burguesa, gentry elite
élite corporativa, corporate elite
élite del poder, power-elite
elitismo étnico, ethnic elitism
elocuente, fluent
emancipación, emancipation
emancipar, emancipate
embajador, ambassador
embalsamamiento, embalming
embalse, reservoir
embarcación, craft
embarcación nórdica, Norse long ship
embargo, embargo
embargo de armas, arms embargo
embargo de bienes muebles, embargo of personal property
embargo petrolero árabe, Arab oil embargo
embaucar, bluff
emigración, emigration
emigrante, emigrant
emigrar, emigrate
Emiratos Árabes Unidos, United Arab Emirates

emires, emirs
emisión atmosférica,
    airborne emission
empaquetado de carne,
    meat packing
empaquetamiento,
    court packing
empatía, empathy
emperador, emperor
    Emperador Aurang-
    zeb, Emperor
    Aurangzeb
    emperador Kangxi,
    Kangxi emperor
    emperador Qianlong,
    Qianlong emperor
empírico, empirical
empirismo, empiricism
empleado, employee
empleador, employer
empleo, employment
    empleo friccional,
    frictional employment
emprendedor,
    entrepreneurial
emprendimiento eco-
nómico, economic
    venture
empresa,
    business firm, firm
    empresa con perso-
    nal sindicalizado y
    no sindicalizado,
    open shop
    empresa Crédit Mobi-
    lier, Credit Mobilier
    empresa de con-
    tenedores,
    container company
    empresa de servicio
    público,
    public service utility
    empresa grande,

large firm
    empresa individual,
    sole proprietorship
    empresa Pacific Rail-
    road, Pacific Railroad
    empresa U.S. Steel,
    United States Steel
    Corporation
    empresa virtual,
    virtual company
empresarial, corporate
empresario,
    entrepreneur
    empresarios de la
    nueva economía,
    new economy entre-
    preneurs
    empresarios morales,
    moral entrepreneurs
empresas municipales y
    comunales, township
    and village enterprises
    (TVEs)
encabezados de capítulo,
    chapter headings
encarcelamiento,
    imprisonment
encenagamiento, silting
enciclopedia, encyclopedia
enclave, enclave
    enclave étnico,
    ethnic enclave
encomendero holandés,
    patroon
encuentro, encounter
    Encuentro europeo,
    European Encounter
encuesta, survey
enemigos del Estado,
    enemies of the state
energética, energy
energía, energy
    energía geotérmica,

geothermal energy
energía nuclear, nuclear energy, nuclear power
energía solar, solar energy, solar power
enfermedad, disease
    enfermedad contagiosa, contagious disease
    enfermedad epidémica, epidemic disease
    enfermedad infecciosa, infectious disease
    enfermedades transmisibles, communicable diseases
enfoque empírico, empirical approach
enfoque estructuralista, structuralist approach
enfoque sistémico, systemic approach
enlace, linkage
enmendar, amend
enmienda, amendment
    enmienda del asesino, killer amendment
    enmienda sobre igualdad de derechos, Equal Rights Amendment
    enmiendas constitucionales, constitutional amendments
    enmienda de la Guerra Civil, Civil War amendment
    enmiendas de la Reconstrucción, Reconstruction amendments
ensayo, essay

ensenada, inlet, creek
ente semi-autónomo, quangos
entender, comprehend, understand
entidad humana, human entity
entidad política, political entity
entonces, then
entorno intercultural, cross-cultural setting
entrenamiento, training
    entretenimiento cultural, high culture entertainment
entrevistas de campo, field interviews
enumeración, enumeration
envase de carne, meat packing
envejecimiento de la población, population aging
enviado, envoy
epidemia, epidemic
epístola, epistle
época, era
    época antigua, ancient time
    época de la India antigua, Indian time
    época de los judíos, Jewish time
    Época de Terror, Reign of Terror
    época de transición, Age of Transition
    época del hambre, Starving Time
    Época Dorada, Gilded Age

época egipcia,
Egyptian time
época glacial,
Ice Age
época musulmana,
Muslim time
épocas históricas,
historical eras
epopeya, epic
   Epopeya de Gilga-mesh, Epic of Gilga-mesh
equidad, equity
   equidad social,
   social equity
equilibrio, equilibrium,
balance
   equilibrio de poder,
   balance of power
   equilibrio económico,
   economic equilibrium
   equilibrio presupues-tario, balanced budget
equinoccio, equinox
equipo de capital,
capital equipment
era, era, age
   Era de buenos senti-mientos, Era of Good Feelings
   Era de la informa-ción, Information Age
   Era de los Descu-brimientos,
   Age of Exploration, Age of Discovery
   Era del hombre común, Age of the Common Man
   Era del Jazz,
   Jazz Age
   era industrial,
   industrial age

   Era Jacksoniana,
   Jacksonian era
   Era Progresista,
   Progressive Era
Eric el Rojo, Eric the Red
erosión,
   erosion, weathering
   erosión del suelo,
   soil erosion
erosionar, erode
erradicación,
   eradication
error, fault
   error de muestreo,
   sampling error
   error de tipo I,
   Type 1 error
   error de tipo II,
   Type 2 error
   error muestral,
   sampling error
erudito, scholar
esbirros, henchmen
escala, scale
   escala de salarios,
   wage rate
   escala de un mapa,
   map scale
   escala espacial,
   spatial scale
   escala local,
   local scale
escalada, escalation
escándalo, scandal
   escándalo de Water-gate, Watergate Scandal
   Escándalo del Teapot Dome, Teapot Dome Scandal
   escándalo Irán-Con-tra, Iran-Contra affair
   escándalos políticos,

political scandals
Escandinavia,
Scandinavia
escapismo, escapism
escarpa, escarpment
escasez,
scarcity, shortage
escasez de recursos,
resource scarcity
escaso, scarce
escenario del conflicto,
theater of conflict
escenario físico,
physical setting
esclavitud, slavery
**esclavitud institu-
cional,** institutional
slavery
esclavizado, enslaved
esclavo, slave
esclavo fugitivo,
escaped slave
esclavo africano,
African slave
esclusa, lock
escocés, Scotch
escocés de Ulster,
Scots-Irish
Escocia, Scotland
escriba, scribe
escritos clásicos,
classical writings
escritura,
charter document,
scripture
escritura alfabética,
alphabetic writing
**escrutinio nominal mayo-
ritario,** single member
plurality
escudero, squire
Escudo canadiense,
Canadian Shield

escuela, school
escuela parroquial,
parochial school
escultor, sculptor
escultura, sculpture
esfera, sphere
**esfera de coprosperi-
dad de Asia Oriental,**
East Asian Co-Prospe-
rity Sphere
esfera de influencia,
sphere of influence
esfera privada,
private sphere
esferoide achatado,
oblate spheroid
esfuerzo del viaje,
travel effort
eslogan, slogan
**eslogan de prospe-
ridad del Partido
Republicano,**
full dinner pail
esmog, smog
espacial, spatial
espacio verde, greenway
España, Spain
esparcimiento, recreation
especia de la India,
Indian spice
especialización,
specialization
**especialización
del trabajo,** speciali-
zation of labor
**especialización eco-
nómica,** economic
specialization
**especialización
ocupacional,**
occupational speciali-
zation
especializarse, specialize

especies en peligro,
endangered species
especies vegetales,
plant species
especismo, speciesism
espectro político,
political spectrum
especulación, profiteering,
speculation
esperanza, hope
esperanza de vida,
life expectancy
espionaje, espionage
espionaje soviético,
Soviet espionage
espíritu del capitalismo,
spirit of capitalism
**espíritu del individua-
lismo,** spirit of indi-
vidualism
espíritu emprendedor,
entrepreneurial spirit
espíritu pionero,
pioneer spirit
esquimal, Inuit
esquirol, scab
estabilidad cultural,
cultural stability
estabilidad de precios,
price stability
estabilidad económica,
economic stability
establecerse, settle
establecido, established
establecimiento colonial,
colonial establishment
**establecimiento comer-
cial en una colonia,**
trading post
estación[1], station
**estación de bombe-
ros,** fire station
estación terminal,
railhead
estación[2], season
estadio deportivo,
sports stadium
estadística, statistics
**estadística inferen-
cial,** inferential statistics
**estadísticamente signi-
ficativo,** statistically
significant
estadístico[1], statistic
estadístico[2], statistical
estado, state
estado absoluto,
absolutist state
estado civil,
marital status
estado clave,
keystone state
estado comunista,
communist state
**estado corporativis-
ta,** corporatist state
estado de bienestar,
welfare state
estado de derecho,
law-based state, rule
of law
estado de hecho,
rule of men
**estado de la naturale-
za,** state of nature
estado de sitio,
state of seige
estado desarrollista,
developmental state
estado esclavista,
slave state
estado hegemónico,
hegemonic state
Estado inacabado,
unfinished state

Estado inconcluso, unfinished state
estado islámico, Islamic state
estado libre, free state
Estado mahdista, Mahdist state
estado papal, papal state
estado patrimonial, patrimonial state
estado rentista, rentier state
Estado satélite, satellite state
estado secular, secular state
estado soberano, sovereign state
estado totalitario, totalitarian state
Estado unitario, unitary government, unitary state
Estado-nación, nation-state
Estados Confederados de América, Confederate States of America
Estados de la Llanura, Plains States
estados del Ganges, Gangetic states
estados del norte, Northern states
estados fronterizos, border states
Estados Generales, Estates-General
Estados Generales franceses, French Estates-General

estados independientes, independent states
estados sureños, Southern states
Estados Unidos, United States
Estados Unidos de América, United States of America
estadounidense, American
estalinismo, Stalinism
estamento, estate
estándar, standard
estancamiento, stalemate
estancamiento de los salarios, stagnation of wages
estanflación, stagflation
Estatua de la Justicia, Statue of Justice
Estatua de la Libertad, Statue of Liberty
estatus, status
estatus social, social status
estatuto, charter document, law
estatuto del banco, bank recharter
este, east
Este de los Estados Unidos, eastern United States
estepa, steppe
estepas de Asia Central, Central Asian steppes
estereotipo, stereotype
estigma, stigma
estilo arquitectónico, architectural style
estilo de vida, lifestyle

estilo de vida agrícola, agricultural lifestyle
estilo del edificio, building style
estilos de los hogares, style of homes
estímulo, stimuli
estrategia, strategy
estrategia de guerra, war strategy
estrategia de reubicación, relocation strategy
estratégico, strategic
estratificación, stratification
estrecho, strait
estrecho de Malaca, Strait of Malacca
estrecho de Tacoma, Tacoma Strait
estribaciones, foothills
estructura bicameral del Congreso, bicameral structure of Congress
estructura de la población, population structure
estructura de mercado, market structure
estructura de oportunidades, opportunity structure
estructura de parentesco, kinship structure
estructura demográfica, demographic structure
estructura interna, internal structure
estructura social, social structure
estructura tributaria, tax structure
estructuras y funciones de la Corte Suprema, structures and functions of the Supreme Court
estudio de caso, case study
estudio de cohorte, panel study
estudio y experimentación con cohetes, rocketry
estudios autoinformados, self-report studies
estudios longitudinales, longitudinal studies
estudios organizacionales, organizational studies
etapa de vida, stage of life
ética empresarial, business ethics
ética judeocristiana, Judeo-Christian ethic
ética protestante del trabajo, Protestant work ethic
ética puritana del trabajo, Puritan work ethic
ética social, social ethics
Etiopía, Ethiopia
etnicidad, ethnicity
étnico, ethnic
etnocéntrico, ethnocentric
etnocentrismo, ethnocentrism
etnografía, ethnography
etnógrafo, ethnographer
eugenesia, eugenics
Eurafrasia, Afro-Eurasia
Eurasia, Eurasia
Eurasiáfrica, Afro-Eurasia
eurocéntrico, Eurocentric

Europa, Europe
   Europa Central,
   Central Europe
   Europa cristiana,
   Christian Europe
   Europa del Este,
   Eastern Europe
   Europa del Sur,
   Southern Europe
   Europa medieval,
   Medieval Europe
   Europa Occidental,
   Western Europe
europeo, European
eutrofización,
   eutrophication
evaluación, evaluation
evaluar, evaluate
evangelio, gospel
   evangelio de la rique-
   za, gospel of wealth
   evangelio social,
   social gospel
evangelismo, evangelism
   evangelismo
   religioso, religious
   evangelism
evangelizar, evangelize
evaporación, evaporation
evasión, escapism
evasores al reclutamien-
to, draft evaders
eventos históricos,
   historical develop-
   ments
evidencia, evidence
   evidencia arqueoló-
   gica, archaeological
   evidence
   evidencia biológica,
   biological evidence
   evidencia empírica,
   empirical evidence

   evidencia textual,
   textual evidence
evolución, evolution
evolucionar, evolve
evolucionario,
   evolutionary
evolucionista, evolutionary
evolutivo, evolutionary
exactitud, accuracy
exacto, accurate
examen de alfabetismo,
   literacy test
examinación del servicio
   civil, civil service
   examination
excavaciones, excavations
excavar, excavate
exceso de población,
   overpopulation
exceso de producción,
   overproduction
excedente económico
   economic surplus
excedente, surplus
excomulgación,
   excommunication
excomulgar,
   excommunicate
excrex, bride price
exención de impuestos,
   tax exemption
exento, enfranchised
exilio, exile
existencialismo,
   Existentialism
éxodo, exodus
   éxodo rural,
   rural exodus, rural-to-
   urban migration
exoneración, acquittal
expansión, expansion
   expansión agrícola,
   agricultural expansion

expansión de Occidente, western expansion

expansión exagerada, overexpansion

expansión hacia el oeste, westward expansion

expansión industrial, industrial expansion

expansión territorial, territorial expansion

expansionismo, expansionism

expatriados, expatriates, displaced persons

expectativas de grupo, group expectations

expedición, expedition

expediciones marítimas de Zheng He, Zheng He maritime expeditions

expedientes, briefs

experiencia de conversión, conversion experience

experiencia de vida, life experience

experiencia directa, direct experience

experiencia laboral, work experience

experiencia previa, prior experience

experimental, experimental

experimentar, experiment

experimento, experiment

explicación, explanation, clarification

explicación cultural, cultural explanation

explicación estructural, structural explanation

explicación funcionalista, functionalist explanation

explicar, explain, clarify

explícito, explicit

exploración, exploration

exploración espacial, space exploration

exploración europea, European Exploration

explorador, explorer, frontiersman

explorador europeo, European explorer

explosión demográfica, population explosion

explosión de natalidad, baby boom

explosión urbana, urban sprawl

explotación, exploitation

explotación a cielo abierto, strip mining

explotación agrícola de carácter familiar, family farm

explotación colectiva, collective farm

explotación del artista, artist exploitation

explotación infantil, child labor

exportación neta, net export

exportadores, exporters

exportar, export

expositor de corrupción, muckraker

expresado, expressed

expresión artística,

artistic expression
expresionismo, Expressionism
expresionismo abstracto, Abstract Expressionism
expropiación, eminent domain, expropriation
expropiar, expropriate
expulsión, expulsion
extensión agraria, agricultural extension
exterminación, extermination
exterminar, exterminate
externalidad, externality
externalidad negativa, negative externality
externalidad positiva, positive
extinción, extinction
extinción de incendios, firefighting
extinto, extinct
extradición, extradition
extracción de madera, timber extraction
extracción de recursos naturales, natural resource extraction
extraditar, extradite
extranjero, alien
extranjero ilegal, illegal alien
extraterritorialidad, extraterritoriality

fábrica, factory
fábrica de papel, paper factory
fábrica opresora, sweatshop
fábula, fable
facción, faction
fácil acceso, accessibility
factor geográfico, geographic factor
factor social, social factor
factores contemporáneos, contemporary factors
factores de atracción, pull factors
factores de empuje, push factors
factores de producción, factors of production
factores económicos, economic factors
faena, chore
falacia del hombre de paja, straw man
falange, phalanx
falla, fault line
falsa política de integración de minorías, token integration
falta, fault
falta de incentivos, disincentive
familia, family
familia estadounidense tradicional, traditional American family

familia extensa, extended family
familia matrilineal, matrilineal family
familia monoparental, single household
familia nuclear, nuclear family
familia real, royal family
familiar, relative
fanático, zealot
fanatismo, bigotry
Faraón, Pharaoh
fasces, fasces
fascismo, fascism
fascista, fascist
fauna, fauna
fauna silvestre, wildlife
fe, faith
fecha, date
fecha de finalización, ending date
federación, federation
Federación Estadounidense del Trabajo, American Federation of Labor (AFL)
federal, federal
federalismo, federalism
federalismo asimétrico, asymmetrical federalism
federalismo cooperativo, cooperative federalism
federalismo dual, dual federalism
federalista, Federalist
felah, fellahin
Felices años Veinte, Roaring Twenties
feminismo, feminism
feminismo liberal, liberal feminism
Fenicia, Phoenicia
fenicios, Phoenicians
fenómenos meteorológicos, weather phenomena
feria, fair
feria comercial, trade fair
feria de muestras, trade fair
Fernando de Magallanes, Ferdinand Magellan
ferrocarril, railroad
ferrocarril subterráneo, Underground Railroad
ferrocarril transcontinental, transcontinental railroad
fértil, fertile
fertilidad del suelo, soil fertility
fertilización, fertilization
fertilización in vitro, in vitro fertilization
fertilizante, fertilizer
fertilizante químico, chemical fertilizer
festival, festival
feudalismo, feudalism
feudo, fief, fiefdom, manor
fiabilidad, reliability
fiable, reliable
fianza, bail
ficción histórica, historical fiction
fiduciario, trustee
fiebre del oro, gold rush
Fiebre del oro de California, California

Gold Rush
fiesta, holiday
    fiesta de la cosecha,
harvest festival
    fiesta nacional,
national holiday
    fiesta religiosa,
religious holiday
    **fiestas conmemora-
tivas,** commemorative
holidays
figura histórica,
historical figure
figura popular,
popular figure
**figuras en terracota de
Nok,** Nok terra cotta
figure
Filadelfia, philadelphia
filantropía, philanthropy
filántropo, philanthropist
filibusterismo, filibustering, filibuster
Filipinas, Philippines
filosofía, philosophy
    **filosofía de los dere-
chos naturales,** natu-
ral rights philosophy
    filosofía política,
political philosophy
    filosofía social,
social philosophy
filosófico, philosophical
filósofo, philosopher
    filósofo griego,
Greek philosopher
financiación, funding
financiamiento,
financing, funding
financiero, financial
finanzas, finance
Finlandia, Finland
fiordo, fjord

firma, signature
fiscal, fiscal
físico(a), physical
fisiografía, physiography
fisiográfico, physiographic
flaquezas, weaknesses
flora, flora
flota, armada
**fluctuación de tempe-
ratura,** temperature
fluctuation
fluido, fluent
flujo de dirección,
directional flow
flujo de energía,
flow of energy
flujo de mercancías,
commodity flow
folklore, folklore
**Fondo de las Naciones
Unidas para la Infan-
cia (UNICEF),**
United Nations
Children's Fund
(UNICEF)
**Fondo Monetario Interna-
cional (FMI),**
International Monetary
Fund (IMF)
fondos, funds, funding
    fondos categóricos,
categorical grants
    **fondos de inversión
mobiliaria,**
mutual funds
forajido, outlaw
**forma de asentamiento
concentrado,**
concentrated settle-
ment form
forma de vida, life form
formación social,
social formation

formaciones, formations
formar una unión más perfecta, form a more perfect union
formas alternativas de gobierno, alternate forms of government
foro público, public forum
fortificación, fortification
forzoso, enforced
fosfato, phosphate
fotografía, photograph, photography
fotografía aérea, aerial photograph
fracción de clase, class fraction
fragata, frigate
fraile, friar
francés, French
Francia, France
franjas y estrellas, stars and stripes
fraternidad, fraternity, fraternal organization
fratricidio, fratricide
fraude, fraud
fraude al consumidor, consumer fraud
Fredericksburgo, Fredericksburg
frente civil, home front
frente interno, home front
Frente Nacional de Liberación de Vietnam, National Liberation Front (NLF)
fricción, friction
fricción de la distancia, friction of distance
frontera, border, boundary, frontier
frontera de malezas, crabgrass frontier
frontera geográfica, geographic border
frontera política, political border
fronteras estatales, state boundaries
fronteras nacionales, national boundaries
fronteras naturales, natural boundaries
fuego griego, Greek fire
fuente, source
fuente de energía, energy source
fuente primaria, primary source
fuentes de energía alternativa, alternative energy source
fuerte, fort
Fuerte Sumter, Fort Sumter
fuerza, force
fuerza de voluntarios, volunteer force
fuerza militar, military force
fuerzas armadas, armed forces
Fuerzas armadas de los Estados Unidos, Armed Forces of the United States
fuerzas encargadas de mantener la paz, peacekeeper
Fuerzas Expedicionarias Estadounidenses, American

Expeditionary Force
fuerzas navales, naval forces
fugitivo, fugitive
función del gobierno, purpose of government
funcionalismo estructural, structural functionalism
funcionario, official
    funcionario público, government employee, public servant
    funcionarios del gobierno local, local government officials
    funcionarios designados, appointed officials
    funcionarios electos, elected officials
funciones gubernamentales, governmental functions
La Fundación de la Herencia, The Haritage Foundation
Fundación de los Oprimidos, Foundation of the Oppressed
fundación de Roma, founding of Rome
fundadores, founders
fundamental, fundamental
fundamentalismo, fundamentalism
    fundamentalismo islámico, Islamic fundamentalism
    fundamentalismo religioso, religious fundamentalism
fundamentalista, fundamentalist
    fundamentalistas islámicos, Islamic fundamentalists
fundamentos, grounds
fundición, smelting
fusión cultural, cultural fusion
fusión de poderes, fusion of powers
fusión vertical, vertical merger
futurista, futurist
futuro, future

G

gabarra, barge
gabinete, cabinet
    gabinete presidencial, president's cabinet
galeón, galleon
Gales, Wales
Galileo, Galileo
gamuza, deerskin
ganadería, cattle raising, livestock, ranching
ganado bovino lechero, dairy cattle
ganador sopresa, dark horse
ganancia, earning, profit
    ganancia económica, economic gain, financial gain
ganar, earn
garantía, warranty, guarantee

garantía constitucional, constitutional guarantee

gases de efecto invernadero, greenhouse gases

gasto, expenditure, expenses, spending

gasto de inversión privada, private investment spending

gasto en defensa nacional, national defense spending

gasto federal, federal spending

gasto fijo, fixed expense

gasto público, national government spending, government spending

gastos corporativos, corporate spending

gastos deficitarios, deficit spending

gastos del Estado, government spending

gastos en bienes de consumo, consumer spending

gastos en defensa, defense spending

gastos médicos, medical expenditure

gastos variables, variable expenses

gauchos, gauchos

géiser, geyser

generación, generation

generación de los baby boomers, baby boom generation

Generación perdida, Lost Generation

Generación X, Generation X

género, gender

Gengis Kan, Genghis Khan

genocidio, genocide

genocidio nazi, Nazi genocide

Génova, Genoa

geografía, geography

geografía cultural, cultural geography

geografía económica, economic geography

geografía física, physical geography

geografía humana, human geography

geografía política, political geography

geográfico(a), geographic

geógrafo, geographer

geología, geology

geólogo, geologist

geomorfología, geomorphology

geopolítica, geopolitics

geopolítica mundial, world geopolitics

Gerónimo, Geronimo

gestión de conflictos, conflict management

gestión de recursos, resource management

gestión de riesgos, risk management

gestión participativa, participatory management

ghetto, ghetto

glaciar, glacier

glasnost, glasnost

global, global

globalismo, globalism

globalización, globalization
globalizar, globalize
globo, globe
gobernador, governor
  gobernadores coloniales, colonial governors
(del/para) gobernador, gubernatorial
gobernante secular, secular ruler
gobernanza, governance
gobernar, govern
gobierno, government, rule
  gobierno burocrático, bureaucratic government
  gobierno central, central government
  gobierno centralizado, centralized government
  gobierno colonial, colonial government
  gobierno confederado, confederate government
  gobierno constitucional, constitutional government
  gobierno de coalición, coalition government
  gobierno de gabinete, cabinet government
  gobierno de la mayoría, majority rule
  gobierno de Lyndon B. Johnson, Lyndon B. Johnson administration
  gobierno de reforma, reform government

gobierno democrático, democratic government
gobierno dividido, divided government
gobierno estable, stable government
gobierno estatal, state government
gobierno fascista, fascist government
gobierno federal, federal government
gobierno ilimitado, unlimited government
gobierno informal, informal government
gobierno limitado, limited government
gobierno local, local government
gobierno mixto, mixed constitution
gobierno oligárquico, oligarchical government
gobierno parlamentario, parliamentary government
gobierno participativo, participatory government
gobierno por el pueblo, rule by the people
gobierno provisional, provisional government
gobierno representativo, representative government
gobierno republicano, republican government

gobierno revolucionario

**gobierno revolucio-
nario**, revolutionary
government
gobierno secular,
secular government
gobierno teocrático,
theocratic government
gobierno títere,
puppet government
gobierno tribal,
tribal government
**gobierno tribal nativo
americano,** American
tribal government
golfo, gulf
Golfo de México,
Gulf of Mexico
Golfo Pérsico,
Persian Gulf
golpe de Estado,
coup d'état
golpe maestro, coup
gótico, gothic
Graco, Gracchi
gradación, gradation
gráfico, graph, chart
gráfico circular,
circle graph
gráfico de barras,
bar graph
gráfico de pastel,
pie graph
gráfico lineal,
line graph
gráfico temático,
thematic graph
gran, grand, great
Gran Alianza,
Grand Alliance
**Gran Barrera de Co-
ral,** Great Barrier Reef
Gran Bretaña,
Great Britain

Gran Canal de China,
Great Canal of China
**Gran Cisma de Occi-
dente,** Great Western
Schism
Gran Compromiso,
Great Compromise
**Gran Cuenca o
Great Basin,**
Great Basin
Gran Depresión,
Great Depression
**Gran Desierto
Americano,**
Great American Desert
Gran Despertar,
Great Awakening
**Gran Ducado de Mos-
cú,** Duchy of Moscow
**Gran esfera de co-
prosperidad de Asia
Oriental,** Greater East
Asia Co-Prosperity
Sphere
Gran Guerra,
Great War
**gran hambruna
irlandesa,**
Irish potato famine
**Gran incendio de
Chicago,**
Great Chicago Fire
gran jurado,
grand jury
Gran Kan Möngke,
Great Khan Mongke
Gran Kan Ogodei,
Great Khan Ogodei
Gran migración,
Great Migration
gran negocio,
big business
Gran Plaga,

Great Plague
Gran Purga,
Great Purge
**Gran Revolución
Cultural Proletaria,**
Great Proletarian Cultural Revolution
Gran Salto Adelante,
Great Leap Forward
gran sello, great seal
Gran Sociedad,
Great Society
**Gran Viejo Partido
(GOP),** Grand Old Party, GOP
Grandes Lagos,
Great Lakes
grandes potencias europeas, Great Powers in Europe
Grandes Llanuras,
Great Plains
granos, grains
granizada, hailstorm
granja, farm
    granja de subsistencia, subsistence farm
    granja familiar,
    homestead
granjero, farmer
    granjero arrendatario, tenant farmer
granujas, scalawags
gravamen, taxation, levy
Grecia, Greece
gremio, craft union, guild, trade union
griego(a), Greek
grieta, crevasse
Groenlandia, Greenland
grupo, group
    grupo caritativo,
    charitable group

grupo cultural,
cultural group, culture group
grupo de interés,
interest group
grupo de interés especial, special interest group
grupo de oposición,
opposition group
grupo de parentesco,
kinship group
grupo de presión,
lobby
grupo de servicio,
service group
**Grupo del Banco
Mundial,**
World Bank Group
grupo demográfico, demographic clustering
grupo étnico,
ethnic group
grupo focal de discusión, focus group
grupo infrarrepresentado, underrepresented group
grupo khoisánido,
Khoisan group
grupo minoritario,
minority group
grupo social,
social group
grupo paritario,
peer group
grupo primario,
primary group
grupo racial,
racial group
grupo religioso,
religious group

grupo secundario, secondary group

grupo separatista, Separatist

grupo socioeconómico, socioeconomic group

grupos derechistas, right-wing groups

grupos indígenas, indigenous groups

grupos paramilitares, vigilantism

Guardia Roja, Red Guard

guerra, war

Guerra Anglo-Bóer en Sudáfrica, South African (Anglo-Boer) War

guerra civil, Civil War

Guerra Civil española, Spanish Civil War

Guerra Civil inglesa, English civil war

Guerra contra la pobreza, War on Poverty

guerra convencional, conventional warfare

Guerra de 1812, War of 1812

Guerra de Black Hawk (halcón negro), Black Hawk War

guerra de caballería, cavalry warfare

Guerra de Corea, Korean War

Guerra de Crimea, Crimean War

guerra de desgaste, war of attrition

guerra de guerrillas, guerilla warfare

Guerra de Independencia de Texas, Texas War for Independence

Guerra de los Bóeres, Boer War

Guerra de los Cien Años, Hundred Years' War

Guerra de los Seis Días, Six Day War

Guerra de los Siete Años, Seven Years' War

Guerra de los Treinta Años, Thirty Years' War

guerra de precios, price war

guerra de trincheras, trench warfare

Guerra de Troya, Trojan war

Guerra de Vietnam, Vietnam War

Guerra del Golfo Pérsico, Persian Gulf War

Guerra del Opio, Opium War

Guerra del Rey Felipe, King Phillip's War

Guerra Franco-India, French and Indian War

Guerra Franco-Prusiana, Franco-Prussian War

Guerra Fría, Cold War

Guerra Hispano-Estadounidense, Spanish-American War

Guerra México–Esta-

dos Unidos, Mexican War, Mexican-American War
guerra mundial, world war
guerra naval, naval warfare
guerra nazi contra los judíos, Nazi war against the Jews
guerra relámpago, blitzkrieg
Guerra Revolucionaria, Revolutionary War
Guerra Sino-Japonesa, Sino-Japanese War
guerra submarina ilimitada, unrestricted submarine warfare
guerra total, total war
Guerras Indígenas, Indian Wars
Guerras Napoleónicas, Napoleon's invasions
Guerras Púnicas, Punic Wars
guerrillero, guerilla soldier
Guillermo el Conquistador, William the Conqueror
gustar, like
gustos de los consumidores, consumer tastes

hábeas corpus, habeas corpus
habilidad innata, innate ability
habilidades, skills
    habilidades cívicas, civic skills
    habilidades geográficas, geographic skills
    habilidades para la participación, participatory skills
habitación, habitation
habitantes, inhabitants
hábitat, habitat
hábito, practice
habladurías, hearsay
hace mucho tiempo, long ago
hacendado, homesteader, landowner
hacer campaña, campaigning
hacer publicidad, advertise
hacer propaganda, advertise
hacienda, hacienda, ranch
hadiz, Hadith
haiku, haiku
Haití, Haiti
halcones de guerra, War Hawks
hambre, hunger, starvation
    hambre masiva, mass starvation
hambruna, famine, mass starvation
harmatán, harmattan
Hawai, Hawaii
Haya, Hague
hebreo, Hebrew
hecho, fact
    hecho cumplir, enforced
    hecho respetar, enforced

hecho social,
social fact
hechos históricos,
historical facts
hegemonía, hegemony
hegemonía de Occidente, Western
hegemony
hegemonía ideológica, ideological
hegemony
hegemónico, hegemonic
hégira, Hegira (Hijrah)
helenismo, Hellenism
helenístico, Hellenistic
hemisferio, hemisphere
Hemisferio Occidental, Western
Hemisphere
Hemisferio Oriental,
Eastern Hemisphere
henequén, sisal
heno, hay
heredabilidad, heritability
heredad, manor
heredar, inherit
hereje, heretic
herejía, heresy
herencia, heredity, heritage
herencia africana,
African heritage
herencia cultural,
cultural heritage
herencia étnica,
ethnic heritage
herético, heretic
hermanas Grimké,
Grimke sisters
Hermano conejo,
Brer Rabbit
Hernán Cortés,
Hernando Cortes
Heródoto, Herodotus

héroe, hero
héroe popular regional, regional folk hero
heroína, heroine
heroísmo, heroism
herramientas, tools
herramientas de navegación,
navigational tools
herramientas geográficas, geographic tools
herramientas de hierro, iron tools
herrero, blacksmith
hezbolá, hezbollahs
hibridación de cultivos,
hybridization of crops
hidrología, hydrology
hidrósfera, hydrosphere
hierro, iron
Hijas de la Libertad,
Daughters of Liberty
Hijos de la Libertad,
Sons of Liberty
hijos de las flores,
flower children,
hippies
hiladora con usos múltiples, spinning jenny
himno, hymn, anthem
himno nacional,
national anthem
hindúes, Hindus
hinduismo, Hinduism
hipoteca, mortgage
hipótesis, hypothesis
hipótesis nula,
null hypothesis
hispanoamericano, Hispanic American, Latino
hippies, hippies, flower
children
historia, history, story

historia antigua,
ancient history
historia cultural,
cultural history
historia del descubri-
miento del petróleo,
history of oil discovery
historia escrita,
recorded history
historia familiar,
family history
historia global,
global history
historia local,
local history
historia mundial,
world history
historia natural,
natural history
historia oral,
oral history
historia personal,
personal history
historias del pasado,
stories from the past
historiador, historian
histórico, historical
hititas, Hittite people
Hodinonhsioni (pueblo
iroqués), Haudeno-
saunee (Iroquois)
hogar, home, household
hogar de asentamien-
to transitorio,
Settlement House
Holanda, Holland
holandés, Dutch
Holocausto, Holocaust
holocausto nazi,
Nazi holocaust
hombre común,
common man
homenaje, tribute

homínido, hominid
homofobia, homophobia
homogeneidad,
homogeneity
homogéneo, homogenous
honestidad, honesty
honesto, honest
hongos, fungi, mushrooms
honor, honor
hora, time
horario, time
Horda de Oro,
Golden Horde
hospicio, asylum
hostilidad, hostility
hoy, today
huelga, strike
huelga de brazos caí-
dos, sit-down strikes
huelga en las minas
de carbón, coal mine
strike
huelga salvaje,
wildcat strike
huertas, truck farms
hueso oracular,
oracle bone
humanismo,
humanism
humanismo italiano,
Italian humanism
humanismo renacen-
tista, Renaissance
humanism
humanistas, humanists
humanitario,
humanitarian
humano, human
humedad, humidity
humedad relativa,
relative humidity
Hungría, Hungary
huracán, hurricane

husos horarios, time zone
hutu, Hutus

I

Ibn Batuta, Ibn Battuta
iceberg, iceberg
icónico, iconic
icono, icon
idea, idea
    idea preconcebida,
    prepossession
    idea principal,
    main idea
ideal, ideal
    ideal constitucional,
    constitutional ideal
    ideal de rehabili-
    tación, rehabilitative
    ideal
    ideales del amor cor-
    tés, courtly ideals
    ideales democráticos,
    democratic ideals
idealismo, idealism
idealista, idealist
identidad, identity
    identidad cultural,
    cultural identity
    identidad cultural
    tradicional,
    traditional cultural
    identity
    identidad de grupo,
    group identity
    identidad estado-
    unidense,
    American identity
    identidad étnica,
    ethnic identity

    identidad nacional,
    national identity
    identidad racial,
    racial identity
    identidad social,
    social identity
    identidad tribal,
    tribal identity
identificación,
    identification
identificación partidaria,
    party identification
identificar, identify
ideográfico, ideographic
ideogramas, ideographs
ideología, ideology
    ideología abolicio-
    nista, antislavery
    ideology
    ideología de una cla-
    se, one class ideology
    ideología leninista,
    Lenin's ideology
    ideología nazi,
    Nazi ideology
    ideología política,
    political ideology
    ideología secular,
    secular ideology
idoneidad del objetivo,
    target suitability
iglesia, church
    iglesia bizantina,
    Byzantine church
    Iglesia católica,
    Catholic Church
    Iglesia Católica
    Romana, Roman
    Catholic Church
    Iglesia de Inglaterra,
    Church of England
    Iglesia de Jesucristo
    de los Santos de los

Últimos Días, Church of Jesus Christ of Latter-Day Saints

iglesia de Laibela, Lalibela church

iglesia kalash, Kalash church

Iglesia latina católica, Latin Catholic church

Iglesia mormona, Mormon Church

iglesia oficial, established church

Iglesia Ortodoxa Cristiana, Orthodox Christian Church

Iglesia Ortodoxa Oriental, Eastern Orthodox

iglesias etíopes talladas en piedra, Ethiopian rock churches

igual, same, peer

igualdad, equality

igualdad de condiciones, equality of condition

igualdad de derechos, equal rights

igualdad de derechos bajo la ley, equal rights under the law

igualdad de oportunidades, equal opportunity, equality of opportunity

igualdad de salarios, pay equity

igualitario, egalitarian

Ilíada, Iliad

Ilustración, Age of Enlightenment, Enlightenment

imagen de Camelot, Camelot image

imagen de satélite, satellite image

imagen pública, public image

imagen satelital, satellite image

imágenes de satélite, satellite imagery

imágenes producidas por satélites, satellite-produced images

imán, imam

impacto, impact

impacto del asentamiento, settlement impact

impacto global, global impact

impacto humano, human impact

impacto social, social impact

imparcial, impartial

imparcialidad, impartiality

impasse, deadlock

imperial, imperial

imperialismo, imperialism

imperialismo británico, British imperialism

imperialismo cultural, cultural imperialism

imperialismo europeo, European imperialism

imperio, empire

Imperio alemán, German Empire

Imperio Antiguo de Egipto, Old Kingdom

Imperio asirio, Assyrian Empire

Imperio Austro-Húngaro, Austro-Hungarian empire

Imperio azteca, Aztec Empire

Imperio babilónico, Babylonian Empire

Imperio bizantino, Byzantine Empire

Imperio británico, British Empire

Imperio carolingio, Carolingian Empire

Imperio celeste, celestial empire

Imperio de los Habsburgo, Hapsburg Empire

Imperio de Mali, Mali Empire

Imperio del mal, evil empire

Imperio euroasiático, Eurasian empire

Imperio franco, Frankish Empire

Imperio gaznávida, Ghaznavid Empire

Imperio Gupta, Gupta Empire

Imperio Han, Han Empire

Imperio ibérico, Iberian Empire

Imperio inca, Incan Empire

Imperio manchú, Manchu Empire

Imperio maurya, Maurya empire

imperio mediterráneo, Mediterranean Empire

Imperio mogol, imperial Mughal, Mughal Empire

imperio mundial, world empire

Imperio musulmán, Muslim Empire

Imperio Nuevo, New Kingdom

Imperio otomano, Ottoman Empire

Imperio persa, Persian Empire

Imperio romano, Roman Empire

Imperio Romano de Occidente, Western Roman Empire

Imperio Romano de Oriente, Eastern Roman Empire

Imperio safávida, Safavid Empire

Imperio sasánida, Sassanid Empire

Imperio selyúcida, Seljuk Empire

Imperio Songay, Songhai Empire

Imperio Tang, Tang Empire

Imperio turco, Turkic Empire

Imperio zulú, Zulu empire

Imperios comerciales de África, African trading kingdoms

Imperios de la India, Indian Empires
implementación de políticas, policy implementation
importación, import
importadores, importers
importante, important
importar, import
importe del servicio, service charge
imprenta, printing press
impresión xilográfica, block printing
Impresionismo, Impressionism
impresionista, Impressionist
imprimir, print
impuesto, duty, tax, levy
    impuesto al consumo, excise tax
    impuesto de capitación, poll tax
    impuesto de importación, import duty
    impuesto de seguridad social, Social Security tax
    impuesto directo, direct tax
    impuesto estatal, state tax
    impuesto federal, federal tax
    impuesto indirecto, indirect tax
    impuesto lineal, flat tax
    impuesto predial, property tax
    impuesto progresivo, graduated income tax,

progressive tax
    impuesto progresivo sobre la renta, progressive income tax
    impuesto proporcional, proportional tax
    impuesto regresivo, regressive tax
    impuesto sobre donaciones, gift tax
    impuesto sobre la herencia, estate tax
    impuesto sobre la propiedad inmobiliaria, property tax
    impuesto sobre la renta, income tax
    impuesto sobre las plusvalías, capital gains tax
    impuesto sobre las ventas, sales tax
    impuesto sobre nómina, payroll tax
    impuesto sobre los salarios, payroll tax
    impuestos estatales sobre la venta, state sales tax
    impuestos externos, external taxes
    impuestos internos, internal taxes
    impuestos sin representación, taxation without representation
    impuestos sobre gasolina, gasoline taxes
inalienable, inalienable
inanición, starvation
incas, Incas
incendiario, incendiary

incendio forestal,
    forest fire
incentivo, incentive
    incentivo económico,
    economic incentive
    incentivo negativo,
    negative incentive
    incentivo positivo,
    positive incentive
incesto, incest
incondicional, stalwart
incorporación,
        incorporation
    **incorporación
    selectiva,** selective
    incorporation
incorporar, incorporate
**incremento de la tem-
    peratura mundial,**
        world temperature
        increase
incremento de precios,
        price increase
incumplimiento de pago,
        default on a loan
indemnizacion, reparation
    **indemnización a los
    trabajadores,**
        workers' compensation
indemnizar, indemnify
independencia,
        independence
    **Independencia de los
    Estados Unidos,**
        American Revolution
    **independencia de los
    tribunales,**
        independent judiciary
    **Independencia de
    Panamá,**
        Panama Revolution
India, India
    India unida,

        unified India
    **Indias Occidentales
    británicas,**
        British West Indies
Indias Orientales,
        East Indies
    **Indias Orientales
    Británicas,**
        British East India
**Indias Occidentales
    Holandesas,**
        Dutch West Indies
indicador económico,
        economic indicator
índice, index, rate
    **índice de alfabetiza-
    ción,** literacy rate
    índice de fertilidad,
        fertility rate
    **Índice de precios al
    consumidor,** Consu-
        mer Price Index (CPI)
    **índice Dow Jones
    (DOW),** Dow Jones
        Industrial Average
        (DOW)
    índice geográfico,
        gazetteer, geographic
        index
indiferencia saludable,
        salutary neglect
indígena, aboriginal,
        indigenous
indio, Indian
indirecto, indirect
individual, individual
individualismo,
        individualism
    **Individualismo
    tosco,** Rugged Indivi-
        dualism
individualista[1],
        individualist

individualista², individualistic
individuo, individual
Indonesia, Indonesia
indulgencias, indulgences
indulto, pardon
    indulto presidencial, presidential pardon
industria, industry
    industria a domicilio, Put Out System
    industria de alta tecnología, high-technology industry
    industria de servicios, service industry
    industria del entretenimiento, entertainment industry
    industria energética, energy industry
    industria familiar, cottage industry
    industria ligera, light industry
    industria maderera, logging
    industria pesada, heavy industry
    industria textil, textile industry
industrial, industrial
industrialización, industrialization
    industrialización por sustitución de importaciones, import substituting industrialization (ISI)
    industrialización rápida, rapid industrialization

industrializado, industrialized
industrializar, industrialize
inevitabilidad histórica, historical inevitability
infanticidio femenino, female infanticide
inferencia, inference
inferir, infer
inflación, inflation
    inflación de costos, cost-push inflation
    inflación de demanda, demand-pull inflation
    inflación de guerra, wartime inflation
    inflación de la posguerra, postwar inflation
    inflación generada por la demanda, demand-pull inflation
inflamatorio, inflammatory
inflar, inflate
influencia, influence
    influencia estadounidense, American influence
    influencia social, social influence
información, information
    información demográfica, demographic information
    información geográfica, geographic information
    información gráfica, graphic data
    información inferida, inferred information

**información obser-
vada,** observed infor-
mation
**información sobre el
uso del suelo,**
land-use data
infracción, infringement
infractor reincidente,
repeat offender
**infractor sin anteceden-
tes penales,**
first-time offender
infraestructura,
infrastructure
infrapoblación,
underpopulation
infringir, infringe
ingeniería genética,
genetic engineering
ingeniero, engineer
Inglaterra, England
**Inglaterra preindus-
trial,** pre-industrial
England
inglés, English
ingreso[1], income
ingreso personal,
personal income
**ingresos del propie-
tario,** proprietor's
income
ingresos disponibles,
disposable income
**ingresos por percep-
ción de alquileres,**
rental income
ingresos salariales,
earned income
ingreso[2], revenue
ingresos estatales,
state revenue
ingresos fiscales,
tax revenue

**ingresos por impues-
tos federales,**
federal tax revenue
iniciativa, initiative
inicio, beginning
injusticia, inequities
inmigración, immigration
inmigración ilegal,
illegal immigration
inmigrante, immigrant
inmigrante irlandés,
Irish immigrant
inmigrar, immigrate
inmovilidad de clases,
class crystallization
**inmovilidad de la mano
de obra,** labor force
immobility
inmunidad, immunity
**inmunidad diplo-
mática,** diplomatic
immunity
innovación, innovation
**innovaciones tecno-
lógicas**, technological
innovations
innovador, innovator
innovar, innovate
inquilino, tenant
Inquisición, Inquisition
inspecciones y balances,
checks and balances
instalación militar,
military installation
instalaciones, facilities
instrucción, training
institución, institution
**institución econó-
mica especializada,**
specialized economic
institution
**institución financie-
ra,** financial institu-

tion
institución peculiar, peculiar institution
institución política, political institution
institución total, total institution
instituciones económicas, economic institutions
instituciones financieras internacionales (IFI), international financial institutions (IFIs)
instituciones gubernamentales, government institutions
instituciones sociales, social institutions
institucional, institutional
institucionalización, institutionalization
instrumentos negociables, commercial paper
insumo, input
insurrección, insurrection
insurrección en Filipinas, Filipino insurrection
integración, integration
integración cultural, cultural integration
integración horizontal, horizontal consolidation, horizontal integration
integración racial, racial integration
integración social,

social integration
integración vertical, vertical consolidation, vertical integration
integrar, integrate
integridad, integrity
intelectualidad, intelligentsia
intención humana, human intention
intendente municipal, mayor
intensificación, escalation
intensificar, escalate
interacción, interaction
interacción cultural, cultural interaction
interacción entre los humanos y el medio ambiente, human-environment interaction
interacción humana, human interaction
intercambio, exchange
intercambio colombino, Columbian Exchange
intercambio cultural, cultural exchange
intercambio de bienes, exchange of goods
intercambio de fauna, exchange of fauna
intercambio de favores, logrolling
intercambio de flora, exchange of flora
intercambio de servicios, exchange of services

intercambio voluntario, voluntary exchange

intercambios económicos, economic exchanges

interdependencia, interdependence

interdependencia cultural, cultural interdependence

interdependencia económica, economic interdependence

interdependencia global, global interdependence

interdependiente, interdependent

interdependiente económicamente, economically interdependent

interés, interest

interés nacional, national interest

interés personal, self-interest

interés propio racional, rational self interest

interés público apremiante, compelling state interest

intereses especiales, special interests

interestatal, intrastate

interior, interior

intermediario, intermediary, middleman, warrant chief

intermedio, intermediate

internacional,

International

Internacional Comunista, Communist International

internalización, internalization

internamiento, internment

Internet, Internet

interpretación, interpretation

interpretación amplia, broad interpretation

interpretación de autor, author's interpretation

interpretación estricta de la Constitución, strict construction of the Constitution

interpretación laxa de la Constitución, loose construction of the Constitution

interpretación liberal, loose constructionist

interpretaciones históricas, historical interpretations

interpretar, interpret

interpretar la ley, interpret law

interrelacionado, interrelated

interrogatorio, interrogation

intervención, intervention

intervención de los Estados Unidos, United States intervention

intervención guber-

namental, govern-
mental interference
intervención militar,
military intervention
intervencionista,
interventionist
Intocables (casta),
Untouchables
**introducción de especies
exóticas,** introduction
of species
intolerancia, bigotry
inundación, flood
    **inundación repenti-
    na,** flash flood
inundar la bomba,
pump-priming
invadir, invade
invalidar, override, nullify
    invalidar un veto,
    override a veto
invasión, invasion
    **invasión a la priva-
    cidad,** invasion of
    privacy
    **invasión francesa de
    Egipto,** French inva-
    sion of Egypt
    **invasión iraquí de
    Kuwait,** Iraq invasion
    of Kuwait
    invasión nórdica,
    Norse invasion
    **invasión soviética
    de Afganistán,**
    Soviet invasion of
    Afghanistan
    **invasión soviética
    de Checoslovaquia,**
    Soviet invasion of
    Czechoslovakia
    **invasiones de los
    hunos,** Hun invasions

invención, inventing
invento, invention
inversión, investment
    **inversión a gran
    escala,** large-scale
    investment
    **inversión de capital
    extranjero,** foreign
    capital investment
    **inversión extranjera
    directa,** foreign direct
    investment
inversionista, investor
invertir, invest
investidura, inauguration
investigación,
    investigation, research
    **investigación arqueo-
    lógica de campo,**
    archaeological field
    survey
    **investigación
    cualitativa,**
    qualitative research
    **investigación
    cuantitativa,**
    quantitative research
    **investigación de
    campo,** field inquiry
    **investigación
    participativa,**
    participatory research
investigar,
    investigate, research
Irán, Iran
Irlanda, Ireland
    Irlanda del Norte,
    North Ireland
irlandés, Irish
iroqueses, Iroquois
irrigación, irrigation
irrigar, irrigate
Isabel I, Elizabeth I

Isfahán o Ispahán

Isfahán o Ispahán, Isfahan
isla, island
    Isla Ángel,
    Angel Island
    isla barrada,
    barrier island
    isla británica,
    British Isle
    isla continental,
    continental island
    isla de calor,
    urban heat island
    Isla Ellis, Ellis Island
islam, Islam
islámico(a), Islamic
islamización, Islamization
Islas del Pacífico,
    Pacific Islands
Islas Vírgenes,
    Virgin Islands
Ismael, Ismail
islote, skerry
Israel, Israel
istmo,
    isthmus, land bridge
Italia, Italy
italiano, Italian
izquierda, left wing
izquierdistas, Leftists

J

Japón, Japan
    Japón de Meiji,
    Meiji Japan
japonés(esa), Japanese
    japonés americano,
    Japanese American
jardín de infantes,
    kindergarten

Jardines colgantes de
    Babilonia, Hanging
    Gardens of Babylon
jaula de hierro, Iron Cage
jazz, jazz
Jean Jaurès, Jean Jaures
jefe, chief
    jefe de tribu, chieftain
    jefe nativo america-
    no, American Indian
    chief
jenízaros, Janissary Corps
jeque, sheikh
jerarquía, hierarchy
jerárquico, hierarchical
jeroglífico[1], hieroglyph
jeroglífico[2], hieroglyphic
Jerusalén, Jerusalem
Jesucristo, Jesus Christ
Jesús de Nazaret,
    Jesus of Nazareth
jingoísmo, jingoism
Jordania, Jordan
José II, Joseph II
José Stalin, Joseph Stalin
Joven Italia, Young Italy
Juan de Piano Carpini,
    John of Piano Carpini
Juan II de Portugal,
    King Joao II
Juana de Arco, Joan of Arc
jubilación, retirement
judaísmo, Judaism
    judaísmo rabínico,
    Rabbinic Judaism
judeocristiano,
    Judeo-Christian
judicatura federal,
    federal judiciary
judicial, judicial
judío[1], Jew
judío[2], Jewish
    judío europeo,

European Jew
judíos como chivos expiatorios,
Jewish scapegoating
jueces de circuito judicial, circuit judges
juego con apuestas,
gambling
juez de primera instancia,
magistrate
juego de rol, role playing
juez de medianoche,
midnight judge
juez presidente,
Chief Justice
juicio, trial
  juicio de acción popular, class action suit
  juicio de Galileo,
  trial of Galileo **juicio de Sacco y Vanzetti,** Sacco and Vanzetti trial
  juicio de Scopes,
  Scopes trial
  juicio imparcial,
  fair trial
  juicio por jurado,
  trial by jury, bench trial
  juicio público,
  public trial
  juicio sumario,
  speedy trial
  juicios de las brujas de Salem,
  Salem witch trials
  juicios de los Rosenburg, Rosenburg trials
  Juicios de Núremberg, Nuremberg Trials

Julio César, Julius Caesar
junta, junta, board, committee
  Junta Agrícola Federal, Federal Farm Board
  Junta de la Reserva Federal, Federal Reserve Board
  Junta de Producción de Guerra, War Production Board
  Junta Laboral de Guerra, War Labor Board
jurado, jury
  jurado de acusación,
  grand jury
juramento, oath
  Juramento de Lealtad, Pledge of Allegiance
  juramento de toma de posesión,
  oath of office
jurisdicción, jurisdiction
  jurisdicción original,
  original jurisdiction
jurisprudencia, case law
jurisprudentes,
  juris prudentes
jurista, jurist
justa, joust
justicia, justice
  justicia correctiva,
  corrective justice
  justicia igualitaria para todos,
  equal justice for all
  justicia penal,
  criminal justice
  justicia social,
  social justice

justificación, justification
Justiniano, Justinian
justo, fair, just
juzgado de lo civil,
 civil court

káiser, kaiser
kan, khans
Kansas sangrante,
 Bleeding Kansas
Kenia, Kenya
Kérenski, Kerensky
keynesianismo,
 Keynesianism
kibutz, kibbutz
kilómetro, kilometer
King's Mountain,
 King's Mountain
kiswahili, Swahili
Ku Klux Klan (KKK),
 Ku Klux Klan (KKK)
kurdos, Kurds

L

laberinto, labyrinth
lago, lake
Lago Erie, Lake Erie
laguna, lagoon
lana, wool
latín, Latin
latitud, latitude
 latitud media,
  midlaltitude
lava, lava

lealtad, allegiance, loyalty
lección de historia,
 lesson of history
legal, legal
legión, legion
legionarios, legionaries
**legislación de "barril de
 tocino",** pork-barrel
 legislation
**legislación de derechos
 civiles,** civil rights
 legislation
**legislación de recompen-
 sas políticas,**
 pork-barrel legislation
legislador,
 law-maker, legislator
legislativo, legislative
legislatura, legislature
 legislatura bicameral,
  bicameral legislature
 **legislatura demo-
 crática,** democratic
  legislature
 legislatura estatal,
  state legislature
 **legislaturas colonia-
 les,** colonial legislatures
legitimidad, legitimacy
Lejano oeste, Far West
lejos, far
lema, motto
lengua, language
 lengua de contacto,
  pidgin language
 lengua franca,
  lingua franca
 lengua indoeuropea,
  Indo-European lan-
  guage
 lengua oral,
  oral language

lengua vehicular, lingua franca

lenguas romances, Romance languages

lenguaje, language

lenguaje escrito, written language

lenguaje universal, universal language

León el Africano, Leo Africanus

letra, letter

letra de cambio, bill of exchange, promissory note

leva, impressment

levantamiento de los criollos, Creole-dominated revolt

levantamiento popular, popular uprising

levantamientos de esclavos, slave uprisings

ley, act, law, statute

Ley Judicial, Judiciary Act

Ley Agraria, Homestead Act

Ley de Atribución de Tierra, Dawes Severalty Act

Ley Dawes, Dawes Severalty Act

Ley de acuartelamiento, Quartering Act

Ley de Ajuste Agrícola, Agricultural Adjustment Act

Ley de Alimentos y Medicamentos Puros, Pure Food and Drug Act

Ley de aranceles Smoot-Hawley, U.S. Smoot-Hawley Tariff

Ley de Arrendamiento de Tierras, Land Lease Act

Ley de Autopistas Interestatales, Interstate Highway Act

Ley de Comercio Interestatal, Interstate Commerce Act

Ley de Derechos Civiles, Civil Rights Act

ley de derechos de autor, copyright law

Ley de Esclavos Fugitivos, Fugitive Slave Law

Ley de Escuelas Libres de Armas, Gun Free School Act

Ley de Escuelas Libres de Drogas, Drug Free Act

Ley de Espionaje, Espionage Act

Ley de estadounidenses con discapacidades, Americans with Disabilities Act

Ley de Expansión Comercial, Trade Expansion Act

ley de extinción de derechos, bill of attainder

ley de gravitación del comercio al por menor, law of retail gravitation

ley de hierro de la oligarquía, Iron Law of Oligarchy

Ley de ingresos, Revenue Act

Ley de Inspección de la Carne, Meat Inspection Act

Ley de Kansas-Nebraska, Kansas-Nebraska Act

ley de la demanda, law of demand

ley de la naturaleza, law of nature

ley de la oferta, law of supply

ley de la oferta y la demanda, law of supply and demand

ley de los rendimientos decrecientes, law of diminishing returns

ley de mascotas, pet bill

Ley de Normas Laborales Justas, Fair Labor Standards Act

Ley de Permanencia en el Cargo, Tenure of Office Act

Ley de Poderes de Guerra, War Powers Act

ley de protección, shield law

Ley de protección ambiental, Environmental Protection Act

Ley de Recuperación Industrial Nacional, National Industrial Recovery Act

Ley de reforma, Great Reform Bill

Ley de Relaciones Del Trabajo, Labor Standards Act

Ley de Remoción de los Indios (Nativos Americanos), Indian Removal Act

Ley de Reorganización de los Indios (Nativos Americanos), Indian Reorganization Act

Ley de sedición, Sedition Act

Ley de seguridad social, Social Security Act

ley de sucesión, inheritance law

ley de utilidad marginal decreciente, law of diminishing marginal utility

Ley de Volstead, Volstead Act

Ley del derecho al voto, Voting Rights Act

Ley del patrón oro, Gold Standard Act

Ley del Té, Tea Act

Ley del Timbre, Stamp Act

ley divina, divine law

Ley ex post facto (efecto retroactivo), ex post facto law

ley islámica, Islamic law

ley marcial,

martial law
ley mordaza,
gag rule
ley municipal,
municipal law
ley natural,
natural law
ley orgánica,
enabling act
**Ley Patriótica de los
Estados Unidos,**
USA Patriot Act
Ley retroactiva,
ex post facto law
Ley Seca,
Prohibition
**Ley Sherman Anti-
trust,** Sherman Anti-
Trust Act
ley suprema,
higher law
Ley Wagner,
Wagner Act
ley y orden,
law and order
leyes antimonopolio,
anti-trust acts
leyes antitrust,
anti-trust acts
leyes de aire limpio,
clean air laws
leyes de cuotas,
quota laws
**Leyes de Cuotas de
Inmigración,** Immi-
gration Quota Acts
**leyes de derechos ci-
viles,** civil rights laws
Leyes de Embargo,
Embargo Acts
**Leyes de Extranjería
y Sedición,**
Alien and Sedition

Acts
**Leyes de inmigra-
ción,** immigration
laws, immigration acts
Leyes de Jim Crow,
Jim Crow Laws
Leyes de Navegación,
Navigation Acts
**leyes de protección
en casos de viola-
ción,** rape shield laws
leyes de reforma,
reform legislation
**Leyes de Seguridad
Nacional,** National
Security Acts
Leyes de Townshend,
Townshend Acts
Leyes Granger,
Granger laws
Leyes Intolerables,
Intolerable Acts
leyes marítimas,
admiralty laws
**leyes sobre coloca-
ción de estudiantes,**
student placement
laws
leyenda de foto, caption
Leyenda negra,
Black Legend
leyenda popular, folktale
Líbano, Lebanon
liberal, liberal
liberalismo, liberalism,
laissez-faire
liberalismo clásico,
classical liberalism
liberalización,
deregulation
libertad, freedom, liberty
libertad condicional,
probation

libertad de asociación, freedom of association

libertad de conciencia, freedom of conscience

libertad de contraer matrimonio con quien uno elija, freedom to marry whom one chooses

libertad de contratación, freedom to enter into contracts

libertad de elección, freedom of choice

libertad de elegir trabajo, freedom to choose employment

libertad de emigrar, freedom to emigratc

libertad de expresión, freedom of expression, freedom of speech

libertad de la necesidad, freedom from want

libertad de la prensa, freedom of the press

libertad de residencia, freedom of residence

libertad de viajar libremente, freedom to travel freely

libertad del temor, freedom from fear

libertad económica, economic freedom

libertad individual, individual liberty

libertad personal, personal liberty

libertad política, political freedom

libertad religiosa, freedom of religion, religious freedom

Libertad, Igualdad y Fraternidad, Liberty, Equality, Fraternity

libertades civiles, civil liberties

libertario, Libertarian

libertarismo, libertarianism

libertos, freedmen

libre comercio, free trade

libre empresa, free enterprise

Libro blanco sobre Palestina, White Paper Reports on Palestine

libro de referencia, reference book

Libia, Libya

licencia poética, artistic license

licores, spirits

líder, leader

líder de la mayoría, majority leader

líder de la minoría, minority leader

líder mundial, world leader

líderes representativos, representative leaders

liderazgo, leadership

Lido Anthony "Lee" Iacocca, Lee Iaccoca

liga, league

Liga árabe, Arab League

Liga de Antidifamación, Anti-Defamation

League
Liga de mujeres votantes, League of Women Voters
Liga musulmana, Muslim League
Liga Urbana, Urban League
limitacion, limitation
limitación de armas, arms limitations
limitación de poderes, limitation of powers
limitación del mandato, term limitation
límite, limit, boundary
límite del arbolado, timberline
límite del tiempo, timeframe
límite regional, regional boundary
límites de clase, class boundaries
límites políticos, political boundaries
limpieza de tierras, land clearing
limpieza étnica, ethnic cleansing
linaje, lineage
linchamiento, lynching
linchar, lynch
línea, line
línea cronológica, time line
línea cronológica de varios niveles, multiple-tier time line
línea cronológica en imágenes, picture time line

línea de cascadas, fall line
línea de cascadas de los montes Apalaches, fall line of the Appalachians
línea de demarcación, demarcation
línea de tiempo cronológica, chronology timeline
línea de tiempo paralela, parallel timeline
línea divisoria de aguas, watershed
línea internacional de cambio de fecha, International Date Line
Línea Mason-Dixon, Mason-Dixon Line
línea principal, principal line
líneas costeras, coast lines
líneas de longitud, lines of longitude
lino, flax
liquidez, liquidity
lista de candidatos, slate
lista negra, black list
literatura, literature
literatura barata, pulp fiction
literatura basura, pulp fiction
literatura del siglo XIX, nineteenth-century literature
literatura occidental, Western literature
litigación, litigation
litigante, litigant

litigar, litigate
litósfera, lithosphere
llamamiento para formar parte de un jurado, jury duty
llanura, plain, flatland
    llanura aluvial, alluvial plain
    llanura costera, coastal plain
    llanura costera del Atlántico, Atlantic Coastal Plain
    llanura de Erie, Erie Plain
    llanura desértica, outback
    llanura interior, outback
    llanura indogangé-tica, Indo-Gangetic plain
llevar dinero, carrying money
lluvia, rainfall
    lluvia ácida, acid rain
lluvia de ideas, brainstorm
local, local
localizador, locator
locomotora, locomotive
    locomotora de vapor, steam locomotive
logia, lodge
lógica[1], logic
lógico(a)[2], logical
Londres, London
longitud, longitude
lucha de clases, class conflict
lugar, place, site
    lugar central, central place
    lugar de origen, place of origin
    lugar de producción, production site
    lugar de trabajo, workplace
    lugar de culto, house of worship
Luis XIV, Louis XIV
Luisiana, Louisiana
lujos, luxuries

macadán, macadam road
macartismo, McCarthyism
macroeconomía, macroeconomics
madera, lumber, timber
madre patria, mother country
Madres de la Plaza de Mayo, Mothers of the Plaza De Mayo
maestro, teacher
mafia, mafia
magistrado, magistrate
magma, magma
magnate, baron
Mahoma, Muhammad
maíz, maize
majlis, majles
mal equipado, poorly equipped
mala cosecha, crop failure
mala distribución, maldistribution
malaria, malaria
Malasia, Malaysia
malayo-polinesio,

Malayo-Polynesia
malla geográfica,
geographic grid
manada de ganado,
cattle drove
mañana, tomorrow
manantial, water spring
mancomunidad,
commonwealth
Mancomunidad de naciones,
Commonwealth of Nations
mandato, mandate, writ
Mandato británico,
British rule
mandato de hábeas corpus,
writ of habeas corpus
mandato de la Sociedad de Naciones,
League of Nations mandate
Mandato del cielo,
Mandate of Heaven
mandato,
arbitrary rule
mandato popular directo,
direct popular rule
mandatos sin financiamiento,
unfunded mandates
mandioca, manioc, cassava
manejo de desechos peligrosos, hazardous waste handling
manejo de desechos tóxicos, toxic waste handling
manglar, mangrove
manifestación,
demonstration

manifestación pacífica, peaceful demonstration
Manifiesto comunista,
Communist Manifesto
Manifiesto de octubre,
October Manifesto
mano de obra,
workforce, labor force
mano de obra barata,
cheap labor
mano invisible,
Invisible Hand
mantenimiento de empleos no productivos,
featherbedding
manto, mantle
manufactura,
manufacture, manufacturing
Mao Tse-Tung,
Mao Zedong
mapa, map, chart
mapa acotado,
contour map
mapa complementario, inset map
mapa de altura,
elevation map
mapa de carreteras,
road map
mapa de coropletas,
choropleth map
mapa de flujo,
flow map
mapa de relieve,
relief map
mapa demográfico,
demographic map
mapa especial,
special purpose map
mapa físico,
physical map

mapa histórico, historical map

mapa mental, mental map, mental mapping

mapa político, political map

mapa temático, thematic map

mapa topográfico, contour map

Maquiavelo, Machiavelli

maquila, sweatshop

máquina, machine

    máquina de vapor, steam engine

    maquinaria de Diesel, diesel machinery

    maquinaria para excavaciones, earth-moving machinery

mar, sea

    Mar Blanco, White Sea

    Mar Caspio, Caspian Sea

    Mar Negro, Black Sea

    Mar Rojo, Red Sea

marcha, protest, march

    Marcha de la sal, Salt March

    marchas por la libertad, freedom ride

Marco Aurelio, Marcus Aurelius

marco de muestreo, sampling frame

marea negra, oil slick

marginal, marginal

marisma, marsh

Marruecos, Morroco

Martes negro, Black Tuesday

mártir, martyr

marxismo, Marxism

marxismo-leninismo, Marxism-Leninism

más allá, afterlife

masa, mass

    masa continental, landmass

    masa monetaria, money supply

    masas continentales, landmasses

    masas de agua, bodies of water

masacre, massacre

    masacre de Boston, Boston Massacre

    masacre de los Paxton Boys, Paxton Boys Massacre

masculinización, masculinization

materia prima, raw material, commodity

materiales culturales, cultural materials

materialismo, materialism

    materialismo dialéctico, dialectical materialism

    materialismo histórico, historical materialism

maternidad republicana, republican motherhood

matriarca, matriarch

matriarcado, matriarchy

matriarcal, matriarchal

matrilinaje, matrilineage

matrilineal, matrilinear
matrimonio arreglado,
    arranged marriage
matrimonio interracial,
    interracial marriage
matriz de decisión,
    decision matrix
maya, Mayan
mayor, elder
mayoría, majority
    mayoría cualificada,
    super majority
    mayoría moral,
    moral majority
    mayoría negra,
    black majority
    mayoría silenciosa,
    Silent Majority
Meca, Mecca
mecenazgo, patron-client
    networks, patronage
    mecenazgo político,
    political patronage
    mecenazgo real,
    royal patronage
Medicaid, Medicaid
Medicare, Medicare
medida, measurement
    medida de la delin-
    cuencia, measure of
    crime
    medida económica,
    economic measure-
    ment
    medidas estándar,
    standard measures
    medidas ordinales,
    ordinal measures
medio[1], middle
    Medio Oeste,
    Midwest
    Medio Oriente,
    Middle East

medio[2], means
    medios de comunica-
    ción, mass media
    medios de distri-
    bución, means of
    distribution
    medios de produc-
    ción, means of
    production
  medio ambiente,
    environment
meditar, meditate
Mediterráneo Oriental,
    Eastern Mediterranean
megaciudad, megacity
megalópolis, megalopolis
Mehmet Ali,
    Muhammad Ali
mejoras internas,
    internal improvements
membresía de grupo,
    group membership
mena, ore
menonitas, Mennonites
menor de edad, juvenile
mercader, merchant
    mercaderes de la
    muerte, Merchants of
    Death
mercado,
    market, marketplace
    mercado alcista,
    bull market
    mercado bursátil,
    stock market
    mercado comercial,
    trade market
    mercado competiti-
    vo, competitive market
    Mercado Común,
    Common Market
    mercado de cambio,
    market exchange

mercado de divisas, foreign exchange market
mercado de trabajo primario, primary labor market
mercado de trabajo secundario, secondary labor market
mercado de valores, stock market
mercado exterior, foreign market
mercado global, global market
mercado internacional, international market
mercado interno, national market
mercado laboral, labor market
mercado libre, free market
mercado negro, black market
mercado privado, private market
mercancía, commodity
mercancías comunes, common goods
mercandería comercial, merchandising
mercantilismo, mercantilism
mercenario, mercenary
meridiano, meridian
meridianos de longitud, meridians of longitude
meritocracia, meritocracy
mes, month
mesa, mesa

meseta, plateau, mesa, altiplano
meseta de Allegheny, Allegheny Plateau
mesías, messiah
Mesoamérica, Mesoamerica
mesolítico, Mesolithic
Mesopotamia, Mesopotamia
mestizos, mestizos
metal precioso, precious metal
método, method
método acusatorio, inquisitorial method
método científico, scientific method
método científico social, social scientific method
método de asignación, allocation method
método de producción, production method
método de subsistencia, subsistence method
método empírico, empirical method
método inquisitivo, inquisitorial method
método psicoanalítico, psychoanalytic method
método socrático, Socratic method
métodos de datación, dating methods
métodos de explotación agrícola,

farming methods
**métodos de partici-
pación,** avenues of
participation
metro, subway
metrópoli, metropolis
metropolitano(a),
metropolitan
México, Mexico
mezquita, mosque
Mi lucha, Mein Kampf
microclima, microclimate
microeconomía,
microeconomics
**microorganismo patóge-
no,** disease microorga-
nism
miembro del equipo,
team member
migración, migration
**migración de larga
distancia,** long-dis-
tance migration
**migración del campo
a la ciudad,** rural-to-
urban migration
migración forzada,
involuntary migration
migración global,
global migration
**migración hacia el
exterior,** outward
migration
migración humana,
human migration
**migración mormo-
na hacia el oeste,**
Mormon migration to
the West
migración negra,
black migration
migración rural,
rural migration

migración turca,
Turkic migration
migración voluntaria,
voluntary migration
**migraciones bantúes
en África,** Bantu mi-
grations in Africa
migrar, migrate
milenarismo,
millennialism
milenio, millennium,
(pl. millennia)
milicia, militia
militar, military
militarismo, militarism
militarista, militarist
milla, mile
mina, mine
minas de carbón,
coal mining
minas de extracción,
extractive mining
mineral, mineral, ore
mineral de hierro,
iron ore
minería, mine
mineros, miners
ministro, minister
minoría, minority
minoría étnica,
ethnic minority
minoría racial,
racial minority
misa, mass
misión, mission
misionero, missionary
misionero cristiano,
Christian missionary
misoginia, misogyny
**La mística de la femini-
dad,** The Feminine
Mystique
mitin, rally

mito, myth
mito de la creación,
  creation myth,
    **mito babilónico de
    la creación,** creation
    myths of Babylon
    **mito chino de la
    creación,** creation
    myths of China
    **mito egipcio de la
    creación,** creation
    myths of Egypt
    **mito griego de la
    creación,** creation
    myths of Greece
    **mito sumerio de la
    creación,** creation
    myths of Sumer
mitología, mythology
mocasín, moccasin
moción de censura,
  vote of no confidence
**modalidad artística asiáti-
ca,** Asian art form
**modalidades alternati-
    vas de solución de
    conflictos,**
    alternative dispute
    resolution (ADR)
modelo, model, pattern
    **modelo de compor-
    tamiento,** standard of
    behavior
    **modelo de flujo
    circular,**
    Circular-Flow Model
    modelo de Hoyt,
    sector model
    **modelo de la
    cordillera y el valle,**
    ridge-and-valley
    pattern
    modelo de la élite

    del poder,
    power-elite model
    **modelo de salud
    pública,** public health
    model
    modelo de sector,
    sector model
    **modelo de toma
    decisiones,**
    decision making model
    **modelo de uso del
    suelo,** land-use pat-
    tern
    **modelo de zonas con-
    céntricas,** concentric
    zone model
    **modelos demográ-
    ficos,** demographic
    patterns
    modelo económico,
    economic model
    modelo geocéntrico,
    geocentric model
    **modelo heliocéntri-
    co,** heliocentric model
    modelo residencial,
    residential pattern
    modelo T, model T
módem, modem
moderación, temperance
moderado, moderate
modernidad, modernity
modernista, modernist
modernización,
  modernization
    **modernización de
    Japón,** Japanese
    modernization
moderno, modern
modificación humana,
  human modification
modificar, modify
modo de comunicación,

mode of communication

modo de discurso,
mode of discourse

modo de producción,
mode of production

modo de vida rural,
agricultural lifestyle

mogol, Mongol

mohawk, Mohawk

molibdeno, molybdenum

molino, mill

momento decisivo,
turning point

> **momento decisivo
> en la historia de la
> humanidad,** turning
> point in human his-
> tory

momia, mummy

momificación,
mummification

monacato, monasticism

monarquía, monarchy

> **monarquía absoluta,**
> absolute monarchy
> **monarquía británica,**
> British monarch
> **monarquía centra-
> lizada,** centralized
> monarchy
> **monarquía constitu-
> cional,** constitutional
> monarchy
> **monarquía europea,**
> European monarchy

monasterio, monastery

monástico, monastic

moneda¹, coin, currency

> **moneda de 25 centa-
> vos,** quarter
> **moneda de curso
> legal,** legal tender

> **moneda de diez cen-
> tavos,** dime
> **moneda débil,**
> soft money
> **moneda estable,**
> sound money
> **moneda extranjera,**
> foreign currency
> **moneda fuerte,**
> hard money
> **moneda sólida,**
> sound money

monedas², specie

monetario, monetary

monetarismo, monetarism

monje, monk

> **monje budista,**
> Buddhist monk

monocultivo, monoculture

monocultural,
monocultural

monogamia, monogamy

monopolio, monopoly,
trust

> **monopolio natural,**
> natural monopoly

**monopolizar, monopolize
,corner**

monoteísmo, monotheism

> **monoteísmo cristia-
> no,** Christian mono-
> theism
> **monoteísmo judío,**
> Jewish monotheism

monoteísta, monotheist

montaña, mountain

> **Montañas Apala-
> ches,** Appalachian
> Highlands
> **Montañas Rocallosas,**
> Rocky Mountains

montañeses,
mountain men

Monte Rushmore

Monte Rushmore,
Mt. Rushmore
Montes Apalaches,
Appalachian Mountains
monumento, monument
Monumento a Lincoln, Lincoln Memorial
monumento a los veteranos,
veterans' memorial
monumento histórico, landmark
monumentos megalíticos, megalithic monuments
monzón, monsoon
moral, moral
moralidad privada,
private morality
morfología urbana,
urban morphology
mormón, Mormon
mormona, Mormon
moro, moor
morrena, moraine
mosaico, mosaic
mosca tsé-tsé, tsetse fly
mosquete, musket
motín, mutiny, uprising
Motín de los Cipayos, Sepoy Mutiny
Motín del té de Boston, Boston Tea Party
motín en protesta del reclutamiento,
draft riot
motivaciones, grounds
motivo, motive
movilidad, mobility
movilidad ascendente, upward mobility

movilidad social,
social mobility
movilización, mobilization
movilización militar,
military mobilization
movilizar, mobilize
movimiento, movement
movimiento abolicionista, Abolitionist Movement, antislavery movement
movimiento antichino, anti-Chinese movement
movimiento anticomunista, anticommunist movement
Movimiento antiderechista, Anti-Rightist Campaign
movimiento artístico, artistic movement
movimiento bhakti, Bhakti movement
movimiento cartista, Chartist movement
movimiento ciudadano, citizen movement
movimiento conservacionista, conservation movement
Movimiento Grange, Grange Movement
movimiento de arena, sand movement
Movimiento de cercamiento, Enclosure Movement
movimiento de conservación, conservation movement
movimiento de derechos civiles, civil

rights movement
movimiento de Garvey, Garvey movement
movimiento de independencia, independence movement
movimiento de independencia de Brasil, Brazilian independence movement
Movimiento de liberación femenina, Women's Liberation Movement
Movimiento de Liberación Homosexual, Gay Liberation Movement
movimiento de los Jóvenes Turcos, Young Turk movement
movimiento de paz, peace movement
movimiento de población, population movement
movimiento de protección ambiental, environmental protection movement
movimiento de reforma, reform movement
movimiento de resistencia, resistance movement
movimiento de resistencia africano, African resistance movement
movimiento de resistencia europeo, European resistance

movement
movimiento de resistencia judía, Jewish resistance movement
movimiento de resistencia marroquí, Moroccan resistance movement
movimiento de trabajadores agrícolas, farm labor movement
movimiento de veteranos de guerra, Bonus Army
Movimiento del Cuatro de Mayo, May Fourth movement
movimiento del evangelio social, social gospel movement
movimiento evangélico, evangelical movement
Movimiento evangélico cristiano, Christian evangelical movement
movimiento feminista, feminist movement, women's movement
movimiento filosófico, philosophical movement
Movimiento hacia el Oeste, westward movement
movimiento laboral, labor movement
movimiento literario, literary movement

movimiento naciona- lista africano, African nationalist movement

Movimiento Nacio- nalista Indio, Indian Nationalist Movement

movimiento progre- sista, Populist Move- ment

Movimiento por los derechos civiles de los asiáticos, Asian Civil Rights Mo- vement

movimiento pro- gresista, Progressive Movement

movimiento religioso militante, militant religious movement

movimiento revo- lucionario chino, China's revolutionary movement

movimiento sepa- ratista, separatist movement

movimiento sindical, union movement

movimiento sionista, Zionist Movement

movimiento social, social movement

movimiento sufragis- ta, suffrage movement

Muchachos de la Montaña Verde, Green Moun- tain Boys

mudéjar, Mudejar Muslim

muela abrasiva, grinding stone

muerte civil, bill of attainder

muestra, sample

muestra probabilísti- ca, probability sample

muestra representa- tiva, cross section

muestreo, sampling

mujeres en el clero, women in the clergy

mulato, mulatto

multicultural, multicultural

multiculturalismo, multiculturalism

multilateral, multilateral

multilateralismo, multilateralism

multilingüe, multilingual

multinacional, multinational

mundo, world

mundo eslavo, Slavic world

mundo moderno, modern world

municipal, municipal

municipalidad, municipality, township

municipio, township, city council, council

mural, mural

Muro de Berlín, Berlin Wall

museo, museum

musulmán, Moslem, Muslim

N

nacimiento de un río,
source of a river
nación, nation
nación acreedora,
creditor nation
nación deudora,
debtor nation
**nación en vías de
desarrollo econó-
mico,** economically
developing nation
**nación nativa ameri-
cana,** American Indian
nation
nación soberana,
sovereign nation
Naciones Unidas,
United Nations
**naciones en vías de
desarrollo,**
developing nations
nacional,
national, domestic
nacionalismo, nationalism
**nacionalismo
económico,** economic
nationalism
nacionalista, nationalist
nacionalización,
nationalization
nacionalsocialismo,
national socialism
Napoleón Bonaparte,
Napoleon Bonaparte
narcotráfico,
drug trafficking
narración literaria,
literary narrative

narrativa esclavista,
slave narrative
narrativa histórica,
historical narrative
NASDAQ,
National Association
of Security Dealers
Automated Quotations
(NASDAQ)
nativismo, nativism
nativista, nativist
nativo, native
nativo americano,
Native American,
American Indian
**nativos americanos
de Delaware,**
Delaware Indians
**nativos americanos
de los bosques,**
Woodland Natives
natural, natural
naturaleza humana,
human nature
naturalización,
naturalization
nave, craft
nave vikinga,
Viking longboat
navegable, navigable
navegación, navigation
navegar, navigate
Navidad, Christmas
**navío musulmán de
comercio,** Muslim
trading vessel
nazi, Nazi
nazismo, Nazism
Neandertal, Neanderthal
necesidad,
necessity, need
necesidades básicas,
basic needs

necesidades humanas, human needs
necesidades ilimitadas, unlimited needs
neerlandés, Dutch
negociación, negotiation
negociación del contrato, contract negotiation
negociaciones colectivas, collective bargaining
negociar, negotiate
negocio, business
neocolonialismo, neocolonialism
neoconfucianismo, neo-Confucianism
neoconservadurismo, neo-conservatism
neoliberalismo, neo-liberalism
neolítico, Neolothic
neopatrimonialismo, neopatrimonialism
nepotismo, nepotism
Nerón, Nero
neuropsicología, neuropsychology
neutral, neutral
neutralidad, neutrality
neutralista, neutralist
Nez Percé, Nez Perce
niebla tóxica, smog
NIMBY (no en mi patio trasero), NIMBY (Not In My Backyard)
nirvana, nirvana
nitrato de sodio, sodium nitrate
nivel de aguas abajo, tail water
nivel de alimentación, feeding level
nivel de precios promedio, average price level
nivel de vida, standard of living
nivel del mar, sea level
niveles de medida, level of measurement
no alineación, nonalignment
no alineado, nonaligned
no exclusión, nonexclusion
no ficción, nonfiction
no homínido, nonhominid
no intervencionismo, noninterference
no lucrativo, not-for-profit
no-partidiario, nonpartisan
no-violencia, non-violence
noble, noble
nobleza, nobility
nodo de transportes, transportation hub
nómada[1], nomad
nómada[2], nomadic
nombrado, appointed
nombramiento, appointment, nomination
nombramiento político, political appointment
nombrar, appoint
non bis in idem, double jeopardy
nordeste, Northeast
noreste, Northeast
norma, norm, rule, regulation, standard
norma cultural, cultural norm
norma de trabajo, work rule
norma laboral,

work rule
norma moral,
moral standard
normas de producto,
product standards
**normas de responsa-
bilidad,** liability rules
normas éticas,
ethical standards
normas sociales,
social norms
normalidad, normalcy
normativa, regulation
noroeste, northwest
Noroeste Pacífico,
Pacific Northwest
norte, north
Norte global,
Global North
Norte industrial,
industrial North
Norteamérica,
North America
Noruega, Norway
Nosotros, el pueblo...,
We the People ...
nota al pie de página,
footnote
nota diplomática,
diplomatic note
noticia de periódico,
newspaper account
**notificación razonable de
una audiencia,**
fair notice of a hearing
novato, newcomer
Novena enmienda,
Ninth Amendment
nuclear, nuclear
neutralismo, neutrality
Nueva Amsterdam,
New Amsterdam
Nueva Delhi, New Delhi

Nueva Escocia,
Nova Scotia
Nueva Frontera,
New Frontier
Nueva Granada,
New Granada
Nueva Guinea, New Guinea
Nueva Inglaterra,
New England
Nueva Izquierda, New Left
Nueva Jersey, New Jersey
**Nueva Jersey contra
T.L.O.,** New Jersey v.
T.L.O.
Nueva Libertad,
new freedom
Nueva Mujer, New Woman
Nueva Orleans,
New Orleans
**Nueva política Económi-
ca,** New Economic
policy
**nueva política Económica
de Lenin,** Lenin's New
Economic Policy
nueva repartición,
reapportionment
Nueva York, New York
Nueva Zelanda,
New Zealand
Los Nueve de Little Rock,
Little Rock Nine
Nuevo Federalismo,
New Federalism
Nuevo Imperialismo,
New Imperialism
nuevo institucionalismo,
new institutionalism
nuevo Klan, New Klan
Nuevo México, New Mexico
nuevo mundo, New World
nuevo nacionalismo,
new nationalism

**nuevo racionalismo
científico,** new scientific rationalism
Nuevo Sur, New South
Nuevo Testamento,
New Testament
Nuevo Trato, New Deal
nuevo urbanismo,
New Urbanism
nuevos inmigrantes,
new immigrants
**número de seguridad
social,** Social Security
number

oasis, oasis
obispo, bishop
objetividad, objectivity
objetivo, objective
objetivos económicos, economic goals
objetor por conciencia,
conscientious objector
óblast, oblast
obligación,
commitment, duty
obligación civil,
civic duty
obligación moral,
moral obligation
obras escritas, writings
obras públicas,
public works
observación, observation
observar, observe
obsidiana, obsidian
obstruccionismo,
filibustering, filibuster

occidentalización,
westernization
Oceanía, Oceania
océano, ocean
océano Antártico,
Southern Ocean
océano Ártico,
Arctic Ocean
Océano Atlántico,
Atlantic Ocean
Océano Índico,
Indian Ocean
Océano Pacífico,
Pacific Ocean
ocupación, occupation
ocupación japonesa de Manchuria,
Japanese occupation
of Manchuria
**ocupación romana
de Bretaña,** Roman
occupation of Britain
ocupación secuencial, sequence
occupance
ocupante ilegal, squatter
Odisea, Odyssey
oeste, west
**Oeste de los
Estados Unidos,**
American West
ofensiva de Tet,
Tet Offensive
oferta, supply, proposition
oferta agregada,
aggregate supply
oferta de dinero,
money supply
oferta y demanda,
supply and demand
oficial, official
oficial militar,
military officer

oficina central, home office
Oficina de Asuntos de Nativos Americanos, Bureau of Indian Affairs
Oficina de libertos, Freedmen's Bureau
Oficina de Oportunidades Económicas, Office of Economic Opportunity
Oficina de Presupuesto del Congreso, Congressional Budget Office
Oficina de Presupuesto y Gestión, Office of Budget and Management
Oficina de Recaudación Fiscal (IRS), Internal Revenue Service (IRS)
Oficina Federal de Investigaciones (FBI), Federal Bureau of Investigation (FBI)
oficinista, white-collar worker
oficio, craft
ókrug, okrug
oleoducto, pipeline
oleoducto Trans-Alaska, Alaska pipeline
oligarca, oligarch
oligarquía, oligarchy
oligopolio, oligopoly
Olimpiadas Especiales, Special Olympics
ombudsman, ombudsman
OPA (Oficina de Administración de Precios), Office of Price Administration (OPA)
Ópera de Sídney, Opera House (Sydney, Australia)
operación encubierta, covert action
operacionalización, operationalization
opinión argumentada, reasoned judgment
opinión editorial, op-ed
opinión pública, public opinion
oponerse, oppose
oportunidad de beneficio, profit opportunity
oportunidad de empleo, employment opportunity
oportunidad de intervención, intervening opportunity
oportunista político, carpetbagger
oposición, opposition
oposición leal, loyal opposition
opresión, oppression
opulencia, affluence
oración diaria, daily prayer
oráculos, oracles
orador, orator
orden, order, writ
orden cronológico, chronological order
orden de asistencia, writs of assistance
orden de los acontecimientos, order of events
orden de registro, search warrant

orden ejecutiva, executive order
orden judicial, general warrant, warrant
orden moral, public morality
orden social, social order
Órdenes Fundamentales de Connecticut, Fundamental Orders of Connecticut
ordenanza, ordinance
Ordenanza del Noroeste, Northwest Ordinance
ordenanza local, local ordinance
Oregón, Oregon
organismo de control, regulatory agency
organismo de control independiente, independent regulatory agency
organización, organization
organización de ayuda multilateral, multilateral aid organization
Organización de Estados Americanos (OEA), Organization of American States (OAS)
Organización de Países Exportadores del Petróleo (OPEP), Organization of Petroleum Exporting Countries (OPEC)
Organización para la Cooperación Económica Europea
(OEEC), Organization for European Economic Cooperation (OEEC)
organización fraternal, fraternal organization
organización multilateral, multinational organization
Organización Mundial de la Salud (OMS), World Health Organization (WHO)
Organización Nacional de las Mujeres (ONM), National Organization of Women (NOW)
organización no lucrativa, nonprofit organization
Organización para la Liberación de Palestina (OLP), Palestinian Liberation Organization (PLO)
organización política, political organization
Organización del Tratado del Atlántico Norte (OTAN), North Atlantic Treaty Organization (NATO)
organización Tweed Ring, Tweed Ring
organizaciones civiles, civil organizations
organizaciones gubernamentales internacionales, international governmental organizations

orientación, orientation
oriental, Oriental
Oriente, Orient
origen, source
    origen étnico,
    ethnic origin
    origen nacional,
    national origin, origen
    orígenes constitucio-
    nales, constitutional
    origins
    orígenes históricos,
    historical origins
Orosio, Orosius
Oscurantismo, Dark Ages
otorgar, grant
    otorgar poderes,
    empower

Pablo el Apóstol,
    Paul the Apostle
Pacífico, Pacific
    Pacífico Sur,
    South Pacific
pacifismo, pacifism, non-
    violence
pacifista, pacifist
pacto, covenant, pact
    pacto Briand-Kellog,
    Kellogg-Briand Pact
    pacto comercial,
    trade pact
    pacto de caballeros,
    Gentleman's Agree-
    ment
    Pacto de la Sociedad
    de Naciones,
    Covenant of the Lea-

gue of Nations
pacto de no agresión,
nonaggression pact
Pacto de no agre-
sión germano-so-
viético, Nazi-Soviet
Non-Aggression Pact
pacto de no agresión
soviético, Soviet non-
aggression pact
Pacto de Varsovia,
Warsaw Pact
Pacto del Eje,
Axis Pact
Pacto del Mayflower,
Mayflower Compact
Pacto del Medio Ca-
mino, Halfway Cove-
nant
pacto verbal,
Gentleman's Agree-
ment
padre de la Patria,
    father of our country
padre del Egipto moder-
    no, father of modern
    Egypt
Padres fundadores,
    Founding Fathers,
    framers
padrón electoral,
    voter registration
pagaré, promissory note
pago, payment
    pago de indemni-
    zación, reparation
    payment
    pago de intereses,
    interest payment
    pago de transferen-
    cia, transfer payment
    pago diferido,
    deferred payment

país, country
    país capitalista,
    capitalist country
    país comunista,
    communist country
    país de origen,
    country of origin,
    home country
    país desarrollado,
    developed country
    país en desarrollo,
    developing country
    país europeo,
    European country
    país musulmán,
    Muslim country
    país neutral,
    neutral nation, buffer
    país sancionado,
    sanctioned country
    país satélite,
    satellite nation
    **país sin salida al
    mar,** landlocked
    country
    país tapón,
    buffer state, buffer
    **países del tercer
    mundo,** Third World
    countries
    **países recientemen-
    te industrializados
    (NIC),** newly industria-
    lizing countries (NICs)
    **países tercermun-
    distas,** Third World
    countries
paisaje, landscape
    paisaje cultural,
    cultural landscape
los Países Bajos,
    Netherlands
Pakistán, Pakistan

    **palabras con carga emo-
    cional,** loaded words
palafitos, houses on stilts
Paleolítico, Paleolithic Era,
    Paleolithic
Palestina, Palestine
palio, canopy
Pallava, Pallavas
panafricanismo,
    Pan-Africanism
Panamá, Panama
panarabismo, Pan-Arabism
pancracio, pancratium
pandemia,
    disease pandemic
    **pandemia mundial
    de influenza,** world
    influenza pandemic
    pandemia recurrente,
    recurrent pandemic
pandémico, pandemic
pandilla callejera,
    street gang
paneslavismo,
    Pan-Slavism
pánico financiero,
    financial panic
pánico moral, moral panic
pantano, swamp, bayou
    pantanos naturales,
    natural wetlands
panteón, pantheon
Panteras negras,
    Black Panthers
Papa, Pope
papado, papacy
papel[1], paper, money
    papel de periódico,
    newsprint
    papel moneda,
    paper money
papel[2], role
    papel del gobierno en

la economía, role of government in the economy
papeleta, ballot
papiro, papyrus
par, peer
para el bien público, pro bono
parábolas, parables
paracaidista, squatter
paraestatales, para-statals
parafrasear, paraphrase
paráfrasis, paraphrase, paraphrasing
paralelo, parallel
    paralelo principal, major parallel
    paralelos de latitud, parallels of latitude
    paralelos principales, principal parallels
parcelación, allotment
parcialidad, bias
parentesco, kinship
paridad industrial, industrial parity
pariente, relative
París, Paris
parlamento, parliament
    Parlamento inglés, English Parliament
    parlamento modelo, Model Parliament
parlamentario(a), parliamentary
parque, park
    parque municipal, city park
    parque nacional, national park
    parque público, city park
párrafo, paragraph

parroquia, parish
parroquial, parochial
partes intercambiables, interchangeable parts
participación, involvement
    participación cívica, civic participation
    participación en beneficios, profit incentive
    participación política, political participation
participar, participate
partidarios del régimen, Loyalist
partido, party
    Partido Antifederalista, Anti-Federalist Party
    Partido Antimasónico, Anti-Masonic Party
    Partido Comunista, Communist Party
    Partido Comunista de China, Chinese Communist Party, Communist Party in China
    Partido Comunista de la Unión Soviética, Communist Party of the Soviet Union (CPSU)
    Partido Comunista de los Estados Unidos, American Communist Party, U.S. Communist Party
    Partido de la anulación, Nullifier Party
    Partido de la Libertad, Liberty Party

Partido de la Prohibición, Prohibition Party
Partido de la Tolerancia, Toleration Party
Partido de la Unión Constitucional, Constitutional Union Party
partido de oposición, Opposition Party
partido de vanguardia, vanguard party
Partido Demócrata, Democratic Party
Partido Demócrata-Republicano, Democratic-Republican Party
Partido Democrático Nacional, National Democratic Party
Partido Federalista, Federalist Party
Partido Know Nothing, Know Nothing Party
Partido Laboral Greenback, Greenback Labor Party
Partido Laborista, Labor Party
Partido Libertario, Libertarian Party
partido nacional, national party
partido político, political party
Partido Populista, Populist Party
Partido Progresista, Progressive Party
Partido Republicano, Republican party
Partido Republicano Americano, American Republican Party
Partido Republicano Nacional, National Republican Party
Partido Socialista, Socialist Party
Partido Socialista Nacional de los Trabajadores Alemanes (NSDAP), National Socialist German Workers Party (NSDAP)
Partido Tierra Libre, Free Soil Party
Partido Unión Nacional, National Union Party
Partido Verde, Green Party
Partido Whig, Whig Party
partido-estado comunista, communist party-state
partidos independientes, independent parties
pasado, past
pasado reciente, recent past
pasaje, passage
pasajeros (jinetes) de la libertad, freedom riders
pasaporte, passport
paso de Khyber, Khyber Pass
paso del Brennero, Brenner Pass
paso del huracán,

hurricane tracks
Paso del Noroeste,
Northwest Passage
paso elevado,
water crossing,
causeway
paso peatonal,
pedestrian walkway
pastar, pasture
pastor, herder
pastores de rebaño,
cattle herders
pastoreo excesivo,
overgraze
pastos, pasture
patente, patent
patógeno, pathogen
patriarcado, patriarchy
patriarcas, patriarchs
patricio, patrician
patrimonialismo,
patrimonialism
patrimonio,
heritage, patrimony
patrimonio cultural,
human-built heritage
patriota, patriot, nativist
patriótico, patriotic
patriotismo,
patriotism, nativism
patrocinador, patron
patrocinio, patronage
patrón, pattern
patrón climático,
climatic pattern
patrón de asentamiento,
settlement pattern
patrón de cambio,
pattern of change
patrón de comportamiento,
behavior pattern

patrón de comportamiento aprendido,
learned behavior pattern
patrón de flujo,
flow pattern
patrón de inundación, flooding pattern
patrón de migración global, global migration pattern
patrón oro,
gold standard
patrones de actividad económica, economic activity patterns
patrones de cultivo agrícola de subsistencia, cultural subsistence agriculture patterns
patrones del comercio global,
global trade patterns
patrones espaciales,
spatial patterns
patrones físicos,
physical patterns
patrones mundiales de la actividad económica,
World Patterns of Economic Activity
paz defectuosa,
flawed peace
paz del Rey, king's peace
"paz por fuerza" de Reagan, Reagan's "Peace Through Strength"
Paz Romana, Pax Romana
peaje, toll
Pearl Harbor, Pearl Harbor
pedernal, flint

Pedro el Grande,
Peter the Great
Peligro Rojo, Red Scare
Peligro Amarillo,
Yellow Peril
pena, punishment, penalty
pena capital,
capital punishment
pena de muerte,
death penalty, capital
punishment
península, peninsula
**Península de
Yucatán,** Yucatan
Peninsula
penique, penny
**pensamiento democráti-
co moderno,** modern
democratic thought
pensamiento moderado,
moderate thinking
**pensamiento político
occidental,** Western
political thought
**pensamiento reaccio-
nario,** reactionary
thinking
Pensilvania, Pennsylvania
pensión, pension
Pentágono, Pentagon
pequeña burguesía,
petite bourgeoisie
Pequeña Italia, Little Italy
pequeña nobleza, gentry
pequeño propietario rural,
yeoman farmer
percepción espacial,
spatial perception
**percepciones de las
mujeres,** women's
perceptions
**percepciones de los
hombres,** men's per-

ceptions
pérdida, loss
pérdida de capital,
capital loss
**pérdida de mano
de obra en tiempos
de guerra,**
wartime manpower
losses
peregrinación,
Hajj, pilgrimage
peregrino, pilgrim
perestroika, perestroika
perfil, contour, profile
perfil de elevación,
elevation profile
pergamino, parchment
periférico, peripheral
periódico, journal
periodismo amarillista,
yellow journalism
**periodista sensacional-
ista,** muckraker
periodizar, periodize
período, period
período antebellum,
antebellum period
período Ashikaga,
Ashikaga period
período clásico,
classical period
período colonial,
colonial period
período de Heian,
Heian period
**período de Kamaku-
ra,** Kamakura period
**período de la posgue-
rra,** postwar period
período helenístico,
Hellenistic period
período histórico,
period of history

período meroítico, Meroitic period
período Muromachi, Ashikaga period
período napoleónico, Napoleonic period
período posterior a la Guerra Civil, post-Civil War period
período posterior a la Guerra Fría, post-Cold War era
período posterior a la Primera Guerra Mundial, post-World War I
período posterior a la Segunda Guerra Mundial, post-World War II
período de tiempo, time period
perjurio, perjury
permafrost, permafrost
persecución, persecution
persecución religiosa, religious persecution
perseguir, persecute
persona jurídica, juristic person
personas desplazadas, displaced persons
personalidad, personality
perspectiva, perspective
perspectiva histórica, historical perspective
perspectivas multilaterales, multiple perspectives
pertenencia tribal, tribal membership
Perú, Peru
pesca, fishing
pesos estándar, standard weights
peste, plague
peste bubónica, bubonic plague
peste negra, Black Death
pesticida, pesticide
petición, petition
Petición de derechos, Petition of Right
Petición de la Rama de Olivo, Olive Branch Petition
petróleo, oil, petroleum
petróleo crudo, crude oil
petroquímico, petrochemical
Piamonte, Piedmont
PIB per cápita, per capita GDP
PIB real, real GDP
pictográfico, pictograph
pidgin, pidgin language
pie de foto, caption
piedad filial, filial piety
piedra caliza, limestone
piedra pulida, ground stone
piedra termofracturada, fire-cracked rock
piel de ciervo, deerskin
pieza de bronce fundido, bronze casting
piezas uniformes, interchangeable parts
pilares de la fe, pillars of faith
pintura rupestre, cave painting
pintura rupestre del Paleolítico, Paleolithic cave painting

pionero¹, pioneer
pioneros², charter groups
piquete, picket
piragua, dugout
Phoenician ship
pirámide, pyramid
    pirámide de población, population
pyramid
    pirámides mayas,
Mayan pyramids
piratería aérea, hijacking
pista, lead
pizarra bituminosa,
oil shale
Pizarro, Pizarro
placa, plate
    placa tectónica,
tectonic plate
plan, plan
    plan 401 (k), 401 K
    plan Anaconda,
Anaconda Plan
    plan de acción,
action plan
    plan de empaquetamiento de la Corte,
court-packing plan
    plan de Nueva Jersey, New Jersey Plan
    plan de rellenar la corte, court packing
    Plan de Townshend,
Townshend Plan
    Plan de Unión de Albany, Albany Plan of
Union
    Plan de Virginia,
Virginia Plan
    plan económico,
economic plan
    plan hipodámico,
grid system

    Plan Marshall,
Marshall Plan
    Plan quinquenal,
Five Year Plan
    Plan Schlieffen,
Schlieffen Plan
planeación regional,
regional planning
planeación urbana,
city planning, urban
planning
planicies, flatlands
plano, chart
planta de manufactura,
manufacturing plant
plantación, plantation
plataforma, platform
    plataforma continental, continental shelf
    plataforma de Omaha, Omaha Platform
    plataforma política,
political platform
plátanos, plantains
Platón, Plato
plaza, piazza, plaza
plebeyo, plebeian
plebiscito, plebiscite
Plena Edad Media,
High Middle Ages
pleno empleo,
full employment,
maximum employment
pluma, pen
    pluma de águila,
eagle feather
pluralismo, pluralism
    pluralismo cultural,
cultural pluralism
plusvalías, capital gains
plutocracia, plutocracy
plutocrático, plutocratic
población, population

población aborigen, aboriginal population
población activa, labor force **población civil,** civilian population
población extranjera, migrant population
población mundial, world population
población refugiada, refugee population
poblado, town, settlement
poblador, settler
pobreza, poverty
poder, power
poder absoluto, absolute power
poder adquisitivo, purchasing power
poder aristocrático, aristocratic power
poder autónomo, autonomous power
poder budista-maurya, Mauryan-Buddhist power
poder compartido, shared power
poder de destitución, removal power
poder de veto, veto power
poder del bolsillo, power of the purse
poder económico, economic power
poder ejecutivo, executive power, executive branch
poder hegemónico, hegemonic power
poder hidroeléctrico, hydroelectric power
poder imperial, imperial power
poder judicial, judicial power, judicial branch
poder legislativo, legislative branch, legislative power
poder militar, military power
poder negro, black power
poder para declarar la guerra, power to declare war
poder para gravar, power to tax
poder por el pueblo, power by the people
poder vertical, power vertical
poderes concurrentes, concurrent powers
poderes de gobierno, branches of government
poderes de los estados, states powers
poderes delegados, delegated powers
poderes enumerados, enumerated powers
poderes expresados, expressed powers
poderes gubernamentales, government powers
poderes implícitos, implied powers
poderes inherentes, inherent powers

poderes policiales, police powers

poderes prohibidos, prohibited powers

poderes reservados, reserved powers

poderes soberanos, sovereign powers

poema épico, epic

poesía, poetry

poesía de Kabir, poetry of Kabir

poesía de Mirabai, poetry of Mirabai

pogromos, pogroms

polarización, polarization

polarización de clases, polarization of classes

polarizado, polarized

pólder, polder

policía política, political policing

poligamia, polygamy

Polinesia, Polynesia

politeísmo, polytheism

politeísta, polytheist

política¹, policy, politics

política agraria, land policy

política aislacionista de los Estados Unidos, U.S. isolationist policy

política arriesgada, brinkmanship

política crediticia, credit policy

política de contención, containment policy

política de defensa, defense policy

política de identidad, identity politics

política de puertas abiertas, Open Door policy

política de remoción, removal policy

política de un solo hijo en China, one child policy in China

Política del buen vecino, Good Neighbor Policy

política dinástica, dynastic politics

política energética interna de los Estados Unidos, U.S. domestic energy policy

política exterior, foreign policy

política exterior de EE.UU., U.S. foreign policy

política exterior de los Estados Unidos, American foreign policy, United States foreign policy

política exterior expansionista, expansionist foreign policy

política fiscal, fiscal policy

política gubernamental, government policy

política gubernamental hacia los pueblos indios, federal Indian policy

política imperial, imperial policy

política interna, domestic policy
política interna de los Estados Unidos, American domestic policy, United States domestic policy
política interna de EE.UU., U.S. domestic policy
política de maquinarias, machine politics
política macroeconómica, macroeconomic policy
política migratoria, immigration policy
política militarista, militarist policy
política monetaria, monetary policy
política nacional, national policy
política pública, public policy
política suicida, brinkmanship
políticas distributivas, distributive policies
políticas nucleares, nuclear politics
políticas patrón-cliente, patron-client politics
políticas redistributivas, redistributive policies
politicastro, carpetbagger
político(a)[2], political
politólogo, political scientist
Polo Norte, North Pole

Polo Sur, South Pole
Polonia, Poland
pólvora, gunpowder
Pompeya, Pompeii
pool, pooling
Popol Vuh, Popul Vuh
populismo, populism
populista, populist
portaaviones, aircraft carrier
portar dinero, carrying money
portuario, port
Portugal, Portugal
portugués, Portuguese
posguerra, postwar
posición, status, position
posición de élite, elite status
posición social, social position
posmodernidad, post-modernism
posmoderno[1], postmodern
posmoderno[2], post-modernist
posteridad, posterity
postura, position
postura de Qing con respecto al opio, Qing position on opio
potasa, potash
potencia mundial, world power
Potencias aliadas, Allied Powers
Potencias centrales, Central Powers
Potencias del Eje, Axis Powers
pozos artesianos, artesian wells

práctica, practice
   práctica agrícola, agricultural practice
   práctica comercial, business practice
   práctica de empleo justo, fair employment practice
   práctica guberna- mentales, practices of government
pradera, grassland, prairie
pragmático, pragmatic
pragmatismo, pragmatism
preámbulo, preamble
preámbulo de la Consti- tución de EE.UU., Preamble of the United States Constituion
prebendas, spoils
precedencia, precedence
precedente, precedent
precio, price
   precio de equilibrio, equilibrium price
   precio de equilibrio del mercado, market clearing price
   precio de las mate- rias primas, commodity price
   precio de mercado, market price
   precio máximo, price ceiling
   precio mínimo, price floor
   precio relativo, relative price
   precio tope, price ceiling
   precio vigente, prevailing price

precipitación, precipitation, rainfall
   precipitación orográfica, orographic precipitation
precisión, accuracy
   precisión de la infor- mación, accuracy of information
preciso, accurate
precolombino, pre-Columbus
predecir, predict
predicción, prediction
predisposición, bias
prefijo telefónico, telephone area code
pregunta, question
   preguntas económi- cas fundamentales, fundamental economic questions
prehistoria, prehistory
prehistórico, prehistoric
prejuicio, prejudice, prepossession, bias
   prejuicio de género sexual, gender bias
Premio Nobel de la Paz, Nobel Peace Prize
prensa, printing press, press
   prensa amarillista, yellow press
preparación militar, military preparedness
presa, dam, quarry
presagio, omen
presente, present
preservación, preservation
   preservación cultu- ral, cultural preserva-

tion
preservación de la Unión, preservation of the Union
preservación histórica, historic preservation
presidencia de John F. Kennedy, John F. Kennedy presidency
presidencia imperial, imperial presidency
presidencial, presidential
presidente, president
presidente de salida, lame duck
presidente del Congreso, Speaker of the House
Presidente provisional del Senado, President Pro-tempore of the Senate
presidio, presidio
prestaciones extras, fringe benefit
préstamo[1], borrowing
préstamo cultural, cultural borrowing
préstamo[2], lending
préstamo y alquiler, lend and lease
prestar, borrow
presunción de inocencia, presumption of innocence
presupuestario, budgetary
presupuesto, budget
presupuesto limitado, limited budget
prevención del delito situacional, situational

crime prevention
primado, primate
primario, primary
Primer Congreso, First Congress
Primer Congreso Continental, First Continental Congress
primer habitante, first inhabitant
primer magistrado, chief magistrate
primer meridiano, prime meridian
primer ministro, prime minister
Primer Nuevo Trato, First New Deal
primera dama, First Lady
Primera Guerra Mundial, World War I
primera infracción, first-time offense
primera persona, first person
primeros auxilios, first aid
primeros habitantes, early inhabitants
primeros habitantes de América, First Americans
primigenio, primeval
primogenitura, primogeniture
Principado de Moscú, Duchy of Moscow
principal, lead
principio, principle, beginning
principio de imposición sobre beneficios, benefit principle

principio de ubicación, location principle
principio inquisitivo, inquisitorial system
principios básicos, basic principles
principios cívicos, civic principles
principios constitucionales, constitutional principles
principios democráticos, principles of democracy
principios fundamentales de la democracia estadounidense, fundamental principles of American democracy
Prisco, Priscus
prisión por deuda, debtor's prisons
privado(a), private
privacidad, privacy
privación del derecho a voto, disenfranchisement
privación relativa, relative deprivation
privado del derecho a voto, disenfranchised
privatización, privatization
privatización desde dentro, insider privatization
privatización espontánea, spontaneous privatization
privatizar, privatize
privilegio, privilege

privilegio del Ejecutivo, executive privilege
privilegio postal, franking privilege
probabilidad, probability
problema, problem, issue
problema de conservación, conservation issue
problema social, social issue
procedimiento penal, criminal procedure
procedimiento Siemens-Martin, open hearth process
procedimientos civiles, civic procedures
procesable, indictable
procesado de alimentos, food processing
procesos, processes
proceso Bessemer, Bessemer process
proceso contencioso, adversarial process
proceso de enmienda, amendment process
proceso de mareas, tidal process
proceso de rusificación, process of Russification
proceso debido, procedural due process
proceso democrático, democratic process
proceso emprendedor, entrepreneurship
proceso físico, physical process

proceso humano, human process

proceso legislativo, legislative process

procesos geológicos, geological processes

procesos mundiales, world processes

proclamación, proclamation

Proclamación de Emancipación, Emancipation Proclamation

procurador general, solicitor general

producción, production

producción de alimentos, food production

producción de alimentos básicos, staple crop production

producción de oro, gold production

producción de plata, silver production

producción en cadena, assembly line

producción en masa, mass production

producción en serie, mass production

producir, produce, yield

productividad, productivity

productivo, productive

producto, product

producto complementario, complementary product

Producto Interno Bruto (PIB), Gross Domestic Product (GDP)

Producto Interno Bruto nominal, nominal Gross Domestic Product

Producto Nacional Bruto (PNB), Gross National Product (GNP)

producto que no es rival, nonrival product

producto sustituto, substitute product

producto terminado, finished product

productor, producer

productos industriales, industrial products

profesor, teacher

profeta, prophet

programa, program

programa agresivo de reclutamiento, aggressive recruitment program

programa de ajuste estructural, structural adjustment program (SAP)

programa de asistencia familiar, family assistance program

programas de ayuda social, entitlement programs

programa de extensión rural, agricultural extension

programas de intervención social, social intervention programs

**programas de recu-
peración,** remedial
programs
**programas de sub-
vención estatal,**
grant-in-aid programs
**programas de trato
preferencial,**
preferential treatment
programs
programa nacional,
domestic program
progresismo, Progressivism
progresista, progressive
progreso, progress
Prohibición, Prohibition
prohibir, outlaw
proletariado, proletariat
proliferación, proliferation
promulgar, enact
promulgar leyes,
enact laws
**propagación de una
enfermedad,**
spread of disease
propaganda[1], propaganda
propaganda[2], advertising
propiedad, property,
ownership
**propiedad de los
bienes,** property
ownership
**propiedad del in-
dividuo,** individual
ownership
propiedad privada,
private property
propiedad pública,
public property
propietario, proprietor
**propietario de
tierras,** patroon
proposición, proposition

propuesta, proposal,
proposition
prorratear, apportion
prorrateo, apportionment
prosperidad, prosperity
**prosperidad repenti-
na,** boom
protección del suelo,
soil conservation
protección igualitaria,
equal protection
**protección igualitaria
de la ley,** equal pro-
tection of the law
proteccionismo,
protectionism
proteccionista,
protectionist
protectorado,
mandate system,
protectorate
protesta, protest
**protesta de la Pla-
za de Tiananmen,**
Tiananmen Square
protest
protesta sentada,
sit-in
protestante, Protestant
protestantismo,
Protestantism
protestar, protest
proveedor, supplier
proverbio, proverb
provincia, province, county
provincial, provincial
provisión, provision
proyección, projection
proyección acimutal,
Azimuthal projection
**proyección cartográ-
fica,** flat-map projec-
tion, map projection

**proyección de merca-
tor,** mercator projec-
tion
proyecto comunitario,
community project
**proyecto de control de
inundaciones,**
flood-control project
**proyecto de la Admi-
nistración para el
Progreso del Empleo,**
WPA project
proyecto de ley, bill
**proyecto de ley sobre
asuntos distintos,**
omnibus bill
Proyecto Manhattan,
Manhattan Project
proyecto público,
public project
prueba de lectura,
literacy test
prueba indirecta, hearsay
prueba religiosa,
religious test
psicolingüística,
psycholinguistics
psicodrama, role playing
psicología, psychology
psicología aplicada,
applied psychology
psicología clínica,
clinical psychology
**psicología de la re-
ligión,** psychology of
religion
**psicología de la sa-
lud,** health psychology
**psicología de la tor-
tura,** psychology of
torture
**psicología evolucio-
nista,** evolutionary

psychology
**psicología experi-
mental,** experimental
psychology
psicología fisiológica,
physiological psycho-
logy
psicología freudiana,
Freudian psychology
**psicología paranor-
mal,** abnormal psy-
chology
psicología política,
political psychology
psicología popular,
popular psychology
psicología social,
social psychology
psicológico, psychological
psicólogo, psychologist
psicópata, psychopath
psicoterapia,
psychotherapy
psique, psyche
psiquiatría, psychiatry
publicación, publication
publicanos, publicans
publicidad, advertising
público, public
publicidad comercial,
commercial adverti-
sing
publicidad masiva,
mass advertising
**Publio Cornelio Escipión
el Africano,**
Scipio Africanus
pueblo, town, village
**pueblo basado en el
comercio,**
market town
**pueblo de la compa-
ñía,** company town

Pueblo del libro,
People of the Book
pueblo escita,
Scythian society
pueblo fantasma,
ghost town
pueblo indoario,
Indo-Aryan people
pueblo minero,
mining town
pueblo minero de Colorado (siglo XIX),
Colorado mining town (19th century)
pueblo nómada dedicado al pastoreo, pastoral nomadic people
pueblo xiongnu,
Xiongnu society
pueblos aborígenes,
aboriginal peoples
pueblos de pastores,
herding societies
pueblos germanos,
Germanic peoples
pueblos germánicos,
Germanic peoples
pueblos indígenas,
indigenous people
pueblos norteamericanos constructores de montículos, North American mound-building people
pueblos sajones,
Saxon peoples
puente, bridge
puente aéreo de Berlín, Berlin Airlift
puente de Beringia,
Bering land bridge
Puente Golden Gate,
Golden Gate Bridge

puercos, hogs
Puerta a Occidente,
Gateway to the West
Puerta Dorada,
Golden Door
puertas abiertas,
open door
puerto, harbor, port
puerto de entrada,
port of entry
puerto de montaña,
mountain pass
puerto fluvial,
inland port
puerto franco,
free port
Puerto Rico, Puerto Rico
puestos del Noroeste,
Northwest posts
punto crítico,
turning point
punto de equilibrio,
equilibrium point
punto de vista,
point of view
punto de vista de la primera persona, first person point of view
punto de vista de la tercera persona, third-person point of view
punto muerto,
stalemate, deadlock
puntos cardinales,
cardinal directions
puntos cardinales intermedios,
intermediate directions
puntos de vista en conflicto, conflicting viewpoints
purgas de Stalin,
Stalin's purge

puritanismo, Puritanism
puritano, Puritan

Q

Quebec francés,
    French Quebec
queroseno, Kerosene
quiebra, bankruptcy
química, chemistry
quipu, quipas
quórum, quorum

R

rabino, rabbi
racial, racial
racionalismo griego,
    Greek rationalism
racionalización,
    rationalization
racionamiento, rationing
racismo, racism
    racismo científico,
    scientific racism
racista, racist
radiación solar,
    solar radiation
radical, radical
    radical político,
    political radical
radicalismo, radicalism
radio, radio
ramadán, Ramadan
Ramsés II, Ramses II
rancho, ranch
rango diplomático,
    diplomatic rank
rápido, rapid
rascacielos, skyscraper
rasgo de personalidad,
    character trait
rasgo físico,
    physical feature
rasgo humano,
    human feature
rasgos culturales,
    cultural exchange
Rasputín, Rasputin
rastra, travois
ratificación, confirmation,
    ratification
    **ratificación de
    un tratado,**
    treaty ratification
ratificar, ratify
Raymond Poincaré,
    Raymond Poincare
raza, race
razón[1], ratio
    **razón de dependen-
    cia,** dependency ratio
    **razón de costo-bene-
    ficio,** cost-benefit ratio
razón[2], reason
    razones morales,
    moral reasons
razonado, reasoned
razonamiento circular,
    circular reasoning,
    circular thinking
razonamiento deductivo,
    deductive reasoning
razonamiento inductivo,
    inductive reasoning
**razonamiento jurispru-
dencial**, jurispruden-
    tial thinking
razonamiento práctico,
    practical reasoning

razonar

razonar, reason, argue
reacción blanca,
white backlash
reaccionario, reactionary
reactivación económica,
economic recovery
reactivar la economía,
pump-priming
realeza, royalty
realidad, reality
realineación partidista,
party realignment
realismo, Realism
  realismo de izquier-
  da, left realism
  realismo idealizado,
  idealized realism
  realismo político,
  realpolitik
  realismo racial,
  racial realism
  realismo socialista,
  Socialist Realism
realista jurídico,
judicial realist
realpolitik, realpolitik
reasentamiento,
resettlement
rebelde, rebel
rebelión, rebellion
  Rebelión de Bacon,
  Bacon's rebellion
  rebelión de esclavos,
  slave rebellion
  rebelión de la
  Bandera del oso,
  Bear Flag Revolt
  Rebelión de la India,
  Indian uprising
  rebelión de Leisler,
  Leisler's Rebellion
  Rebelión de los
  bóxers,

Boxer Rebellion
  rebelión de los indios
  Pueblo, Pueblo Revolt
  Rebelión de Pontiac,
  Pontiac's Rebellion
  Rebelión de Shays,
  Shay's Rebellion
  Rebelión de Stono,
  Stono Rebellion
  Rebelión Decembris-
  ta, Decembrist uprising
  Rebelión del
  whiskey,
  Whiskey Rebellion
  rebelión Taiping,
  Taiping Rebellion
rebrote, regrowth
recesión, recession
reciclaje,
recycling, reclamation
reciclar, recycle
recién llegado, newcomer
recinto religioso,
religious facility
reciprocidad, reciprocity
reclamar, reclaim
reclamo de tierra,
land claim
reclutamiento,
draft, conscription
recobrar, recover
recolector, gatherer
recompensa, reward
  recompensas políti-
  cas, pork barrel
recomposición de la
corte, court packing
reconcentración,
reconcentration
reconciliación,
reconciliation
reconocimiento diplo-

mático, diplomatic recognition
reconquista de España, reconquest of Spain
Reconstrucción, Reconstruction
Reconstrucción negra, Black Reconstruction
recreo, recreation
recuerdo, memento
recuperación, repossession, reclamation
recuperación económica, economic recovery
recuperar, recover, reclaim
recurso, resource
    recurso capital, capital resource
    recurso de flujo, flow resource
    recurso escaso, scarce resource
    recurso humano, human resource
    recurso importado, imported resource
    recurso legal, legal recourse
    recurso local, local resource
    recurso mineral, mineral resource
    recurso natural, natural resource
    recurso no renovable, nonrenewable resource
    recurso renovable, renewable resource
    recursos bibliotecarios, library resources
    recursos capitales, capital resources
    recursos comunes, pooled resources
    recursos limitados, limited resources
    recursos mundiales, world resources
    recursos no renovables, non-renewable resources
red, network
    red alimentaria, food web
    red comercial económica contemporánea, contemporary economic trade network
    red de arrastre, trawl
    red de autopistas interestatales, interstate highway system
    red de carreteras, road system
    red de carreteras romanas, Roman system of roads
    red de comunicación, communication network
    red de crimen, crime net
    red de transporte, transportation network
    red global, global grid
    red social, social network
    red trófica, food web
    redes de carreteras, systems of roads
redistribución de la riqueza, redistribution of wealth

redistribución de los distritos electorales, redistricting

redistribución del ingreso, redistribution of income

reduccion, reduction

reducción de impuestos, tax reduction

reducción de la diversidad de especies, reduction of species diversity

reducción de las aguas subterráneas, groundwater reduction

reducción de los bosques tropicales de África Central, depleted rain forests of central Africa

reducción de riesgos, risk reduction

reducción del daño, harm reduction

reduccionismo psicológico, psychological reductionism

reducir, reduce

reembolso, rebate

reencarnación, reincarnation

reestructuración, restructuring

referencia, reference

referendo, referendum

reforestación, reforestation

reforma, reform

Reforma católica, Catholic Reformation

reforma del financiamiento de campañas electorales, campaign finance reform

reforma del mercado, market reform

reforma del servicio civil, civil service reform

reforma educativa, educational reform

Reforma en Europa, European Reformation

reforma moral, moral reform

reforma penitenciaria, prison reform

Reforma protestante, Protestant Reformation, Reformation

reforma social, social reform

reforma utópica, utopian reform

reformas económicas, economic reforms

reformador, reformer

reformador social, social reformer

reformadores religiosos, religious reformers

refuerzo, reinforcement

refugiado, refugee

refugiado judío, Jewish refugee

refugiados del mar vietnamitas, Vietnamese boat people

refugio, shelter, lodge

refugios de huracanes, hurricane shelter

refugio de vida sil-

vestre, wildlife refuge
refutabilidad, refutability, falsifiability
régimen, regime
  régimen autoritario, authoritarian rule
  régimen colonial europeo, European colonial rule
  régimen de Diem, Diem regime
  régimen fascista, fascist regime
  régimen señorial, manorialism
  régimen totalitario, totalitarian regime
región, region
  región andina, Andean region
  región autónoma, autonomous region
  región báltica, Baltic region
  región climática, climate region, climatic region
  región compuesta, composite region
  región cultural, cultural region
  región de contacto, region of contact
  región de cordillera y valle, ridge and valley region
  región de los Grandes Lagos, Great Lakes region
  región de percepción, perceptual region
  región de Piamonte, Piedmont Region

  región de suelos, soil region
  región de vegetación, vegetation region
  región del Atlántico central, Middle Atlantic Region
  región del Cabo, Cape region
  región del Egeo, Aegean region
  región demográfica, population region
  región económica, economic region
  región formal, formal region
  región funcional, functional region
  región lingüística, language region
  región local, local region
  región manufacturera, manufacturing region
  región mediterránea, Mediterranean region
  región panorámica, scenic area
  región pobre en energía, energy-poor region
  región política, political region
  región rural, rural region
  regiones del mundo, world regions
  regiones físicas, physical regions
  regiones geográficas, geographic regions

regionalismo

regionalismo, sectionalism, regionalism
regionalista, sectionalist
regionalización,
regionalization
registro, record
**registro e incau-
tación,** search and
seizure
registro escrito,
written record
**registro y confisca-
ción ilegal,**
illegal search and
seizure
registros del pasado,
records from the past
regla, rule, regulation
regla arbitraria,
capricious rule, arbi-
trary rule
regla de exclusión,
exclusionary rule
**regla del peligro
claro e inminente,**
clear and present
danger rule
regreso a la normalidad,
return to normalcy
**regreso al ámbito domés-
tico,** return to domes-
ticity
regulación, regulation
regulación de zonas,
zoning regulation
**regulación del
crecimiento,**
growth management
**regulación del uso
de suelo,** land use
regulation
**regulación guberna-
mental,** government

regulation
**reguladores de
Carolina,** Carolina
regulators
regular, regulate
rehén, hostage
reina, queen
reina Hatshepsut,
Queen Hatshepsut
reinado, reign
reinar, reign
reino, kingdom
reino de Saba,
Sheba
reino ermitaño,
Hermit Kingdom
Reino Medio,
Middle Kingdom
Reino Unido, Britain
reivindicar, reclaim
reja de arado de acero,
steel-tipped plow
relajación de tensión,
détente
rejilla, grid
relación, relationship
**relación entre el
Sol y la Tierra,** Earth-
sun relationship
relación especial,
special relationship
**relación humana
con un lugar,**
human connection to
place
relación social,
social relationship
relaciones de raza,
race relations
**relaciones del trián-
gulo de hierro,** iron
triangle relationships
relaciones entre cla-

ses, class relations

relaciones exteriores, foreign relations

relaciones geopolíticas, geopolitical relationships

relaciones Iglesia-Estado, church-state relations

relaciones industriales, industrial relations

relaciones interestatales, interstate relations

relaciones internacionales, international relations

relaciones laborales, labor relations

relaciones políticas, political relationships

relativismo cultural, cultural relativism

relativo, relative

relato bíblico del Génesis, biblical account of Genesis

relato histórico, historical account

releer, reread

relevancia, relevance

relieve, land form

relieve geográfico, landform relief

religión, religion

religión maya, Mayan religion

religión oficial, established religion

religiones del mundo, world religions

religiosidad, religiosity

religioso, religious

reliquias, relics

relojes, clocks

remedio legal, legal remedy

remisión, cross-reference

remitir a un tribunal inferior, remand

remoción de los chickasaw, Chickasaw removal

remoción de los choctaw, Choctaw removal

remoción de los cree, Cree removal

remoción de los cri, Cree removal

remoción de los indios (nativos americanos), Indian removal

remoción de los semínolas, Seminole removal

remuneración, wages

Renacimiento, Renaissance

Renacimiento de Harlem, Harlem Renaissance

Renacimiento italiano, Italian Renaissance

renacimiento religioso, religious revival, revival

Renacimiento en Europa, European Renaissance

rendición incondicional, unconditional surrender

rendimiento, output, yield

rendimiento de la cosecha, crop yield
rendimiento de la inversión, return on investment
rendimiento de producción, production output
rendimiento por hora, output per hour
rendimiento por máquina, output per machine
rendimiento por trabajador, output per worker
rendimiento por unidad de tierra, output per unit of land
rendir, yield
rendirse, surrender
reno, reindeer
renta, rent, income
renta fija, fixed income
renta per cápita, per capita income
rentabilidad, profitability
reparacion, reparation
reparación de agravios, redress of grievances
repartir, allocate, apportion
repartir de nuevo, reapportion
reparto, partition, allotment, allocation, apportionment
reparto de África, partition of Africa, scramble for Africa
reparto de tierras por

cabeza, headright
registro de electores, voter registration
repertorio, repertoire
repliegue, retreat
represalia, retaliation
representación, representation
representación geográfica, geographic representation
representación proporcional, proportional representation
representación virtual, virtual representation
representante, representative
representante electo, elected representative
representativo, representative
represión, repression
república, republic
república autónoma, autonomous republic
Republica Centroafricana, Central African Republic
República Checa, Czech Republic
república clásica, classical republic
República de la Estrella Solitaria, Lone Star Republic
república de la unión, union republic
República de Platón, Plato's Republic
República de Texas, republic of Texas

resolución presupuestaria

República de Weimar, Weimar Republic
República Dominicana, Dominican Republic
república federal, federal republic
República Federal Alemana, German Federal Republic
República Holandesa, Dutch Republic
república islámica, Islamic republic
República Popular China, People's Republic of China
República Romana, Roman Republic
republicanismo, republicanism
republicanismo clasico, classical republicanism
republicanismo del siglo XVIII, 18th century republicanism
republicanismo moderno, modern republicanism
republicano, Republican
republicanos radicales, Radical Republicans
repudiar, repudiate
requerimiento judicial, injunction
requisar, impress
requisición, impressment
requisito, qualification, requirement
requisito por estatuto, statutory requirement
rescatar, rescue
rescate, rescue
reserva, reservation
Reserva federal, Federal Reserve
reserva natural, nature preserve
reservas de fosfatos, phosphate reserves
reservas indias, reservations
reservas mínimas, reserve requirement
reservación, reservation
residencia, residency
residente, resident
residuo común, common refuse
resignación, resignation
resistencia, resistance
resistencia no violenta, nonviolent resistance
resistencia pasiva, passive resistance
resocialización, resocialization
resolución, resolution
resolución de conflictos, conflict resolution
resolución de la ONU, UN resolution
resolución de litigios, dispute resolution
resolución de problemas, problem solving
resolución del Golfo de Tonkín, Gulf of Tonkin Resolution
resolución presupuestaria, budget resolution

resolver, resolve
respeto, respect
  respeto ciego,
  blind respect
  **respeto del indivi-
  duo,** individual
  respect
  **respeto por el
  derecho ajeno,**
  respect for the rights
  of others
  respeto por la ley,
  respect for law
  **respeto por los
  demás,** respect for
  others
  **respeto por los dere-
  chos de los demás,**
  respect for the rights
  of others
responsabilidad,
  liability, responsibility,
  accountability
  **responsabilidad
  absoluta,**
  absolute liability
  responsabilidad civil,
  civic responsibility
  **la responsabilidad
  del hombre blanco,**
  White Man's Burden
  **responsabilidad del
  Estado hacia los na-
  tivos americanos,**
  trust responsibility
  **responsabilidad em-
  presarial,** corporate
  responsibility
  **responsabilidad ilimi-
  tada,** absolute liability
  **responsabilidad in-
  condicional,**
  absolute liability
  **responsabilidad
  individual,** individual
  responsibility
  **responsabilidad
  moral,** moral
  responsibility
  **responsabilidad sin
  fundamentos,**
  unfunded liability
  **responsabilidad
  personal,** personal
  responsibility
  **responsabilidad polí-
  tica,** political
  accountability
restauración, restoration
  Restauración Meiji,
  restoration
**restaurante de comida
  rápida,** fast-food
  restaurant
**restricción gubernamen-
  tal,** government
  restriction
restricción judicial,
  judicial restraint
**restricción presupuesta-
  ria,** budget constraint
restricción previa,
  prior restraint
**restricciones de tiempo,
  lugar y manera,**
  time, place, manner
  restrictions
resultados no previstos,
  unintended results
resultados previstos,
  intended results
resumen, outline
  resumen estadístico,
  statistical abstract
resumir, summarize,
  abbreviate

retaguardia, home front
retención de la seguridad social, social security withholding
retirada, retreat
retirarse, retreat
retiro, retirement
retórica, rhetoric
   retórica moral, moral rhetoric
retractarse, recant
retribución en especie, fringe benefit
reubicación de japoneses, Japanese relocation
reubicación forzada, forced relocation
reubicar, relocate
reunificación, reunification
reunión municipal, town meeting
reuniones públicas, public meetings
reunirse, assemble
reutilizable, reusable
reutilizar, reuse
reverencia, reverence
revisión de aduana, customs search
revisión de inmigración, immigration screening
revisión de la Corte Suprema, higher court review
revisionismo, revisionism
revocar, repeal
revolución, revolution
   Revolución agraria, Agrarian Revolution
   revolución agrícola neolítica, Neolithic Agricultural Revolution
revolución armada, armed revolution
Revolución china, Chinese Revolution
revolución científica, scientific revolution
Revolución comercial, Commercial Revolution
Revolución comunista, Communist Revolution
Revolución comunista china, Chinese Communist Revolution
Revolución cubana, Cuban Revolution
Revolución cultural proletaria, Cultural Revolution
Revolución de los transportes, Transportation Revolution
Revolución de Octubre, October Revolution
revolución de Reagan, Reagan revolution
Revolución de Texas, Texas Revolution
Revolución estadounidense, American Revolution
Revolución francesa, French Revolution
Revolución Gloriosa, Glorious Revolution
Revolución haitiana, Haitian Revolution

Revolución húngara,
Hungarian revolt
Revolución Indus-trial, Industrial Revolution
Revolución informática, Computer Revolution
Revolución inglesa,
English Revolution
revolución latinoamericana, Latin American revolution
revolución mercantil,
market revolution
Revolución mexicana, Mexican Revolution
revolución neolítica,
Agricultural Revolution
Revolución polaca,
Polish rebellion
Revolución puritana,
Puritan Revolution
Revolución republicana china, China's Republican Revolution
Revolución rusa,
Russian Revolution
Revolución verde,
Green Revolution
Revuelta de Haymarket,
Haymarket Rebellion
rey Alfonso I del Congo, King Afonso I of Kongo
rey Alfredo de Inglaterra, King Alfred of England
rey Algodón, King Cotton
rey Jacobo I, King James I
rey Mansa Musa,
Monarch Mansa Musa

reyerta familiar,
blood feud
reyes sacerdotes,
priest-kings
rezo en las escuelas,
school prayer
rezo en las escuelas públicas, prayer in public schools
riachuelo, creek
Riad, Riyadh
riesgo, risk
    riesgo económico,
    economic risk
    riesgo natural,
    natural hazard
    riesgo tecnológico,
    technological hazard
río, river
    río abajo,
    downstream
    río Allegheny,
    Allegheny River
    río arriba,
    upstream
    río Colorado,
    Colorado River
    río Columbia,
    Columbia River
    río de barro,
    mud slide
    río Delaware,
    Delaware River
    río Grande (río Bravo), Rio Grande River
    río Misisipi,
    Mississippi River
    río Misuri,
    Missouri River
    río navegable,
    navigable river
    río Níger, Niger River
    río Ohio, Ohio River

río Ruhr, Ruhr
ríos navegables, navigable rivers
riqueza, wealth, affluence
riqueza de las naciones, Wealth of Nations
rito de iniciación, rite of passage
ritual, ritual
rivalidad de las superpotencias, superpower rivalry
rol de género, gender role
rol de raza, racial role
rol familiar, family role
Roma, Rome
romance, ballad
romanización de Europa, Romanization of Europe
romanticismo, Romanticism
rompeolas, sea wall
rosa, rose
rosa de los vientos, compass rose
rotación de cultivos, crop rotation
Ruanda, Rwanda
rueca, spinning wheel, wheel
rueda de la vida, Wheel of Life
Rumanía, Romania
runas, runes
rural, rural
Rusia, Russia
Rusia de Kiev, Kievan Russia
ruso blanco, White Russian
rusos rojos, Red Russian

ruta, route
ruta comercial, trade route
ruta comercial marítima, maritime trade route
ruta comercial por tierra, overland trade route
rutas comerciales internacionales, international trade routes
ruta de evacuación, evacuation route
ruta de exploración, exploration route
ruta de la seda, Silk Road
ruta de suministro, supply route
ruta de transporte, transportation route
ruta del comercio triangular, triangular trade route
ruta histórica, historical route
ruta marítimas, seaway

sábado (judíos), sabbath
sabana, savanna
sabbat, sabbath
sacar conclusiones, drawing conclusions
sacerdote, priest

sachem, Sachem
sacramentos, sacraments
sacrificio ritual,
  ritual sacrifice
saga, saga
sagrado, sacred
  **Sagrado de los sagra-
  dos,** holy of holies
salario, salary, wage
  salario mínimo,
  minimum wage
saldo, balance
salinización de Ruanda,
  Rwanda salinization
salinización del suelo,
  soil salinization
Salomón, Solomon
salón de clases, classroom
Salón francés, French salon
salud, health
  salud pública,
  public health
Samarcanda, Samarkand
Samori Turé, Samori Ture
samurái, samurai
San Agustín, St. Augustine
sanción, sanction
  **sanciones económi-
  cas,** economic sanc-
  tions
Sandinistas, Sandinistas
sangre azul, blue blood
Santísima Trinidad,
  Holy Trinity
santo, saint
santuarios, shrines
Sargón, Sargon
satélite, satellite
sección, section
seccional, sectional
secesión, secession
secta, sect
sector de cuello blanco,

  white-collar sector
sector informal,
  informal sector
sector privado,
  private sector
sector profesional,
  professional sector
secuaces, henchmen
secuencia, sequence
secuestro, hijacking
secular, secular
secularismo, secularism
secularización,
  secularization
secundario, secondary
seda, silk
sedición, sedition
sedicioso, seditious
sedimento, sediment
segadora mecánica,
  mechanical reaper
segregación, segregation
  segregación de facto,
  de facto segregation
  segregación de jure,
  de jure segregation
  segregación racial,
  racial segregation
seguidores de Shays,
  Shaysites
Segunda Guerra Mundial,
  World War II
**segunda revolución indus-
  trial,** second indus-
  trial revolution
segunda vuelta, runoff
**segundas elecciones
  primarias,**
  runoff primary
**Segundo Congreso Conti-
  nental,** Second Conti-
  nental Congress
segundo frente,

second front
segundo Gran Despertar, Second Great Awakening
segundo Nuevo Trato, Second New Deal
seguridad, safety, security
  seguridad colectiva, collective security
  seguridad de los productos de consumo, consumer product safety
  seguridad de los trabajadores, worker safety
  seguridad económica, economic security
  seguridad nacional, national security
  seguridad pública, public safety
  seguridad social, Social Security
seguro, insurance
  seguro de salud, health care
selección, choice
  selección por méritos, merit selection
selva, forest
  selva de Malasia, Malaysian rain forest
  selva tropical, rain forest, tropical rain forest
semáforos, traffic lights
semana, week
sembradora, seed drill
semejanzas, similarities
semiexperimento, quasi-experiment
Sena, Seine

Senado, Senate
senador, senator
  senador estatal, state senator
sendero, trail
  Sendero de lágrimas, Trail of Tears
  Sendero de lágrimas cherokee, Cherokee Trail of Tears
Séneca, Seneca
senescal, seneschal
señor, squire, lord
  señor feudal, feudal lord
  señor independiente, independent lord
señorío, manor
sentada, sit-in
sentencia declarativa, declaratory judgment
sentido común, common sense
separación, separation
  separación de la Iglesia y el Estado, separation of church and state
separados pero iguales, separate but equal
separar del Estado, disestablish
separarse, secede
sequía, drought
Ser Supremo, Supreme Being
servicio, service
  servicio al cliente, customer service
  servicio civil, civil service
  servicio comunitario, community service

servicio consular, consular service

Servicio de Impuestos Internos (IRS), Internal Revenue Service (IRS)

Servicio de Parques Nacionales, National Park Service

Servicio de Salud Pública, Public Health Service

servicio de transmisión de facsímil, facsimile transmission service

Servicio Exterior de los Estados Unidos, Foreign Service

servicio militar, military draft

servicio público, public service

servicio selectivo, selective service

Servicios de Inmigración y de Naturalización, Immigration and Naturalization Services

servicios del gobierno local, local government services

servicios fiduciarios, trusteeship

servicios sanitarios, health services

servicios sociales, social services

servidumbre, serfdom

servidumbre por contrato, indentured servitude

servil, subservient

sesgo, bias

sexismo, sexism

sexo, sex

shogunato Tokugawa, Tokugawa shogunate

Siberia, Siberia

Sicilia, Sicily

sida, AIDS

siderurgia, iron metallurgy

Sierra Nevada, Sierra Nevada

siervo, serf

siglo, century

siglo veinte, twentieth century

signos convencionales, legend

signos convencionales del mapa, map key

sij, Sikh

sílex, flint

Silo, Shiloh

silueta, contour

silvicultura, forestry

sima, mantle

simbiótico, symbiotic

simbolismo, symbolism

símbolo, symbol

símbolo cultural, cultural symbol

símbolo estadounidense, American symbol

símbolos del estado, state symbols

símbolos patrios, patriotic symbols

similar, alike

simultáneo, concurrent

sin fuerza legal, null and void

sin hogar, homeless
sin salida al mar,
  landlocked
sin techo, homeless
sinagoga, synagogue
sindicato, trade union,
  organized labor
  **Sindicato America-
  no de Ferrocarriles,**
  American Railway
  Union
**síndrome del sobrevivien-
  te,** survivor syndrome
sinergia, synergy
Singapur, Singapore
sinocéntrico, Sinocentric
sintetizar, Synthesize
sintoísmo, Shintoism
sionismo, Zionism
Siria, Syria
siroco, sirocco
sirviente contratado,
  indentured servant
sirviente por contrato,
  indentured servant
sismo, earthquake
sistema, system
  sistema acusatorio,
  adversary system
  sistema adversarial,
  adversary system
  **sistema alfanumé-
  rico,** alphanumeric
  system
  Sistema Americano,
  American System
  sistema autoritario,
  authoritarian system
  **sistema bipartidis-
  mo,** two-party system
  sistema cosmético,
  cosmetic system
  sistema cultural,

culture system
sistema de alianzas,
system of alliances
**sistema de aporte y
dispersión,**
hub-and-spoke
sistema de canales,
canal system
sistema de castas,
caste system
sistema de clases,
class system
sistema de comités,
committee system
**sistema de comuni-
cación contemporá-
neo,** contemporary
system of communica-
tion
**sistema de comuni-
cación por satélite,**
satellite-based com-
munications system
**sistema de consig-
nación,** consignment
system
**sistema de contro-
les y contrapesos,**
system of checks and
balances
sistema de cuotas,
quota system
**sistema de derecho
de retención de cose-
cha,** crop lien system
**sistema de enco-
mienda,** encomienda
system
sistema de escritura,
writing system
**sistema de escritura
chino,** Chinese writing
system

sistema de fábrica,
factory system
sistema de gabinete,
cabinet system
sistema de gobierno,
government system,
polity
**sistema de impren-
ta de tipos móviles,**
moveable type printing
machines
**Sistema de Informa-
ción Geográfica (SIG),**
Geographic Informa-
tion Systems (GIS)
**Sistema de la Reser-
va Federal,** Federal
Reserve System
**sistema de libre em-
presa,** free enterprise
system
**sistema de libre em-
presa estadouniden-
se,** U.S. Free Enter-
prise System
**sistema de libre
mercado,** free-market
system
**sistema de New
Lanark de Robert
Owen,**
Robert Owen's New
Lanark System
sistema de partidos,
party system
**sistema de pesos
y medidas,**
system of weights and
measures
**sistema de plan-
tación,** plantation
system
sistema de preben-

das, prebendalism,
spoils system
**sistema de privile-
gios políticos,**
spoils system
**sistema de registro
de la propiedad rural,**
land-survey system
**sistema de reparto
de tierras por cabeza,**
headright system
**sistema de reser-
vación,** reservation
system
**sistema de respon-
sabilidad doméstica,**
household responsibi-
lity system
sistema de satélites,
satellite system
**sistema de sentencia
obligatoria,** manda-
tory sentencing system
**sistema de servicio
civil,** civil service system
**sistema de tesore-
ría independiente,**
Independent Treasury
System
**sistema de trabajo li-
bre,** free labor system
**sistema de transpor-
te,** transport system,
transportation system
**sistema de trans-
porte rápido,** rapid
transit
**sistema de trenes
ligeros,** tight-rail
system
**sistema de tribuna-
les federales,** federal

court system
sistema de Westminster, Westminster model
sistema decimal, decimal system
sistema dinámico, dynamic system
sistema distributivo, distributive system
sistema doméstico, Put Out System
sistema ecológico, ecological system
sistema económico, economic system
sistema económico de mercado, market economic system
sistema económico internacional, international economic system
sistema económico mixto, mixed economic system
sistema económico tradicional, traditional economic system
sistema educativo, education system
sistema electoral, electoral system
sistema electoral de escrutinio nominal mayoritario, single-member plurality electoral system
sistema electoral donde el ganador se lleva todo, winner-

take-all system
sistema federal, federal system
sistema feudal, feudal system
sistema feudal japonés basado en la lealtad, feudal Japanese loyalty
sistema fluvial, river system
sistema humano, human system
sistema monárquico, monarchial system
sistema monetario, medium of exchange
Sistema Monetario Europeo (EMS), European Monetary System (EMS)
sistema parlamentario, parliamentary system
sistema político confederado, confederal political system
sistema político de poderes compartidos, shared powers political system
sistema político estadounidense, American political system
sistema político parlamentario, parliamentary political system
sistema presidencial estadounidense, American presidential system

sistema proporcional, proportional system

sistema rígido de clases sociales, rigid social class system

sistema señorial, manor system

sistema señorial europeo, European manorial system

sistema social hereditario, hereditary social system

sistema solar, solar system

sistema totalitario, totalitarian system

sistema tribal, tribal system

sistema unitario, unitary system

sistemas de creencias, belief systems

sistemas de gobernanza, governance systems

sistemas de intercambio, exchange systems

sistemas éticos, ethical systems

sistemas políticos, political systems

sistemas políticos comparados, comparative government systems

sistémico, systemic

sitio¹, site, place

sitio arqueológico, archaeological site

sitio histórico, historic site

sitio², siege

sitio de Troya, siege of Troy

situación, situation

siux, Sioux

soberanía, sovereignty

soberanía del consumidor, consumer sovereignty

soberanía del individuo, individual ownership

soberanía estatal, state sovereignty

soberanía parlamentaria, parliamentary sovereignty

soberanía popular, popular sovereignty

soberano(a), sovereign

sobornar, bribe

soborno, bribery, kickbacks

sobrecarga, surcharge

sobregeneralización, over-generalization

sobrepesca, overfishing

sobrepoblación, overpopulation

sobrerrepresentación, overrepresentation

sobresimplificación, oversimplification

sobresimplificar, over simplify

social, social

socialista, socialist

socialización, socialization

socialización política, political socialization

sociedad, society, partnership

sociedad agraria, agricultural society

sociedad agrícola, agrarian society

sociedad agrícola neolítica, Neolithic agricultural society

Sociedad Americana de Colonización, American Colonization Society

sociedad anónima, joint stock company

sociedad cimarrona, Maroon Society

sociedad cívica, civic society

sociedad civil, civil society

sociedad comanditaria simple, limited partnership

sociedad cristiana medieval, medieval Christian society

sociedad de clases, class system

sociedad de consumo, consumer society

sociedad de masas, mass society

Sociedad de Naciones, League of Nations

sociedad de participación financiera, holding company

sociedad democrática, democratic society

sociedad dual, dual society

sociedad estadounidense, American society

sociedad euroasiática, Eurasian society

sociedad feudal, feudal society

sociedad feudal japonesa, Japanese feudal society

sociedad industrial, industrial society

sociedad moderna temprana, early modern society

sociedad móvil, mobile society

sociedad patriarcal, patriarchal society

sociedad por acciones, joint stock company

sociedad posindustrial, post-industrial society

sociedad primitiva, primitive society

sociedad rural, folk society

sociedad sin clases, classless society

sociedades acéfalas, acephalous societies

sociedades de ayuda mutua, mutual aid societies

sociedades europeas occidental y oriental, Western and Eastern European societies

socioeconómico, socioeconomic

sociología, sociology

sociología política, political sociology

sociólogo, sociologist

Sócrates

Sócrates, Socrates
sofisticado,
sophisticated
sogún, shogun
sol de medianoche,
midnight sun
soldado, soldier
soldado afroamericano de la Unión,
African-American
Union soldier
soldado cristiano,
Christian soldier
soldados búfalo,
Buffalo Soldiers
soldados de Hesse,
Hessians
soldados hessianos,
Hessians
solidaridad, solidarity
solidaridad colectiva,
collective solidarity
solidaridad mecánica, mechanical
solidarity
solidaridad orgánica,
organic solidarity
Solón, Solon
solsticio de invierno,
winter solstice
solsticio de verano,
summer solstice
solución, solution
solución de conflictos, dispute resolution
Solución final,
Final Solution
soluciones alternativas, alternative solutions
sombra pluviométrica,
rain shadow
sondeo, survey

sondeo de opinión,
public opinion poll
sorgo, sorghum
sostenible, sustainable
sotavento, leeward
soviético(a), Soviet
spot publicitario,
advertisement
status quo, status quo
suajili, Swahili
subconsumo,
underconsumption
subcontinente,
subcontinent
subcontratación,
outsourcing
subcontratar, outsource
subcultura, subculture
subcultura carcelaria, prison subculture
súbditos, subject
subdividido,
partitioned
subida al trono de Isabel I de Inglaterra, accession of Elizabeth I
subjetividad, subjectivity
subjetivismo, subjectivism
subjetivo, subjective
submarino, submarine
subsidio, subsidy
subsidio gubernamental, government subsidy
subtitulaje, captioning
suburbanización,
suburbanization
suburbano, suburban
suburbio, suburb
suburbios de tranvía,
streetcar suburbs
subversión, subversion
subversivo, subversive

suceso, event
  suceso aleatorio,
  chance event
sucesor, dauphin
  sucesos críticos,
  critical events
Sudáfrica, South Africa
Sudamérica,
  South America
Sudán, Sudan
sudoeste, Southwest
  Sudoeste asiático,
  Southwest Asia
Suecia, Sweden
sueco, Swedish
sueldo, wage
suelo, soil, sod
  suelo agrícola,
  agricultural soil
sueño americano,
  American dream
sufismo, Sufism
sufragio, suffrage
  sufragio femenino,
  woman suffrage
  sufragio universal
  para los hombres
  blancos,
  universal white male
  suffrage
Suiza, Switzerland
Suleimán el Magnífico,
  Suleiman the Magni-
  ficent
suministro, provision
  suministros medicos,
  medical provisions
  suministros navales,
  naval supplies
sunismo, Sunnism
sunita, Sunni
superávit comercial,
  trade surplus

superávit presupuestario,
  budget surplus
supercarretera de la información, information
  superhighway
superdelegados,
  superdelegates
superficie, yard size
superioridad, superiority
superpoblación,
  overpopulation
superpotencias,
  superpowers
superstición,
  superstition
supervisión legislativa,
  legislative oversight
supervisor, overseer
suposición, assumption
supremacía federal,
  federal supremacy
supremacía legislativa,
  legislative supremacy
supremacía parlamen-
  taria, parliamentary
  supremacy
supuesto, assumption
sur, south
  sur de la India,
  South India
  sur de la Penínsu-
  la Ibérica,
  Southern Iberia
  Sur global,
  Global South
surcos, furrows
Sureste asiático,
  Southeast Asia
surrealismo, Surrealism
surrealista, Surrealist
sustentable, sustainable
swahili, Swahili

tabaco, tobacco
tabernáculo,
    holy of holies
tabla, grid
    tabla de contenido,
    table of contents
    tabla de millaje,
    mileage table
    tabla plana,
    flat board
tabú, taboo
táctica, tactic
    **táctica de tierra
    quemada,**
    scorched-earth policy
    táctica militar,
    military tactic
taiga, taiga
Tailandia, Thailand
Taiwán, Taiwan
tala, logging
    tala de árboles,
    timber cutting
    **tala excesiva de los
    bosques de pinos,**
    overcutting of pine
    forest
**talladura de herramientas
    en bronce,** bronze
    tool-making techno-
    logy
taller cerrado,
    closed shop
taller no sindicalizado,
    open shop
**tamaño promedio del
    hogar,** average family
    size

Tamerlán, Timur the Lame
    (Tamerlane)
Tammany Hall,
    Tammany Hall
tanino, tannin
taoísmo, Daoism,Taoism
tarea, chore
tarifa, tariff
    tarifa de ingresos,
    revenue tariff
    Tarifa Underwood,
    Underwood Tariff
tarjeta de crédito,
    credit card
tasa, rate
    **tasa anual equivalen-
    te,** annual percentage
    rate
    **tasa bruta de
    mortalidad,**
    crude death rate
    **tasa bruta de natali-
    dad,** crude birth rate
    **tasa de accidentali-
    dad,** casualty rate
    **tasa de consumo
    de recursos,** rate of
    resource consumption
    **tasa de crecimiento
    demográfico,** popula-
    tion growth rate
    **tasa de crecimien-
    to natural,** rate of
    natural increase
    tasa de descuento,
    discount rate
    tasa de desempleo,
    unemployment rate
    tasa de fertilidad,
    fertility rate
    tasa de inflación,
    inflation rate
    tasa de interés,

interest rate

tasa de interés corriente, current interest rate

tasa de interés fija, fixed rate of interest

tasa de interés nominal, nominal interest rate

tasa de interés real, real interest rate

tasa de mortalidad, death rate, mortality rate

tasa de mortalidad infantil, infant mortality rate

tasa de natalidad, birth rate

tasa porcentual anual, annual percentage rate

tasa prevista de inflación, expected rate of inflation

taurocatapsia, bull leaping

tazón de arroz de hierro, iron rice bowl

teatro de operaciones del Pacífico, Pacific Theater

teatro europeo, European theater

teatro griego, Greek drama

teatro noh japonés, Noh drama

techo de cristal, glass ceiling

técnica de investigación, investigative technique

técnica de irrigación central, center-pivot irrigation

técnica de pintura china, brush painting

técnicas de explotación agrícola, farming techniques

técnicas propagandísticas, propaganda techniques

tecnócratas, technocrats

tecnología, technology

  tecnología agrícola, agricultural technology

  tecnología de comunicación, communication technology

  tecnología geográfica, geographic technology

  tecnología informática, computer technology

  tecnología marítima, maritime technology

  tecnología nuclear, nuclear technology

tecnológico, technological

tectónica de placas, plate tectonics

Texas, Texas

tejido, weaving

telar mecánico, power loom

telecomunicación, telecommunication

teledemocracia, teledemocracy

teledetección, remote sensing

telégrafo, telegraph

Telegrama de Ems, Ems telegram

telescopio, telescope
teletrabajo, telecommuting
tema, theme
temazcal, sweat lodge
temblor, earthquake
temperatura, temperature
templanza, temperance
templo, temple
   templo de Madurai, temple of Madurai
temporada, season
tendencia, bias, trend
   tendencia de la globalización, globalizing trend
   tendencias de población, population trends
   tendencias económicas, economic trends
Tenochtitlán, Tenochtitlan
tensión, tension
   tensión étnica, ethnic tension
   tensiones sociales, social tensions
teocracia, theocracy
teocrático, theocratic
teología, theology
   teología de la liberación, liberation theology
   teología medieval, medieval theology
teoría, theory
   teoría crítica, critical theory
   teoría de custodia, stewardship theory
   teoría de "divide y vencerás" de Joseph François Dupleix, Joseph Francois Dupleix's theory of "divide and rule"
   teoría de economía política, political economy theory
   teoría de intercambio social, exchange theory
   teoría de la acción, action theory
   teoría de la elección racional, rational choice theory
   teoría de la modernización, modernizational theory
   teoría de la relatividad, theory of relativity
   teoría de la ventaja comparada, theory of comparative advantage
   teoría de los lugares centrales, central place theory
   teoría depost-control, post-control theory
   teoría del conflicto, conflict theory
   teoría del contrato social, social contract theory
   teoría del control social, social control theory
   teoría del desarrollo moral, moral development theory
   teoría del dominó, Domino Theory

teoría del estilo de vida, lifestyle theory
teoría del etiquetamiento, labeling theory
teoría del sitio central, central place theory
teoría del suicidio del estado, state suicide theory
teoría del territorio conquistado, con-quered territory theory
teoría del valor-trabajo, labor theory of value
teoría económica, economic theory
teoría económica clásica, classical economic theory
teoría feminista, feminist theory
teoría interpretativa, interpretative theory
teoría laboral del valor, labor theory of value
tepe, sod
terapia de choque, shock therapy
tercer mundo, Third World
tercera persona, third party
tercero, third party
terciario, tertiary
termal, thermal
Terranova, Newfoundland
terrateniente, landowner
terraza, terrace

terremoto, earthquake
terreno, terrain
terreno abierto, open range
terreno inundable, floodplain
terrenos pantanosos, swamp lands
territorio, territory
territorio aborigen, aboriginal territory
territorio cedido, ceded territory
territorio de los Estados Unidos, U.S. territory
territorio de Oregón, Oregon territory
Territorio del Noroeste, Northwest Territory, Old Northwest
territorio en fideicomiso, trust territory
territorio reclamado, claimed territory
territorio reivindicado, claimed territory
terrorismo, terrorism
tesis, thesis
tesorero de la ciudad, city manager
testimonio del testigo presencial, eyewitness account
textil, textile
textiles chinos, Chinese textile
texto de información, informational text
Tiberio Graco, Tiberius Gracchus
tiempo[1], weather

tiempo², time, weather
    tiempo de calendario, calendar time
    tiempo de duplicación, doubling time
tierra, land, sod
    tierra adentro, back country
    tierra arable, arable land
    tierra baja, lowland
    tierra de dominio público, public land
    tierra fértil, fertile land, fertile soil
    tierra interior, hinterland
    Tierra Santa, Holy Land
    tierras altas, highland
    tierras ancestrales, ancestral lands
    tierras bajas costeras, coastal lowlands
    tierras bajas del interior, Interior Lowlands
    tierras de labranza, farmland
    tierras de pantanos, wetlands
    tierras tribales, tribal lands
tifón, typhoon
timón, rudder
Timor Oriental, East Timor

Tío Sam, Uncle Sam
tipi, tepee
tipificado como delito, indictable
tipo, rate
    tipo de cambio, exchange rate
tipología, typology
tiradero, landfill
tiranía, tyranny
tirarse un farol, bluff
título¹, title, caption
    título del mapa, map title
    Título IV, Title VII
título², security
    títulos del Estado, government security
todos los hombres son creados iguales, all men are created equal
Tokio, Tokyo
toldo, canopy
tolerancia, tolerance
tolerante, tolerant
tolerar, tolerate
toltecas, Toltecs
toma de Constantinopla, seizure of Constantinople
toma de decisiones, decision-making
toma de decisiones económicas, economic decision making
toma de decisiones racionales, rational decision-making process
toma de posesión, inauguration
Tombuctú, Timbuktu
topografía, topography

topógrafo, surveyor
toque de queda, curfew
Torá, Torah
tormenta, storm
    tormenta de polvo, dust storm
    tormenta de viento, wind storm
    Tormenta del desierto, Desert Storm
tornado, tornado
torrecilla, turret
totalitario, totalitarian
totalitarismo, totalitarianism
    totalitarismo estalinista, Stalinist totalitarianism
tótem, totem pole
trabajador, worker
    trabajador cualificado, skilled worker
    trabajador de cuello azul, blue-collar worker
    trabajador extranjero, migrant
    trabajador indio, Indian laborer
    trabajador indocumentado, undocumented worker
    trabajador migratorio, migrant worker
    trabajador no cualificado, unskilled worker
    trabajador no sindicalizado, nonunion worker
    trabajador socialista, socialist worker
    trabajadores chinos, Chinese workers
    Trabajadores Industriales del Mundo, Industrial Workers of the World
trabajar, work
trabajo, job, labor, work
    trabajo a distancia, telecommuting
    trabajo agrícola, farm labor
    trabajo con predominancia masculina, male-dominated job
    trabajo contratado, contract labor
    trabajo de medio tiempo, part-time employment
    trabajo de tiempo completo, full-time employment
    a trabajo igual salario igual, equal pay for equal work
    trabajo organizado, organized labor
    trabajos forzados, coerced labor
tradición, tradition
    tradición cultural, cultural tradition
    tradición étnica, ethnic tradition
    tradición oral, oral tradition
tradicionalismo, traditionalism
tradicionalista, traditionalist
tradiciones culturales, culture traditions
tráfico de opio en Europa, European opium trade

tráfico urbano,
urban commuting
tragafuegos, fire eater
tragedia, tragedy
tragedia griega,
Greek tragedy
traición, treason
traidor, traitor
tranquilidad doméstica,
domestic tranquility
transbordador,
ferry, shuttle
transbordador espacial, space shuttle
transcontinental,
transcontinental
transferencia de competencias, devolution
transformación,
transformation
Transiberiano,
Trans-Siberian
railroad
transición demográfica,
demographic transition
tránsito público,
public transit
transmisión de creencias,
transmission of beliefs
transmisión de la cultura,
transmission of
culture
transmisión subcultural,
subculture transmission
Trans-Misisipi,
trans-Mississippi
region
transmitir, transmit
transportación,
transportation
transportar, transport

transporte, transportation
transporte ferroviario, rail transportation
transporte marítimo,
marine transportation
transporte por tierra,
portage
transporte público,
public transportation
transporte refrigerado, refrigerated
trucking
transporte vecinal,
neighborhood transportation
trascendentalismo,
Transcendentalism
trascendentalistas,
Transcendentalists
trasfondo,
background cause
trata, slave trade
trata de esclavos de África,
African slave trade
trata de esclavos del Atlántico,
Atlantic slave trade
tratado, treatise,
agreement, treaty
Tratado Antártico,
Antarctic Treaty
Tratado de Guadalupe Hidalgo,
Treaty of Guadalupe
Hidalgo
Tratado de Jay,
Jay's Treaty
Tratado de Jay-Gardoqui, Jay Gardoqui
Treaty
Tratado de Libre Comercio de

América del Norte (TLCAN), North Atlantic Free Trade Agreement (NAFTA)

Tratado de Nanking, Treaty of Nanking

Tratado de París, Treaty of Paris

tratado de paz, peace treaty

Tratado de Portsmouth firmado por Roosevelt, Roosevelt's Treaty of Portsmouth

Tratado de prohibición parcial de ensayos nucleares, Nuclear Test Ban Treaty

Tratado de Shimonoseki, Treaty of Shimonoseki

Tratado de Versalles, Conference of Versailles, Treaty of Versailles

tratado desigual, unequal treaty

Tratado SALT I, SALT I Treaty

Tratado Sykes-Picot, Sykes-Picot Agreement

Trato Justo, Fair Deal

travesía, journey, passage, voyage

travesía intermedia, Middle Passage

a través del tiempo y el espacio, across time and place

trazado reticular, gridiron pattern

trece colonias, thirteen colonies

trece virtudes, thirteen virtues

tregua, truce

tren de vagones, wagon train

tres poderes del gobierno, three branches of government

tríada, triad

triángulo de comercio, trading triangle

triángulo de hierro, Iron triangle

tribalismo, tribalism

tribu, tribe

tribu Coeur d'Alene, Coeur d'Alene tribe

tribu kutenai, Kootenai tribe

tribu Nez percé, Nez Perce Tribe

tribuna, tribune,

tribunal, court, tribunal

tribunal colegiado, collegial court

tribunal de apelación, appellate jurisdiction, court of appeals

tribunal de circuito judicial, circuit-court

tribunal de primera instancia, lower court

tribunal del Almirantazgo, admiralty court

tribunal estatal, state court

tribunal federal, federal court

tribunal federal de distrito, federal district court

tribunal imparcial, impartial tribunal

tribunal judicial, judicial court

tribunal militar, military court

tribunal municipal, municipal court, civic court

Tribunal Supremo, High Court

tribus de las llanuras de América del Norte, North American plains society

tribus nómadas qizilbash, Qizilbash nomadic tribesmen

tribus shoshones y bannock, Shoshone-Bannock tribe

tribus shoshones y paiutes, Shoshone-Paiute tribe

tributación, taxation

tributación directa, direct taxation

tributación indirecta, indirect taxation

tributación progresiva, progressive taxation

tributación proporcional, proportional taxation

tributación regresiva, regressive taxation

tributación sobre donaciones, gift taxation

tributación sobre la propiedad inmobiliaria, property taxation

tributario, tributary

tributo, tribute

trigo, wheat

trimestre, quarter

trincheras, trenches

Triple Alianza, Triple Alliance

Triple Entente, Triple Entente

tripulación, crew

trirremes, triremes

triunvirato, triumvirate

tropas federales, federal troops

trópico de Cáncer, Tropic of Cancer

trópico de Capricornio, Tropic of Capricorn

trópicos, tropics

trovadores, minstrel show, troubadours

trueque, barter

trueque silencioso, silent barter

tsunami, tsunami

tuberculosis, tuberculosis

tucupí, tucupi

tundra, tundra

tungsteno, tungsten

turba, peat

Turkestán, Turkestán

turnarse, take turns

turno, shift

turquesa, turquoise

Turquestán, Turkestan

Turquía, Turkey

tutela de los juristas islámicos, jurist's guardianship

Tutmosis III, Thutmose III

U

U.R.S.S., U.S.S.R.
uadi, wadi
ubicación, location
    ubicación absoluta,
    absolute location
    ubicación relativa,
    relative location
Ucrania, Ukraine
Última Frontera,
    Last Frontier
umbral, threshold
    umbral de la pobreza,
    poverty line
    umbral de población,
    threshold population
un hombre un voto,
    one man one vote
ungido, anointed
unicameral, unicameral
único, unique
unidad, unity
    unidad cultural,
    cultural unity
    unidad de análisis,
    unit of analysis
    unidad militar,
    military unit
    unidad política,
    political unit
unificación, unification
    unificación de Alemania, unification of
    Germany
    unificación de Italia,
    unification of Italy
unificar, unify, unite
unión, union, linkage
    Unión Europea,
    European Union
    **Unión Internacional
    de Costureras,**
    International Ladies
    Garment Workers
    Union
    **Unión Soviética
    (URSS),** Soviet Union
    (USSR)
unitario, unitary
universalidad, universality
universidad, university
    **universidades agro-
    nómicas,** land grant
    colleges
Upanisad, Upanishad
Upton Sinclair,
    Upton Sinclair
urbanidad, civility
urbanismo, urbanism
urbanización,
    urbanization, housing
    development
urbanizar, urbanize
urbano, urban
urna, ballot
uso, use, practice
    uso de explosivos,
    use of explosives
    uso de recursos,
    resource use
    uso de suelo,
    land use
    uso público,
    public use
usurpación, usurpation
    **usurpación de identi-
    dad,** identity theft
utilidad, utility, benefit
    utilidad marginal,
    marginal benefit
    utilidades públicas,
    public utilities

utilitarismo, utilitarianism

utilización, utilization

utopía, utopia

vaca lechera, dairy cow

vacuna, vaccine

vagón de tren refrigerado, refrigerated railroad car

validez, validity
    validez interna, internal validity

valla publicitaria, billboards

valle, valley
    Valle de la Muerte, Death Valley
    valle del Indo, Indus Valley
    valle del Nilo, Nile Valley
    valle del río Ganges, Ganges River Valley
    valle del Tigris y el Éufrates, Tigris-Euphrates Valley
    valle fértil, fertile valley
    valle fluvial, river valley

valor[1], value, courage
    valor comparativo, comparative value
    valor de cambio, exchange value
    valor de las tierras, land value

valor fundamental, fundamental value

valor total de mercado, total market value

valores cívicos, civic values

valores democráticos, democratic values

valores democráticos fundamentales, core democratic values

valores intrínsecos, embedded values

valores morales, moral values

valores occidentales, Western values

valores personales, personal values

valores puritanos, Puritan values

valores victorianos, Victorian values

valores[2], stocks, securities
    valores bursátiles, securities
    valores del Estado, government security

vapor de agua, water vapor

vaquero, cowboy

variable, variable
    variable dependiente, dependent variable
    variable independiente, independent variable

variación física, physical variation

variado, diverse

vasallo, vassal

Vaticano, Vatican

vecindad, neighborhood, tenement

vecindario étnico,
ethnic neighborhood
vecino, neighbor
vedas, vedas
vegetación, vegetation
vegetación marina,
marine vegetation
vegetación natural,
natural vegetation
vehículo eléctrico,
electric car
vehículo motorizado,
motorized vehicle
vehículo no motorizado,
nonmotorized vehicle
vela latina, lateen sails
vencedor[1], victory
vencedor[2], victorious
vendaje de pies,
foot binding
vendedor, seller
vendedor inesperado,
dark horse
vender, sell
vendetta, blood feud
Venecia, Venice
venta, sale
venta con señuelo,
bait and switch
ventaja, advantage
ventaja absoluta,
absolute advantage
ventaja comercial,
trade advantage
ventaja comparativa,
comparative advantage
ventaja inicial,
Head Start
ventajoso, advantageous
ventilación, fanning
ventisca, blizzard
verdad, truth
verdades manifies-

tas, self-evident truths
vernáculo, vernacular
verosímil, credible
Versalles, Versailles
vertedero, landfill
vertedero tóxico,
toxic dumping
vetar, veto
veteranos, veteran
veto, veto
veto absoluto,
absolute veto
veto de bolsillo,
pocket veto
**veto de partidas
específicas,**
line-item veto
veto selectivo,
line-item veto
vía de comunicación,
communication route
vía verde, greenway
viajar, travel
**viajar todos los días
para ir al trabajo,**
commute
viaje, journey, passage,
voyage
viajero, voyageur
**viajes de descubri-
miento,** voyages of
discovery
vicegobernador,
Lieutenant Governor
vicepresidente,
vice president
victoria, victory
victoria arrolladora,
landslide victory
victorioso, victorious
vida, life
vida cívica,
civic life

vida comunitaria y familia regulada, regulated family and community life

vida comunitaria y familiar reguladas, regulated family and community life

vida contemporánea, contemporary life

vida cotidiana, daily life

vida después de la muerte, afterlife

vida diaria, daily life

vida en común, communal life

vida familiar, family life

vida intelectual, intellectual life

vida política, political life

vida privada, personal life, private life

vida pública, public life

vida rural en África, African village life

Vida, libertad y búsqueda de la felicidad, life, liberty, and the pursuit of happiness

Viejo Imperialismo, Old Imperialism

Viejo Nogal, Old Hickory

viento, wind

(en) la dirección del viento, downwind

viento dominante, prevailing wind

viento local, local wind

viento monzón, monsoon wind

vientos alisios, trade wind

Viernes negro, Black Friday

Vietnam, Vietnam

vietnamita, Vietnamese

vietnamización, Vietnamization

VIH, HIV

vikingos, Vikings

vilipendio, mudslinging

villa global, global village

villas Hoover, Hoovervilles

Vincennes, Vincennes

vinculant, binding

vínculo social, social bond

vínculos religiosos, religious ties

violación, violation, rape

violaciones históricas de la dignidad humana, historical violations of human dignity

violencia, violence

violencia sexual, sexual assault

virrey, viceroy

virtud cívica, civic virtue

virtud personal, personal virtue

viruela, smallpox

visa, visa

visir, vizier

vivienda, housing

vivienda de interés social, public housing

**vivienda multifami-
liar,** tenement housing
Vladimiro de Kiev,
Vladimir of Kiev
vocación, vocation
volcán, volcano
volumen, volume
voluntad general,
general will
voluntad popular,
popular will
voluntariado, volunteerism
voluntario, volunteer
votación, polling, voting,
ballot
votar, vote
voto, vote
    voto concurrente,
concurring opinion
    voto de censura,
vote of no confidence
    voto dividido,
split-ticket rating
    voto popular,
popular vote
    **voto por correspon-
dencia,** absentee vote
    voto secreto,
secret ballot
vulcanismo, volcanism

W

Wall Street, Wall Street
Washington, Washington
Watergate, Watergate
wigwam, wigwam

xenofobia, xenophobia

yacimiento petrolífero,
oil field
yihad, jihad
(el) yo, self
yo mismo, myself
yuca, cassava
yurta, yurt
yute, jute

Z

zaibatsu, zaibatsu
zar, czar
    Zar Nicolás I,
Czar Nicholas I
    Zar Nicolás II,
Czar Nicholas II
zen, zen
zigurat, ziggurat
zona, zone, area, district
    **zona central de nego-
cios,** central business
district
    **zona comercial del
centro de la ciudad,**
downtown business
area

zona costera,
coastal area
**zona costera de
inundación,**
coastal flood zone
**zona de asistencia
escolar,** school atten-
dance zone
**zona de bajos
ingresos,**
low-income area
**zona de calmas
ecuatoriales,**
doldrums
zona de latitud alta,
high-latitude place
**zona de libre comer-
cio,** free trade zone
zona de subducción,
zone of subduction
zona desmilitarizada,
Demilitarized Zone
(DMZ)
**zona económica
especial,** special
economic zone
zona franca,
free port
zona horaria,
time zone
zona metropolitana,
metropolitan zone
zona minera,
mining area
zona postal,
postal zone
zona selvática,
wilderness area
zona semiárida,
semiarid area
zona sísmica,
earthquake zone
zona tapón,

buffer zone
zona urbana,
urban area
zona virgen,
wilderness area
zonificación, zoning
**zonificación de uso
del suelo,** zoned use
of land
zoología, zoology
zoroastrismo,
Zoroastrianism
zuñi, Zuni

Section II
English - Spanish

1

401 K, plan 401 (k)

A

A.D., A.D. (Anno Domini)
abbreviate,
    abreviar, resumir
abbreviation, abreviatura,
    abreviación
abdicate, abdicar
abdication, abdicación
abnormal psychology,
    psicología paranormal
abolish, abolir
abolishment, abolición
abolition, abolición
abolitionism,
    abolicionismo
abolitionist, abolicionista
    **Abolitionist Move-
    ment,** movimiento
    abolicionista
aboriginal,
    aborigen, indígena
    aboriginal peoples,
    pueblos aborígenes
    **aboriginal
    population,**
    población aborigen
    aboriginal territory,
    territorio aborigen
abortion, aborto
absence of rules and laws,
    ausencia de reglas y
    leyes
absentee ballot,
    voto por correspon-

dencia
absolute, absoluto
    absolute advantage,
    ventaja absoluta
    absolute liability,
    responsabilidad abso-
    luta, responsabilidad
    ilimitada, responsabili-
    dad incondicional
    absolute location,
    ubicación absoluta
    absolute monarchy,
    monarquía absoluta
    absolute power,
    poder absoluto
    absolute veto,
    veto absoluto
absolutism, absolutismo
absolutist state,
    estado absoluto
**Abstract Expression-
    ism,** expresionismo
    abstracto
Abstractionism,
    Abstraccionismo
abuse, abuso
    abuse of power,
    abuso de poder
acceptable behavior,
    comportamiento
    aceptable
access, acceso
accessibility,
    accesibilidad, fácil
    acceso
accession of Elizabeth I,
    subida al trono de
    Isabel I de Inglaterra
accommodate, alojar,
    albergar, adaptar
accommodation, acuerdo
accountability,
    responsabilidad

accounting, contabilidad
acculturate, aculturar
acculturation,
     aculturación
accuracy,
     exactitud, precisión
     accuracy of informa-
     tion, precisión de la
     información
accurate, preciso, exacto
accused, acusado
acephalous societies,
     sociedades acéfalas
acid rain, lluvia ácida
acquit, absolver
acquittal, absolución,
     exoneración
acropolis, acrópolis
across time and place,
     a través del tiempo y el
     espacio
act, ley, decreto, acta
     Act of Settlement,
     Acta de establecimien-
     to o Ley de instau-
     ración
     Act of Supremacy,
     Acta de Supremacía
action, acción
     action plan,
     plan de acción
     action theory,
     teoría de la acción
acupuncture, acupuntura
adapt, adaptar
adaptation, adaptación
adequate,
     adecuado, aceptable
administration,
     administración
admiralty court,
     tribunal del Almiran-
     tazgo

admiralty laws,
     leyes marítimas
adobe, adobe
advantage, ventaja
advantageous, ventajoso
adversarial process,
     proceso contencioso
adversary system,
     sistema acusatorio o
     adversarial
advertise,
     anunciar, hacer publi-
     cidad o propaganda
advertisement,
     anuncio, spot publici-
     tario
advertising,
     publicidad, propagan-
     da
advice and consent,
     consejo y consen-
     timiento
advisory opinion,
     dictamen consultivo
Aegean region,
     región del Egeo
aerial photograph,
     fotografía aérea,
     aerofotografía
aerospace, aeroespacial
affirmative action,
     discriminación posi-
     tiva, acción afirmativa
affix, afijo
affluence,
     riqueza, opulencia
Afghanistan, Afganistán
AFL-CIO, AFL-CIO (Feder-
     ación Estadounidense
     del Trabajo y Congreso
     de Organizaciones
     Industriales)
Africa, África

African American, afroamericano
African American community, comunidad afroamericana
African civilization, civilización africana
African heritage, herencia africana
African National Congress, Congreso Nacional Africano
African nationalist movement, movimiento nacionalista africano
African resistance movement, movimiento de resistencia africano
African slave, esclavo africano
African slave trade, trata de esclavos de África
African trading kingdoms, imperios comerciales de África
African village life, vida rural en África
African-American Union soldier, soldado afroamericano de la Unión
Afro-Eurasia, Eurafrasia, Eurasiáfrica o continente euroasiático africano
afterlife, más allá, vida después de la muerte
age, edad, era
Age of Discovery, Era de los Descubrimientos
Age of Enlightenment, Ilustración
Age of Exploration, Era de los Descubrimientos
Age of Faith, Era de la Fe
Age of Reason, Edad de la Razón
Age of the Common Man, Era del hombre común
Age of Transition, época de transición
agency, agencia
aggregate, agregado
aggregate demand, demanda agregada
aggregate supply, oferta agregada
aggressive recruitment program, programa agresivo de reclutamiento
agitators, agitadores
agora, ágora
agrarian, agrario
agrarian civilization, civilización agraria
agrarian community, comunidad agraria
Agrarian Revolution, Revolución agraria
agrarian society, sociedad agrícola
agree, acordar
agreement, acuerdo, tratado
agribusiness, agroindustria
agricultural, agricola
Agricultural Adjust-

ment Act, Ley de Ajuste Agrícola
agricultural area, área agricola
agricultural economy, economía agrícola
agricultural expansion, expansión agrícola
agricultural extension, extensión agraria, programa de extensión rural
agricultural lifestyle, estilo de vida agrícola, modo de vida rural
agricultural practice, práctica agrícola
Agricultural Revolution, revolución neolítica
agricultural society, sociedad agraria
agricultural soil, suelo agrícola
agricultural technology, tecnología agrícola
agriculture, agricultura
Agustin de Iturbide, Agustín de Iturbide
Aid to Families with Dependent Children, Ayuda a Familias con Niños Dependientes (AFDC)
AIDS, sida
air conditioning, aire acondicionado
air pollution, contaminación atmosférica
airborne emission, emisión atmosférica

aircraft carrier, portaaviones
air-mass circulation, circulación atmosférica
airport, aeropuerto
Akhenaton (Amenhotep IV), Akenatón o Ajenatón (Amenhotep IV)
Alamo, Álamo
Alaska pipeline, oleoducto Trans-Alaska
Albany Plan of Union, Plan de Unión de Albany
alchemy, alquimia
Alexander, Alejandro
Alexander of Macedon, Alejandro de Macedonia
Alfred the Great, Alfredo el Grande
algebra, álgebra
Alger Hiss case, caso Alger Hiss
Algeria, Argelia
Algonquian, algonquino
alien, extranjero
Alien and Sedition Acts, Leyes de Extranjería y Sedición
alienation, alienación
aligned, alineados
alignment, alineación
alike, similar
all men are created equal, todos los hombres son creados iguales
Allegheny Plateau, meseta de Allegheny
Allegheny River, río Allegheny

allegiance, lealtad
alliance, alianza
Alliance for Progress,
    Alianza para el
    progreso
Allied Powers,
    Potencias aliadas
allocate, asignar, repartir,
    distribuir
allocation, asignación,
    reparto, distribución
    allocation method,
    método de asignación
    allocation of power,
    asignación de poder
allot, asignar, adjudicar
allotment, adjudicación,
    parcelación, reparto
alluvial fan,
    abanico aluvial
alluvial plain,
    llanura aluvial
ally¹, aliado
ally², aliarse
almanac, almanaque
almshouse,
    casa de beneficencia
alpha numeric grids,
    cuadrícula alfanu-
    mérica
alphabet, alfabeto
alphabetic writing,
    escritura alfabética
alphanumeric system,
    sistema alfanumérico
Alps, Alpes
**alternate forms of govern-
    ment,** formas alterna-
    tivas de gobierno
**alternative courses of ac-
    tion,** cursos alternati-
    vos de acción
alternative dispute reso-

lution (ADR), modali-
    dades alternativas de
    solución de conflictos
alternative energy source,
    fuentes de energía
    alternativa
alternative solutions,
    soluciones alternativas
alternatives, alternativas
altiplano, altiplano, meseta
altitude, altitud
altruism, altruismo
Amazon, amazona
ambassador, embajador
amend, enmendar
amendment, enmienda
    amendment process,
    proceso de enmienda
America, América
American, estadounidense,
    americano(a)
    **American citizen-
    ship,** ciudadanía
    estadounidense
    **American Coloniza-
    tion Society,**
    Sociedad Americana
    de Colonización
    **American Commu-
    nist Party,**
    Partido Comunista de
    los Estados Unidos
    **American constitu-
    tional democracy,**
    democracia constitu-
    cional estadounidense
    **American domestic
    policy,** política interna
    de los Estados Unidos
    American dream,
    sueño americano
    **American Expedi-
    tionary Force,**

Fuerzas Expedicionarias Estadounidenses
American Federation of Labor (AFL), Federación Estadounidense del Trabajo
American foreign policy, política exterior de los Estados Unidos
American holiday, día festivo estadounidense
American identity, identidad estadounidense
American Indian, amerindio o nativo americano
American Indian chief, jefe nativo americano
American Indian nation, nación nativa americana
American influence, influencia estadounidense
American political system, sistema político estadounidense
American presidential system, sistema presidencial estadounidense
American Railway Union, Sindicato Americano de Ferrocarriles
American Republican Party, Partido Republicano Americano

American Revolution, Independencia de los Estados Unidos o Revolución estadounidense
American society, sociedad estadounidense
American symbol, símbolo estadounidense
American system, Sistema Americano
American tribal government, gobierno tribal nativo americano
American West, Oeste de los Estados Unidos
Americanization, americanización
Americans with Disabilities Act, Ley de estadounidenses con discapacidades
the Americas, las Américas, continente americano
Americentric, americentrista
Amerindian, amerindio
amicus curiae, amicus curiae, amigo de la corte
Amish, amish
Ammianus Marcellinus, Amiano Marcelino
amnesty, amnistía
Amnesty International, Amnistía Internacional
Amsterdam, Ámsterdam

Anaconda Plan,
plan Anaconda
analysis, análisis
analyze, analizar
anarchist, anarquista
anarchy, anarquía
ancestor,
ancestro, antepasado
ancestor worship, culto a
los antepasados
ancestral, ancestral
ancestral lands,
tierras ancestrales
ancestry,
ascendencia, abolengo
ancient, antiguo
ancient civilization,
civilización antigua
ancient Greece,
Antigua Grecia
ancient history,
historia antigua
ancient Rome,
Antigua Roma
ancient time,
época antigua
Andean region,
región andina
Angel Island, Isla Ángel
Anglo-Saxon, anglosajón
animal domestication,
domesticación animal
animism, animismo
Annapolis Convention,
Convención de An-
napolis
annex, anexionar, anexar
annexation, anexión
annual, anual
**anual percentage
rate,** tasa anual equi-
valente, tasa porcen-
tual anual

annually, anualmente
anointed, ungido
Antarctic Circle,
círculo polar antártico
Antarctic Treaty,
Tratado Antártico
Antarctica, Antártica
antebellum period,
período antebellum
anthracite, antracita
anthropologist,
antropólogo
anthropology, antropología
antibiotics, antibiótico
anti-Chinese movement,
movimiento antichino
anticlericalism,
anticlericalismo
**anticommunist move-
ment,** movimiento
anticomunista
Anti-Defamation League,
Liga de Antidifamación
Anti-Federalist,
antifederalista
Anti-Federalist Party,
Partido Antifederalista
anti-immigrant attitude,
actitud antiinmigrante
Anti-Masonic Party,
Partido Antimasónico
Anti-Rightist Campaign,
Movimiento anti-
derechista
anti-Semitism,
antisemitismo
anti-Semitist, antisemita
antislavery ideology,
ideología abolicionista
antislavery movement,
movimiento abolicioni-
sta
anti-terrorism,

antiterrorismo
anti-trust acts,
leyes antitrust o anti-
monopolio
apartheid, apartheid
apologists, apologistas
Appalachia, Apalachia
**Appalachian High-
lands,** Montañas
Apalaches
**Appalachian Moun-
tains,** Montes
Apalaches
appeal, apelar
appeal to emotion,
apelar a la emoción
appeal to ignorance,
apelar a la ignorancia
appease,
apaciguar, aplacar
appeasement,
apaciguamiento
appellate, (de) apelación
appellate jurisdiction,
tribunal de apelación
appendix, apéndice
applied psychology,
psicología aplicada
appoint, nombrar, designar
appointed,
designado, nombrado
appointed officials,
funcionarios designa-
dos
appointment,
nombramiento
apportion,
repartir, prorratear
apportionment,
reparto, prorrateo
apprentice, aprendiz
apprenticeship,
aprendizaje

aqueduct, acueducto
aquifer, acuífero
Arab Caliph, califa árabe
Arab League, Liga árabe
Arab Muslim, árabe
musulmán
Arab oil embargo,
embargo petrolero
árabe
Arab Palestinian,
árabe palestino
Arabic, árabe
Arab-Israeli crisis,
crisis o conflicto ára-
be-israelí
arable land, tierra arable
arbitrary rule,
mandato o regla
arbitraria
arbitrate, arbitrar
arbitration, arbitraje
**archaeological associa-
tion,** asociación ar-
queológica
archaeological evidence,
evidencia arqueológica
**archaeological field sur-
vey,** investigación
arqueológica de campo
archaeological site,
sitio arqueológico
archaeologist, arqueólogo
archaeology, arqueología
archbishops, arzobispos
archipelago, archipiélago
architect, arquitecto
architectural drawings,
dibujos arquitectóni-
cos
architectural style,
estilo arquitectónico
architecture, arquitectura
Arctic, Ártico

Arctic Circle,
círculo polar ártico
Arctic Ocean,
océano Ártico
area, área
argue, argumentar, discutir, razonar
argument, argumento, discusión
argumentation, argumentación, discusión
arid, árido
arid climate, clima árido
aristocracy, aristocracia
aristocrat, aristócrata
aristocratic power, poder aristocrático
Aristotle, Aristóteles
armada, armada, flota
armed control, control armado
armed forces, fuerzas armadas
Armed Forces of the United States, Fuerzas armadas de los Estados Unidos
armed revolution, revolución armada
armistice, armisticio
arms, arma
arms embargo, embargo de armas
arms limitations, limitación de armas
arms race, carrera armamentista
arraignment, comparecencia
arranged marriage, matrimonio arreglado

arroyo, arroyo
arsenal, arsenal
Arsenal of Demoracy, Arsenal de Democracia
art, arte
art for art's sake, el arte por el arte
art of courtly love, arte del amor cortés
artesian wells, pozos artesianos
article, artículo
Articles of Confederation, Artículos de la Confederación
artifact, artefacto
artillery, artillería
artisan, artesano
artist, artista
artist exploitation, explotación del artista
artistic expression, expresión artística
artistic license, licencia poética
artistic movement, movimiento artístico
arts and crafts, artesanía
Aryan culture, cultura aria
Ashikaga period, período Ashikaga o Muromachi
Ashoka, Asoka
Asia, Asia
Asian-American, asiático americano, americano de origen asiático
Asian art form, modalidad artística asiática
Asian Civil Rights Movement, Movimiento por los derechos civiles de

los asiáticos
Asian Pacific settler,
colono del Pacífico
asiático
assassinate, asesinar
assassination, asesinato
assemble,
reunirse, congregarse
assembled, congregado
assembly, asamblea
assembly line,
producción en cadena
Assembly of Experts,
Asamblea de expertos
assets, activos
assimilate, asimilar
assimilation, asimilación
association, asociación
assume, asumir
assumption, suposición,
supuesto, asunción
Assyria, Asiria
Assyrian Empire,
Imperio asirio
astrolabe, astrolabio
astronaut, astronauta
astronomer, astrónomo
astronomical discov-
ery, descubrimiento
astronómico
astronomy, astronomía
asylum, asilo, hospicio
asymmetrical federalism,
federalismo asimétrico
atheism, ateísmo
atheist, ateo
Athenian democracy,
democracia ateniense
Athens, Atenas
Atlanta Compromise,
Compromiso de At-
lanta
Atlantic basin,

Cuenca del Atlántico
Atlantic charter,
Carta del Atlántico
Atlantic Coastal Plain,
llanura costera del
Atlántico
Atlantic Ocean,
Océano Atlántico
Atlantic slave trade,
trata de esclavos del
Atlántico
atlas, atlas
atmosphere, atmósfera
atmosphere bio-
sphere,
biosfera-atmósfera
atmospheric pressure
cells, celdas de
presión atmosférica
atmospheric warming,
calentamiento atmos-
férico
atomic bomb,
bomba atómica
atomic diplomacy,
diplomacia atómica
atonism, atonismo
attack, atacar
attitude, actitude
Augustus, Augusto
austerity, austeridad
Australia, Australia
Austria, Austria
Austro-Hungarian empire,
Imperio Austro-Hún-
garo
author, autor
authoritarian rule,
régimen autoritario
authoritarian system,
sistema autoritario
authoritarianism,
autoritarismo

authoritative, autoritario
authority, autoridad
authorize, autorizar
author's interpretation,
     interpretación de autor
autobahn, autopista
autobiography,
     autobiografía
autocracy, autocracia
autocrat, autócrata
autocratic, autocrático
auto-free zone,
     calle peatonal
automation,
     automatización
autonomous, autónomo
     autonomous power,
     poder autónomo
     autonomous region,
     región autónoma
     **autonomous repub-
     lic,** república autóno-
     ma
autonomy, autonomía
availability, disponibilidad
avenues of participation,
     métodos de partici-
     pación
average family size,
     tamaño promedio del
     hogar
average price level, nivel
     de precios promedio
aviation, aviación
axis, eje
     Axis Pact,
     Pacto del Eje
     Axis Powers,
     Potencias del Eje
ayatollah, ayatolá o ayatola
Azimuthal projection,
     proyección acimutal o
     azimutal

Aztec, azteca
     Aztec Empire,
     Imperio azteca
     **Aztec Foundation of
     Heaven,** Cimientos del
     cielo azteca

B

B.C., Before Christ,
     aC, a. de C. (antes de
     Cristo), a. JC, a. de
     J.C. (antes de Jesu-
     cristo)
baby boom, baby boom o
     explosión de natalidad
     **baby boom genera-
     tion,** generación de los
     baby boomers
Babylon, Babilonia
Babylonian Empire,
     Imperio babilónico
back country,
     tierra adentro
background, antecedente
     background cause,
     trasfondo, antece-
     dentes
     **background knowl-
     edge,** conocimientos
     previos
Bacon's rebellion,
     Rebelión de Bacon
Baghdad, Bagdad
bail, fianza
bailiff, alguacil
bait and switch,
     venta con señuelo
balance,
     balance, saldo,
     equilibrio, contrapeso

balance of payments, balanza de pagos
balance of power, equilibrio de poder
balance of trade, balanza comercial
balanced budget, equilibrio presupuestario
Balfour Declaration, Declaración Balfour
Balkanization, balcanización
Balkans, Balcanes
ballad, romance, balada
ballot, votación, papeleta, boleta electoral, urna
Baltic region, región báltica
bandwagon, efecto de arrastre o amplificación
bank, banco
    bank holiday, asueto (día de fiesta) bancario
bank recharter, estatuto del banco
banking, banca
bankruptcy, quiebra, bancarrota
Bantu, bantú
    Bantu migrations in Africa, migraciones bantúes en África
bar graph, gráfico de barras, diagrama
barbarian, bárbaro
barge, barcaza o gabarra
baron, barón, magnate
baroque art, arte barroco
barrier island, isla barrada
barter, trueque
    barter economy, economía del trueque

bases of power, bases de poder
basic landform, accidente geográfico básico
basic needs, necesidades básicas
basic principles, principios básicos
basin, cuenca
Basin and Range, Cuenca y cordillera
battle, batalla
    Battle for Britain, Batalla de Inglaterra
    Battle of Buena Vista, Batalla de Buena Vista
    Battle of Hastings, Batalla de Hastings
    Battle of New Orleans, Batalla de Nueva Orleans
    Battle of Quebec, Batalla de Quebec
    Battle of the Bulge, Batalla de las Ardenas
    Battle of Tippecanoe, Batalla de Tippecanoe
    Battle of Tours, Batalla de Tours o Batalla de Poitiers
Bavaria, Baviera
bay, bahía
Bay of Pigs, Bahía de Cochinos
bayou, bayou, pantano
bazaar, bazar
Bear Flag Revolt, rebelión de la Bandera del oso
beginning, principio, inicio, comienzo
behave, comportarse
behavior, comportamiento

**behavior conse-
quence,** consecuencia
del comportamiento
behavior pattern,
patrón de compor-
tamiento
behaviorism, conductismo
Belgium, Bélgica
belief, creencia
belief systems,
sistemas de creencias
believe, creer
bell curve, curva normal,
distribución normal,
curva de campana
belligerent,
beligerante, agresivo
bench trial,
juicio sin jurado
benefit, beneficio, utilidad
benefit principle,
principio de im-
posición sobre
beneficios
Benin, Benín
Bering land bridge,
puente de Beringia
Berlin, Berlín
Berlin Airlift,
puente aéreo de Berlín
Berlin blockade,
bloqueo de Berlín
Berlin Wall,
Muro de Berlín
Bessemer process,
proceso Bessemer
Bhakti movement,
movimiento bhakti
Bhutan, Bután
bias, tendencia, predisposición, prejuicio,
sesgo, parcialidad
Bible, Biblia

biblical, bíblico
**biblical account of
Genesis,** relato bíblico
del Génesis
bibliography, bibliografía
bicameral, bicameral
bicameral legislature,
legislatura bicameral
**bicameral structure
of Congress,**
estructura bicameral
del Congreso
bicultural, bicultural
biculturalism,
biculturalismo
bicycle lane,
ciclovía, ciclopista,
bicicarril
big business, gran negocio
big stick diplomacy,
diplomacia de mano
dura
bigotry, fanatismo,
intolerancia
bilateral, bilateral
bilateral agreement,
acuerdo bilateral
bilateralism, bilateralismo
bilingual, bilingüe
bilingual education,
educación bilingüe
bilingualism, bilingüismo
bill, proyecto de ley
bill of attainder,
ley de extinción de
derechos, muerte civil
bill of exchange,
letra de cambio
bill of information,
acta de información
Bill of Rights,
Carta o Declaración de
derechos

billboards,
valla publicitaria
binding, vinculante
binding agreement,
acuerdo vinculante
binding contract,
contrato vinculante
biodiversity, biodiversidad
biographical, biográfico
biography, biografía
biological evidence,
evidencia biológica
biological magnification,
biomagnificación
biology, biología
biome, bioma
biopsychology,
biopsicología
biosphere, biosfera
biotic community,
comunidad biótica
bipartisan, bipartidista
bipartisanship,
bipartidismo
bipolar centers of power,
centros bipolares del
poder
birth rate,
tasa de natalidad
bishop, obispo
**Bismarck's "blood and
iron" speech,**
discurso "hierro y san-
gre" de Bismarck
black codes,
códigos negros
Black Death, peste negra
Black Friday,
Viernes negro
Black Hawk War,
Guerra de Black Hawk
(halcón negro)
Black Legend,

Leyenda negra
black list, lista negra
black majority,
mayoría negra
black market,
mercado negro
black migration,
migración negra
Black Panthers,
Panteras negras
black power, poder negro
Black Reconstruction,
Reconstrucción negra
Black Sea, Mar Negro
Black Tuesday,
Martes negro
blacksmith, herrero
blanket primary,
elección preliminar
comprensiva
Bleeding Kansas,
Kansas sangrante
blind respect,
respeto ciego
blitzkrieg, blitzkrieg
(guerra relámpago)
blizzard, ventisca
block grants,
donaciones globales
block printing,
impresión xilográfica
blockade, bloqueo
blood feud,
vendetta, reyerta
familiar
Bloody Sunday,
Domingo Sangriento
blue blood, sangre azul
blue-collar worker,
trabajador de cuello
azul
bluff, tirarse un farol,
embaucar

board, junta
   board of directors,
   consejo de adminis-
   tración
body of water,
   cuerpo de agua
body politic,
   cuerpo político
Boer, bóer
   Boer War,
   Guerra de los Bóeres
bog, ciénaga
Bolshevik, bolchevique
   Bolshevik Revolu-
   tion, Revolución
   Bolchevique
bond, bono
   bond drives,
   campañas de bonos de
   guerra
Bonus Army, movimiento
   de veteranos de guerra
boom, boom, auge, prosperidad repentina
   boomtown, ciudad
   con rápido desarrollo
bootlegging, edición pirata
border, frontera
   border conflict,
   conflicto fronterizo
   border states,
   estados fronterizos
borrow, prestar
borrowing, préstamo
Bosnia and Herzegovina,
   Bosnia-Herzegovina
Boston Massacre,
   masacre de Boston
Boston Tea Party,
   Motín del té de Boston
botany, botánica
Botswana, Botsuana
boundary, frontera, límite

boundary dispute,
   disputa fronteriza
bourgeois class,
   clase burguesa
bourgeoisie, burguesía
bow and arrow,
   arco y flecha
Boxer Rebellion,
   Rebelión de los bóxers
boyars, boyardos
boycott¹, boicot
boycott², boicotear
Brahmanism,
   brahmanismo
Braille alphabet,
   alfabeto braille
brainstorm, lluvia de ideas
branches of government,
   poderes de gobierno
Brazil, Brasil
   Brazilian indepen-
   dence movement,
   movimiento de inde-
   pendencia de Brasil
bread-and-butter issues,
   asuntos básicos
breakup of Soviet Union,
   desintegración de la
   Unión Soviética
Brenner Pass,
   paso del Brennero
Brer Rabbit,
   Hermano conejo
bribe, sobornar
bribery, soborno
bride price, excrex, dote
bridge, puente
brief, expedientes o actas
brinkmanship,
   política arriesgada,
   política suicida
Britain, Reino Unido
British, británico(a)

British colony, colonia británica
British constitution, Constitución británica
British East India, Indias Orientales Británicas
British East India Company, Compañía Británica de las Indias Orientales
British Empire, Imperio británico
British imperialism, imperialismo británico
British Isle, isla británica
British monarch, monarquía británica
British North America Act, Acta de Norteamérica británica
British rule, Mandato británico
British West Indies, Indias Occidentales británicas
broad constructionism, construccionismo amplio
broad interpretation, interpretación amplia
broadleaf tree, árbol de hoja ancha
Bronze Age, Edad de Bronce
bronze casting, pieza de bronce fundido
bronze tool-making technology, talladura de herramientas en bronce
Brown v. Board of Educa-
tion, Brown contra la Junta Educativa de Topeka
Bruges, Brujas
brush painting, técnica de pintura china
bubonic plague, peste bubónica
Buddha, Buda
Buddhism, budismo
Buddhist beliefs, creencias budistas
Buddhist monk, monje budista
Buddhist-Hindu culture, cultura hindú-budista
budget, presupuesto
  budget constraint, restricción presupuestaria
  budget deficit, déficit presupuestario
  budget resolution, resolución presupuestaria
  budget surplus, superávit presupuestario
budgetary, presupuestario
Buffalo Soldiers, soldados búfalo
buffer, país neutral o tapón
  buffer state, país tapón
  buffer zone, zona tapón
buffering, amortiguamiento
building, edificio
  building style, estilo del edificio
bull leaping, taurocatapsia

bull market,
mercado alcista
bull run,
batallas de Bull Run
buoy, boya
Bureau of Indian Affairs,
Oficina de Asuntos de
Nativos Americanos
bureaucracy, burocracia
bureaucrat, burócrata
bureaucratic government,
gobierno burocrático
burgess, burgués
burghers, burgueses
burgs, burgos
Burma Pass,
Camino de Birmania
Bushido, Bushido
business, negocio
**business organiza-
tion,** organización de
negocios
business cycle,
ciclo económico
business deduction,
deducción de negocio
business ethics,
ética empresarial
business firm,
compañía o empresa
business practice,
práctica comercial
bust, caída, colapso
buy, comprar
buyer, comprador
buying on margin,
compra en descubierto
Byzantine church,
iglesia bizantina
Byzantine Empire,
Imperio bizantino
Byzantium, Bizancio

C

C.E., EC (Era Común)
cabinet, gabinete
cabinet government,
gobierno de gabinete
cabinet system,
sistema de gabinete
cable, cable
cache, alijo
cadre, cuadro
Cairo, El Cairo
calamity, calamidad
calendar, calendario
calendar time,
tiempo de calendario
California Gold Rush,
Fiebre del oro de
California
caliph, califa
caliphate, califato
calligraphy, caligrafía
Cambodia, Camboya
camel, camello
camel caravan,
caravana de camellos
Camelot image,
imagen de Camelot
Camp David Accords,
Acuerdos de Camp
David
campaign, campaña
**campaign
finance reform,**
reforma del financi-
amiento de campañas
electorales
campaigning,
hacer campaña
Canada, Canadá
Canadian Bill of Rights,

Declaración de
Derechos de Canadá
Canadian Shield,
Escudo canadiense
canal, canal
canal system,
sistema de canales
Canberra, Canberra
candidate, candidato
cannon, cañón
canon laws,
derecho canónico
canopy, dosel, palio, toldo
Canton, cantón
canyon, cañón
capacity, capacidad
cape, cabo
Cape region,
Región del Cabo
capital, capital
**capital accumula-
tion,** acumulación de
capital
capital crime,
crimen capital, crimen
con pena de muerte
capital equipment,
equipo de capital, bien
de capital
capital gains,
plusvalías
capital gains tax,
impuesto sobre las
plusvalías
capital goods,
bienes de capital
capital loss,
pérdida de capital
capital offense,
delito capital, delito
con pena de muerte
capital punishment,
pena capital, pena de

muerte
capital resource,
recurso capital
capital resources,
recursos capitales
capital stock,
acción de capital
capitalism, capitalismo
capitalist country,
país capitalista
capitalist economy,
economía capitalista
Capitol Hill, Capitolio
capricious rule,
regla arbitraria
captaincies, capitanías
captains of industry,
capitanes de la
industria
caption, título, leyenda o
pie de foto
captioning, subtitulaje
captors, captores
**capture of Constantino-
ple,** captura de Con-
stantinopla
caravan, caravana
caravel, carabela
carbon cycle,
ciclo del carbono
cardinal directions,
puntos cardinales
career, carrera
career criminal,
criminal de carrera
Caribbean, Caribe
Caribbean Basin,
Cuenca del Caribe
Carolina regulators,
reguladores de
Carolina
Carolingian Empire,
Imperio carolingio

carpetbagger,
aventurero político,
oportunista político,
politicastro
carrying capacity,
capacidad de persis-
tencia o de carga
carrying money,
llevar dinero, portar
dinero
cartel, cartel o cártel
Carthage, Cartago
cartogram, cartograma
cartographer, cartógrafo
cartography, cartografía
cartoon, dibujos animados
Cartouche,
cartucho, cartela
casbah, casba
the Cascades, cascadas
case, caso
    case law,
    jurisprudencia
    case study,
    estudio de caso
cash, dinero en efectivo
    cash crop,
    cultivo comercial
    cash crop economy,
    economía de cultivos
    comerciales
Caspian Sea, mar Caspio
cassava, mandioca, yuca
caste, casta
    caste system,
    sistema de castas
castle, castillo
casualty rate,
tasa de accidentalidad
catacombs, catacumbas
cataract, catarata
categorical grants,
fondos categóricos

category, categoría
Catherine the Great,
Catalina la Grande
Catholic Christianity,
cristianismo católico
Catholic Church,
Iglesia católica
Catholic clergy,
clero católico
Catholic Reformation,
Reforma católica o
Contrarreforma
cattle drove,
manada de ganado
cattle herders,
pastores de rebaño
cattle raising, ganadería
caucus, camarilla política,
asamblea partidista
causality, causalidad
cause, causa
    cause and effect,
    causa y efecto
causeway,
paso elevado, calzada
cavalier, cavalier
cavalry, caballería
    cavalry warfare,
    guerra de caballería
cave painting,
pintura rupestre
cede, ceder
    ceded territory,
    territorio cedido
celebrate, celebrar
celebration, celebración
Celestial Empire,
Imperio celeste
censor, censurar
censorship, censura
census, censo
    census data,
    datos del censo

census district, distrito de censo
center, centro
center-pivot irrigation, técnica de irrigación central
Central Africa, África Central
Central Africa Republic, República Centroafricana
Central America, Centroamérica
Central Asia, Asia Central
Central Asian steppes, estepas de Asia Central
central authority, autoridad central
central business district, zona central de negocios
Central Europe, Europa Central
central government, gobierno central
Central Iberia, centro de la Península Ibérica
Central Intelligence Agency, Agencia Central de Inteligencia
central place, lugar central
central place theory, teoría de los lugares centrales, teoría del sitio central
Central Powers, Potencias centrales
centralized control, control centralizado
centralized government, gobierno centralizado

centralized monarchy, monarquía centralizada
century, siglo
ceremony, ceremonia
certificate of deposit, certificado de depósito
cession, cesión
Ceylon, Ceilán
Chamber of Commerce, Cámara de comercio
chance event, suceso aleatorio
chancellor, canciller
change, cambio
change in demand, cambio en la demanda
change in supply, cambio en la oferta
channel, canal
chapter, capítulo
chapter headings, encabezados de capítulo
character trait, rasgo de personalidad
chariot, carro (de guerra), cuadriga
charitable giving, donación caritativa
charitable group, grupo caritativo
Charlemagne, Carlomagno
Charles II (King of England), Carlos II de Inglaterra
chart, gráfico, carta, mapa, diagrama, plano (geografía)
charter, carta
charter colony, colonia de carta

charter document, estatuto, escritura

charter groups, pioneros

Charter Oath of 1868, Carta de Juramento de 1868

Chartist movement, cartismo o movimiento cartista

chateaux, castillo

chattel, bienes muebles

chauvinism, chovinismo

cheap labor, mano de obra barata

checking account, cuenta corriente, cuenta de cheques

checks and balances, inspecciones y balances, controles y contrapesos

chemical cycle, ciclo químico

chemical fertilizer, fertilizante químico

chemical warfare, arma química

chemistry, química

Chernobyl nuclear accident, accidente nuclear de Chérnobil

Cherokee Trail of Tears, Cherokee, Sendero de lágrimas cherokee

Chickasaw removal, remoción de los chickasaw

chief, jefe

Chief Justice, juez presidente

chief magistrate, primer magistrado

chieftain, cabecilla, cacique, jefe de tribu

child labor, explotación infantil

Chile, Chile

Chimu society, cultura chimú

China, China

China's Republican Revolution, Revolución republicana china

China's population growth, crecimiento de la población china

China's revolutionary movement, movimiento revolucionario chino

Chinatown, Barrio chino

Chinese, chino(a)

Chinese civilization, civilización china

Chinese Communist Party, Partido Comunista de China

Chinese Communist Revolution, Revolución comunista china

Chinese community, comunidad china

Chinese Exclusion Act, Ley de Exclusión de los Chinos

Chinese New Year, Año nuevo chino

Chinese Revolution, Revolución china

Chinese textile, textiles chinos

Chinese workers, trabajadores chinos

Chinese writing system, sistema de

escritura chino
chivalry, caballerosidad, cortesía
chlorofluorocarbons, clorofluorocarbonos
Choctaw removal, remoción de los choctaw
choice, selección
chore, tarea, faena
choropleth map, mapa de coropletas
Chou dynasty, dinastía Chou (Zhou)
Christendom, Cristiandad
Christian, cristiano
   Christian beliefs, creencias cristianas
   Christian community, comunidad cristiana
   Christian denomination, denominación cristiana
   Christian Europe, Europa cristiana
   Christian evangelical movement, Movimiento evangélico cristiano
   Christian missionary, misionero cristiano
   Christian monotheism, monoteísmo cristiano
   Christian religious art, arte religioso cristiano
   Christian soldier, soldado cristiano
Christianity, cristianismo
Christmas, Navidad
Christopher Columbus, Cristóbal Colón
chronological order, orden cronológico
chronology, cronología
chronology timeline, línea de tiempo cronológica
church, iglesia
   Church of England, Iglesia de Inglaterra
   Church of Jesus Christ of Latter-Day Saints, Iglesia de Jesucristo de los Santos de los Últimos Días
   church-state relations, relaciones Iglesia-Estado
Cicero, Cicerón
Cincinnatus, Cincinato
CIO (Committee for Industrial Organizations), Comité de Organizaciones Industriales (CIO)
circle graph, gráfico circular
circuit court district, distrito de tribunal de circuito
circuit judges, jueces de circuito judicial
circuit-court, tribunal de circuito judicial
circular reasoning, razonamiento circular, demostración en círculo
circular thinking, razonamiento circular, demostración en círculo

Circular-Flow Model,
modelo de flujo circular

circulation, circulación
circulation of money,
circulación del dinero,
circulación monetaria

circumnavigate,
circunnavegar

circus, circo

citadel, ciudadela

citation, cita, citación

cite, citar

citizen, ciudadano
citizen movement,
movimiento ciudadano

citizenry, ciudadanía

citizens and subjects,
ciudadanos y súbditos

citizenship, ciudadanía
citizenship by birth,
ciudadanía por
nacimiento

city, ciudad
city center,
centro de la ciudad
city council, ayun-
tamiento, municipio
city manager,
tesorero de la ciudad
city park,
parque público,
parque municipal
city planning,
planeación urbana
**City Upon a Hill
speech,** Discurso "La
ciudad en la colina"
city-state, ciudad-
estado

civic[1], cívico(a)
civic affairs,
asuntos civiles

civic center,
edificios municipales

civic court,
tribunal municipal

civic disposition,
disposición cívica

civic duty,
obligación civil

civic efficacy,
eficacia civil

civic life,
vida cívica

civic participation,
participación cívica

civic principles,
principios cívicos

civic procedures,
procedimientos civiles

civic responsibility,
responsabilidad civil

civic skills,
habilidades cívicas

civic society,
sociedad cívica

civic values,
valores cívicos

civic virtue,
virtud cívica

civic-mindedness,
civismo

civics[2], educación cívica

civil, civil
civil case, caso civil
civil code, código civil
civil court,
juzgado de lo civil
civil disobedience,
desobediencia civil
civil law,
derecho civil
civil liberties,
libertades civiles
civil organizations,

organizaciones civiles
civil rights, derechos civiles
Civil Rights Act, Ley de Derechos Civiles
civil rights laws, leyes de derechos civiles
civil rights legislation, legislación de derechos civiles
civil rights movement, movimiento de derechos civiles
civil service, servicio civil
civil service examination, examinación del servicio civil
civil service reform, reforma del servicio civil
civil service system, sistema de servicio civil
civil society, sociedad civil
civil unrest, descontento civil
Civil War, guerra civil
Civil War amendment, enmienda de la Guerra Civil
Civil Works Administration, Administración de Trabajos Civiles
civilian, civil
Civilian Conservation Corps, Cuerpo Civil de Conservación

civilian control of the military, control civil de los militares
civilian population, población civil
civilian review board, comisión de investigación civil
civility, urbanidad, cortesía
civilization, civilización
civilized, civilizado
claimed territory, territorio reclamado o reivindicado
clan, clan
clarification, explicación, aclaración
clarify, explicar, aclarar
class, clase
class action suit, juicio de acción popular
class analysis, análisis de clases
class boundaries, límites de clase
class conflict, lucha de clases
class consciousness, conciencia de clase
class crystallization, inmovilidad de clases
class fraction, fracción de clase
class relations, relaciones entre clases
class system, sistema de clases
classical, clásico
classical civilization, civilización clásica

classical conditioning, condicionamiento clásico

classical criminology, criminología clásica

classical economic theory, teoría económica clásica

classical Greek art and architecture, arquitectura y arte griego clásico

classical learning, aprendizaje clásico

classical liberalism, liberalismo clásico

classical period, período clásico

classical republic, república clásica

classical republicanism, republicanismo clásico

classical writings, escritos clásicos

classify, clasificar

classless society, sociedad sin clases

classroom, aula, salón de clases

clay pottery, cerámica de arcilla

clean air laws, leyes de aire limpio

clear and present danger rule, regla del peligro claro e inminente

clearing of forest, deforestación

Cleisthenes, Clístenes

clergy, clero

clientelism, clientelismo

cliffs, acantilados

climate, clima

climate changes, cambios climáticos

climate graph (climograph), climograma

climate region, región climática

climatic, climático

climatic pattern, patrón climático

climatic region, región climática

climograph, climograma

clinical psychology, psicología clínica

clipper ship, buque clíper

clocks, relojes

closed primary, elección primaria cerrada

closed shop, taller cerrado

cloture, clausura

cloudburst, chaparrón, aguacero

Clovis, Clodoveo

coal, carbón

coal mine strike, huelga en las minas de carbón

coal mining, minas de carbón

coalition, coalición

coalition government, gobierno de coalición

coalition of the willing, coalición de la voluntad

coast, costa

coast line, líneas costeras

coastal area, zona costera

coastal ecosystem,
ecosistema costero
coastal flood zone,
zona costera de inun-
dación
coastal lowlands,
tierras bajas costeras
coastal plain,
llanura costera
coastal range,
cordillera costera
code, código
code Napoleon,
código napoleónico
code of chivalry,
código de caballería
code of Hammurabi,
Código de Hammurabi
coerced labor,
trabajos forzados
coercion, coacción
coercive, coactivo
Coeur d'Alene tribe,
tribu Coeur d'Alene
coffee trade,
comercio del café
cognition, cognición
cohesion, cohesión
cohesiveness, cohesión
coin, moneda
coining money,
acuñar dinero
cold climate, clima frío
Cold War, Guerra Fría
collapse, colapso
collective bargaining,
negociaciones
colectivas
collective decision,
decisión colectiva
collective farm,
explotación colectiva
collective security,

seguridad colectiva
collective solidarity,
solidaridad colectiva
collectivism,
colectivismo
collectivization,
colectivización
collegial court,
tribunal colegiado
collusion,
colusión, connivencia
colonial, colonial
colonial Africa,
África colonial
colonial America,
América colonial
colonial charters,
cartas coloniales
colonial community,
comunidad colonial
colonial establish-
ment, establecimiento
colonial
colonial government,
gobierno colonial
colonial governors,
gobernadores
coloniales
colonial legislatures,
legislaturas coloniales
colonial period,
período colonial
colonial rule,
dominio colonial
colonialism,
colonialismo
colonies, colonias
colonist, colono,
colonizador
colonization,
colonización
colonize, colonizar
colony, colonia

colony in Massachusetts, colonia en Massachusetts

Colorado mining town (19th century), pueblo minero de Colorado (siglo XIX)

Colorado River, río Colorado

Columbia River, río Columbia

Columbian Exchange, intercambio colombino

Columbus, Colón

Columbus Day, Día de la Raza

combine, combinar

command economic system, economía dirigida o planificada

command economy, economía de planificación

commander, comandante

commander in chief, comandante en jefe

commemorative holidays, fiestas conmemorativas

commerce, comercio

commerce clause, cláusula de comercio

commercial advertising, publicidad comercial

commercial agriculture, agricultura comercial

commercial banking, banca comercial

commercial center, centro comercial

commercial farming, agricultura comercial

commercial paper, efectos comerciales, instrumentos negociables

Commercial Revolution, Revolución comercial

commercialization, comercialización

commitment, compromiso, obligación

commission, comisión

committee, comité, junta

Committee for Industrial Organizations (CIO), Comité de Organizaciones Industriales (CIO)

Committee of Correspondence, Comité de correspondencia

committee system, sistema de comités

Committees of Correspondence, Comités de Correspondencia

commodity, mercancía, artículo, materia prima

commodity flow, flujo de mercancías

commodity price, precio de las materias primas

commodore, comodoro

common, común

common cause, causa común

common good, bien común

common goods, mercancías comunes

common law, derecho consuetudi-

nario
common man, hombre común
Common Market, Mercado Común
common refuse, residuo común
common sense, sentido común
commonwealth, comunidad de naciones, mancomunidad
Commonwealth of Independent States, Comunidad de Estados Independientes
Commonwealth of Nations, Mancomunidad de naciones
communal life, vida en común
commune, comuna
communicable diseases, enfermedades transmisibles
communication, comunicación
communication hub, centro de comunicación
communication network, red de comunicación
communication route, vía de comunicación
communication technology, tecnología de comunicación
Communism, comunismo
communist, comunista

communist country, país comunista
Communist International, Internacional Comunista
Communist Manifesto, Manifiesto comunista
Communist Party, Partido Comunista
Communist Party in China, Partido Comunista de China
Communist Party of the Soviet Union (CPSU), Partido Comunista de la Unión Soviética
communist party-state, partido-estado comunista
Communist Revolution, Revolución Comunista
communist state, estado comunista
communitarian, comunitario
community, comunidad
community characteristics, características de la comunidad
community development, desarrollo comunitario
community project, proyecto comunitario
commute, viajar todos los días para ir al trabajo, conmutar
compact, compacto
company town, pueblo de la compañía

comparative,
   comparativo
   comparative advantage, ventaja comparativa
   comparative advantage tariffs,
   aranceles de ventaja comparativa
   comparative government systems,
   sistemas políticos comparados
   comparative value,
   valor comparativo
compare, comparar
   compare and contrast, comparar y contrastar
comparing the past,
   comparar el pasado
compass, brújula
   compass rose,
   rosa de los vientos
compelling state interest,
   interés público apremiante
competition, competencia
competitive market,
   mercado competitivo
competitive behavior,
   comportamiento competitivo
complementarily,
   complementariamente
   complementary product, producto complementario
complexity, complejidad
composite region,
   región compuesta
comprehend,
   comprender, entender

compromise, compromiso
   Compromise of 1850,
   Compromiso de 1850
compulsory education,
   educación obligatoria
computer, computadora
   Computer Revolution, Revolución informática
   computer technology, tecnología informática
concentrated settlement form, forma de asentamiento concentrado
concentration,
   concentración
   concentration camp,
   campo de concentración
   concentration of services, concentración de servicios
   concentric zone model, modelo de zonas concéntricas
concept, concepto
concubine, concubina
concurrent, concurrente, simultáneo
   concurrent jurisdiction,
   competencia compartida
   concurrent powers,
   poderes concurrentes
concurring opinion,
   voto concurrente
condensation,
   condensación
conditionality,
   condicionalidad
conduct of citizens,

conducta de los ciuda-
danos
Conestoga, conestoga
Conestoga Wagon,
carreta Conestoga
Confederacy,
confederación
**confederal political sys-
tem,** sistema político
confederado
confederate, confederado
Confederate Army,
Ejército Confederado
**confederate govern-
ment,** gobierno con-
federado
**Confederate States
of America,**
Estados Confederados
de América
confederation,
confederación
Conference at San Remo,
Conferencia de San
Remo
conference committee,
comité de conferencia
Conference of Versailles,
Tratado de Versalles
confirmation, ratificación
confiscate, confiscar
conflict, conflicto
**conflict manage-
ment,** gestión de
conflictos
conflict resolution,
resolución de conflic-
tos
conflict theory,
teoría del conflicto
conflicting viewpoints,
puntos de vista en
conflicto

conformity,
conformidad
Confucianism,
confucianismo
Confucius, Confucio
conglomerate,
conglomerado
Congregationalists,
congregacionalistas
Congress, Congreso
**Congress of Racial
Equality (CORE),**
CORE (Congreso de la
Igualdad Racial)
Congress of Vienna,
Congreso de Viena
congressional,
(del) Congreso
**Congressional au-
thority,** autoridad del
Congreso
**Congressional Budget
Office,** Oficina de Pre-
supuesto del Congreso
**Congressional
committee,**
comité del Congreso
**congressional
district,**
distrito electoral
**congressional
election,** elecciones
parlamentarias
**Congressional Indus-
trial Organization
(CIO),** Congreso de
Organizaciones Indus-
triales (COI)
coniferous, conífero
Connecticut Compromise,
Compromiso de Con-
necticut
conquered, conquistado

conquered territory theory, teoría del territorio conquistado
conquest, conquista
conscientious objector, objetor por conciencia
conscription, reclutamiento, alistamiento
consent, consentimiento
consent of the governed, consentimiento de los gobernados
consequences, consecuencias
conservation, conservación
Conservation Day, Día de la Conservación
conservation issue, problema de conservación
conservation movement, movimiento de conservación, movimiento conservacionista
conservation of resources, conservación de recursos
conservationist, conservacionista
conservatism, conservadurismo
conservative, conservador
conserve, conservar
consider the rights and interests of others, considerar los derechos e intereses de otros
consignment system, sistema de consig-
nación
consolidation, consolidación
conspicuous consumption, consumo ostentoso
conspiracy, conspiración
Constantine, Constantino
Constantinople, Constantinopla
constituency, circunscripción, distrito electoral
constituent, elector
constitution, constitución
Constitutional, constitucional
constitutional amendments, enmiendas constitucionales
Constitutional Convention, Convención constitucional
constitutional democracy, democracia constitucional
constitutional differences, diferencias constitucionales
constitutional government, gobierno constitucional
constitutional guarantee, garantía constitucional
constitutional ideal, ideal constitucional
constitutional law, derecho constitucional
constitutional monarchy, monarquía

constitucional
**constitutional
origins,** orígenes
constitucionales
**constitutional prin-
ciples,** principios
constitucionales
**Constitutional Union
Party,** Partido de la
Unión Constitucional
constitutionalism,
constitucionalismo
constitutionality of laws,
constitucionalidad de
las leyes
construction, construcción
consul, cónsul
consular service,
servicio consular
consulate, consulado
consumer, consumidor
consumer credit,
crédito al consumo
consumer culture,
cultura de consumo
**consumer econom-
ics,** aspectos económi-
cos del consumo
consumer fraud,
fraude al consumidor
consumer goods,
bienes de consumo
**Consumer Price
Index (CPI),** Índice de
precios al consumidor
**consumer product
safety,** seguridad de
los productos de con-
sumo
consumer society,
sociedad de consumo
**consumer sover-
eignty,** soberanía del

consumidor
consumer spending,
gastos en bienes de
consumo
consumer tastes,
gustos de los consumi-
dores
consumer's rights,
derechos del consumi-
dor
consumerism,
consumismo
consumer's rights,
derechos del consu-
midor
consumption,
consumo, consunción
contagious disease,
enfermedad contagiosa
container company,
empresa de contene-
dores
containment, contención
containment policy,
política de contención
contemporary,
contemporáneo
contemporary art,
arte contemporáneo
**contemporary de-
mocracy,** democracia
contemporánea
**contemporary eco-
nomic trade net-
work,** red comercial
económica contem-
poránea
**contemporary fac-
tors,** factores contem-
poráneos
contemporary issues,
asuntos contemporá-
neos

contemporary life, vida contemporánea

contemporary system of communication, sistema de comunicación contemporáneo

contempt of court, desacato al tribunal

content, contenido

content analysis, análisis de contenido

context, contexto

context clues, claves contextuales

contextual, contextual

contiguous, contiguo

continent, continente

continental, continental

Continental Army, Ejército Continental

continental climate, clima continental

Continental Congress, Congreso Continental

continental congresses, congresos continentales

continental divide, divisoria o división continental

continental drift, deriva continental

continental island, isla continental

continental shelf, plataforma continental

continentalism, continentalismo

continuity, continuidad

controversy, controversia

contour, contorno, perfil, silueta

contour line, cota, curva de nivel

contour map, mapa acotado o topográfico

contraband, contrabando

contract, contrato

contract labor, trabajo contratado, braceros contratados

contract negotiation, negociación del contrato

contras, contras

contrast, contraste

contribution, contribución

control, control

convent, convento

convention, convención

conventional crime, delito convencional

conventional warfare, guerra convencional

conversion, conversión

conversion experience, experiencia de conversión

convert, convertir, convertirse

cooperate, cooperar

cooperation, cooperación

cooperative, cooperativa

cooperative federalism, federalismo cooperativo

co-optation, cooptación

Copernicus, Copérnico

copper belt, cinturón del cobre

Coptic Christians, cristianos coptos

copyright, derechos de

autor, derechos de reproducción
copyright law, ley de derechos de autor
coral reef, arrecife de coral
core democratic values, valores democráticos fundamentales
corner the market, acaparar el mercado
corollary, corolario
corporate, empresarial, colectivo
   corporate crime, crimen corporativo
   corporate elite, élite corporativa
   corporate responsibility, responsabilidad empresarial
   corporate spending, gastos corporativos
corporation, corporación
corporatism, corporativismo
corporatist state, estado corporativista
corrective justice, justicia correctiva
correlation, correlación
corruption, corrupción
cosmetic system, sistema cosmético
cosmopolitan, cosmopolita
cosmos, cosmos
cost, costo
   cost of production, costo de producción
   cost-benefit analysis, análisis costo-beneficio
   cost-benefit ratio, razón de costo-beneficio
   cost-distance, costo-distancia
   cost-push inflation, inflación de costos
cottage industry, industria familiar
cotton, algodón
   cotton gin, despepitadora de algodón, desmotadora de algodón
council, consejo, ayuntamiento, municipio
Counter Reformation, contrarreforma
counterargument, contraargumento
countercultural, contracultural
counterculture, contracultura
country, país
   country of origin, país de origen
county, condado, provincia
coup, golpe maestro
coup d'état, golpe de estado
courage, valor, coraje
coureur de bois, corredor de los bosques
court, tribunal, corte
   court case, caso ante la corte
   court of appeals, tribunal de apelación
   court of Heian, corte de Heian

court-martial,
corte marcial, consejo
de guerra
court packing,
plan de rellenar la
corte, empaquetamien-
to o recomposición de
la corte
court-packing plan,
plan de empaque-
tamiento de la Corte
courtly ideals,
ideales del amor cortés
courtly love, amor cortés
covenant, pacto, convenio
**covenant commu-
nity,** comunidad
de alianza
**Covenant of the
League of Nations,**
Pacto de la Sociedad
de Naciones
covered wagon,
carromato, carreta con
toldo
covert action,
operación encubierta
cowboy, vaquero
cowboy culture,
cultura de vaqueros
crabgrass frontier,
frontera de malezas
craft, oficio, arte, nave,
embarcación
craft union, gremio
craftsmen, artesano
**creation myths of Baby-
lon,** mito babilónico
de la creación
creation myth,
mito de la creación
**creation myths of
China,** mito chino de
la creación
**creation myths of
Egypt,** mito egipcio de
la creación
**creation myths of
Greece,** mito griego de
la creación
**creation myths of
Sumer,** mito sumerio
de la creación
credibility, credibilidad
credible, creíble, verosímil
credit, crédito
credit card,
tarjeta de crédito
Credit Mobilier,
empresa Crédit
Mobilier
credit policy,
política crediticia
creditor, acreedor
creditor nation,
nación acreedora
Cree removal, remoción de
los cree o cri
creek, arroyo, riachuelo,
cala, ensenada
cremation, cremación
Creole, criollo
**Creole-dominated
revolt,** levantamiento
de los criollos
Crete, Creta
crevasse, grieta
crew, tripulación
crime, crimen
crime net,
red de crimen
Crimean War,
Guerra de Crimea
**crimes against human-
ity,** crímenes contra la
humanidad

criminal courts,
corte penal
criminal justice,
justicia penal
criminal law,
derecho penal
criminal procedure,
procedimiento penal
criminology, criminología
crisis, crisis
critical developments,
desarrollos críticos
critical events,
sucesos críticos
critical text analysis,
análisis crítico de
textos
critical theory,
teoría crítica
Cro-Magnon,
Cro-Magnon o Croma-
ñón
crop, cosecha, cultivo
crop failure,
mala cosecha
crop lien system,
sistema de derecho de
retención de cosecha,
crédito por compra
adelantada de cosecha
crop rotation,
rotación de cultivos
crop yield, rendimiento de la cosecha
Cross of Gold speech,
Discurso de la Cruz
de oro
cross section, muestra
representativa
cross-cultural analysis,
análisis intercultural
cross-cultural contact,
contacto entre cultu-

ras
cross-cultural setting,
entorno intercultural
cross-examination,
contrainterrogación
cross-reference, remisión
cross-section diagram,
diagrama transversal
crown corporation, corporación de la Corona
crude birth rate,
tasa bruta de natali-
dad
crude death rate,
tasa bruta de mortali-
dad
crude oil, petróleo crudo
**cruel and unusual punish-
ment,** castigo cruel e
inusual
crusader, cruzado
Crusades, Cruzadas
crust, corteza
Cuba, Cuba
Cuban Missile Crisis,
Crisis de los misiles en
Cuba
Cuban Revolution,
Revolución cubana
Cubism, cubismo
Cubist, cubista
cult, culto
cult of domesticity,
culto a la domestici-
dad
cultural, cultural
**cultural anthropol-
ogy,** antropología
cultural
cultural borrowing,
préstamo cultural
cultural change,
cambio cultural

cultural characteristics, características culturales

cultural construction, construcción cultural

cultural contact, contacto cultural

cultural continuity, continuidad cultural

cultural contributions, contribuciones culturales

cultural convergence, convergencia cultural

cultural development, desarrollo cultural

cultural differences, diferencias culturales

cultural diffusion, difusión cultural

cultural divergence, divergencia cultural

cultural diversity, diversidad cultural

cultural ecology, ecología cultural

cultural exchange, intercambio cultural, rasgos culturales

cultural explanation, explicación cultural

cultural fusion, fusión cultural

cultural geography, geografía cultural

cultural group, grupo cultural

cultural heritage, herencia cultural

cultural history, historia cultural

cultural identity, identidad cultural

cultural imperialism, imperialismo cultural

cultural integration, integración cultural

cultural interaction, interacción cultural

cultural interdependence, interdependencia cultural

cultural landscape, paisaje cultural

cultural materials, materiales culturales

cultural norm, norma cultural

cultural patterns, modelos (patrones) culturales

cultural pluralism, pluralismo cultural

cultural preservation, preservación cultural

cultural region, región cultural

cultural relativism, relativismo cultural

Cultural Revolution, Revolución cultural proletaria

cultural stability, estabilidad cultural

cultural subsistence agriculture patterns, patrones de cultivo agrícola de subsistencia

cultural symbol, símbolo cultural

cultural tradition, tradición cultural

cultural traits,

características culturales

cultural understanding, comprensión cultural

cultural unity, unidad cultural

culture, cultura

culture group, grupo cultural

culture hearth, cultura madre, crisol cultural

culture of fear, cultura del miedo

culture of shock, cultura del escándalo

culture system, sistema cultural

culture traditions, tradiciones culturales

Cumberland Gap, desfiladero de Cumberland

cuneiform, cuneiforme

curfew, toque de queda

currency, moneda, divisas

currency exchange, cambio de divisas

current, actual

current interest rate, tasa de interés corriente

currently, actualmente

custom, costumbre

customer service, servicio al cliente

customs search, revisión de aduana

cutaway diagram, diagrama en sección

cycle, ciclo

cycle of abuse,

ciclo de violencia

cyclical unemployment, desempleo cíclico o coyuntural

cycling of energy, ciclo de energía

cyclone, ciclón

Cyrus I, Ciro I

czar, zar

Czar Nicholas I, Zar Nicolás I

Czar Nicholas II, Zar Nicolás II

Czech Republic, República Checa

D

Dadaism, dadaísmo

daily life, vida diaria, vida cotidiana

daily prayer, oración diaria

daily survival skill, destreza de supervivencia diaria

daimyo, daimio

dairy cattle, ganado bovino lechero

dairy cow, vaca lechera

dam, presa, dique

Damascus, Damasco

dance, danza

Daoism, taoísmo

Darius I, Darío I

Darius the Great, Darío el Grande

Dark Ages, Oscurantismo

dark horse, vencedor inesperado, ganador sopresa

data, datos
> **data set,**
> conjunto de datos

database, base de datos

date, fecha

dating methods,
> métodos de datación

Daughters of Liberty,
> Hijas de la Libertad

dauphin, sucesor

Dawes Severalty Act,
> Ley Dawes o Ley de
> Atribución de Tierra

day, día
> **day school,**
> colegio sin internado

D-Day, Día D

de facto, de facto
> **de facto segregation,**
> segregación de facto

de jure, de jure
> **de jure segregation,**
> segregación de jure

deadlock,
> punto muerto, im-
> passe

death penalty,
> pena de muerte

death rate,
> tasa de mortalidad

Death Valley,
> Valle de la Muerte

debate, debate

debt, deuda

debtor, deudor
> **debtor class,**
> clase deudora
> **debtor nation,**
> nación deudora
> **debtor's prisons,**
> prisión por deuda

decade, década

Decembrist uprising,
> Rebelión Decembrista

decentralization,
> descentralización

decentralize,
> descentralizar

deciduous, caduco

decimal system,
> sistema decimal

decision, decisión
> **decision-making,**
> toma de decisiones
> **decision making
> model,** modelo de
> toma decisiones
> **decision matrix,**
> matriz de decisión

declaration, declaración
> **Declaration of Inde-
> pendence,**
> Declaración de Inde-
> pendencia
> **Declaration of Senti-
> ments,**
> Declaración de sen-
> timientos
> **Declaration of the
> Rights of Man,**
> Declaración de los
> Derechos del Hombre
> y del Ciudadano
> **Declaration of the
> Rights of Women,**
> Declaración de los
> Derechos de la Mujer y
> de la Ciudadana

declaratory judgment,
> sentencia declarativa

decline, declinar

decolonization,
> descolonización

deductive reasoning,
> razonamiento deduc-
> tivo

deerskin,
piel de ciervo, gamuza
default on a loan,
incumplimiento de
pago
defendant, acusado
defense policy,
política de defensa
defense spending,
gastos en defensa
deferment of loan,
aplazamiento
deferred payment,
pago diferido
deficit, déficit
deficit spending,
gastos deficitarios
defining characteristic,
característica
distintiva
deflation, deflación
deforestation,
deforestación
Deism, deísmo
deist, deísta
Delaware Indians,
nativos americanos de
Delaware
Delaware River,
río Delaware
delegated powers,
poderes delegados
delegates, delegados
delegation, delegación
delta, delta
demagogic, demagógico
demagogue, demagogo
demand, demanda
demand curve,
curva de demanda
demand-pull infla-
tion, inflación de
demanda, inflación

generada por la de-
manda
demarcation,
línea de demarcación
Demilitarized Zone (DMZ),
zona desmilitarizada
demobilization,
desmovilización
democracy, democracia
Democrat, demócrata
democratic,
democrático
democratic central-
ism, centralismo
democrático
democratic despo-
tism, despotismo
democrático
democratic gov-
ernment, gobierno
democrático
democratic ideals,
ideales democráticos
democratic legis-
lature, legislatura
democrática
Democratic nomi-
nee, candidato por el
Partido Demócrata
Democratic Party,
Partido Demócrata
democratic process,
proceso democrático
democratic society,
sociedad democrática
democratic values,
valores democráticos
Democratic-Republi-
can Party,
Partido Demócrata-
Republicano
democratization,
democratización

demographic

demographic, demográfico
  **demographic cluster-
ing,** grupo demográ-
fico
  **demographic infor-
mation,** información
demográfica
  demographic map,
mapa demográfico
  **demographic pat-
terns,** modelos
demográficos
  demographic shift,
cambio demográfico
  **demographic struc-
ture,** estructura
demográfica
  **demographic tran-
sition,** transición
demográfica
demographics, demografía
demography, demografía
demonstration,
manifestación
Denmark, Dinamarca
denomination,
denominación
density, densidad
  **density of popula-
tion,** densidad de
población
department, departamento
  **Department of Agri-
culture,** Departamen-
to de Agricultura
  **Department of Com-
merce,** Departamento
de Comercio
  **Department of De-
fense,** Departamento
de Defensa
  **Department of Edu-
cation,** Departamento
de Educación
  **Department of En-
ergy,** Departamento
de Energía
  **Department of
Health and Human
Services,** Departa-
mento de Salud y
Servicios Humanos
  **Department of
Housing and Urban
Development,** Depar-
tamento de Vivienda y
Desarrollo Urbano
  **Department of Jus-
tice,** Departamento de
Justicia
  Department of Labor,
Departamento de Tra-
bajo
  Department of State,
Departamento de Es-
tado
  **Department of the
Interior,** Departamen-
to del Interior
  **Department of the
Treasury,** Departa-
mento del Tesoro
  **Department of Vet-
eran's Affairs,** Depar-
tamento de Asuntos de
los Veteranos
dependency ratio,
razón de dependencia
dependent, dependiente
  **dependent devel-
opment,** desarrollo
dependiente
  dependent variable,
variable dependiente
**depleted rain forests
of central Africa,**

reducción de los
bosques tropicales de
África Central
deposition, deposición
depreciate, depreciar
depression,
depresión, crisis
deregulation, desregularización, liberalización
derivation, derivación
desalinization, desalinización, desalación
**Descartes' "Discourse on
method",** "Discurso
del método" de Des-
cartes
descendant, descendiente
descent, ascendencia
describe, describir
description, descripción
descriptive, descriptivo
desegregate,
abolir la segregación
desegregation, abolición
de la segregación
desert[1], desertar
desert[2], desierto
Desert Storm,
Tormenta del desierto
desertification,
desertificación, desert-
ización
despotism,
déspota, despotismo
détente,
distensión, rejación de
tensión, détente
**determinants of supply
and demand,** determi-
nantes de la oferta y la
demanda
determinism,
determinismo

deterrence, disuasión
develop, desarrollar
developed country,
país desarrollado
developing, en desarrollo
developing country,
país en desarrollo
developing nations,
naciones en vías de
desarrollo
development, desarrollo,
desarrollos críticos
developmental state,
estado desarrollista
developmentalism,
desarrollismo
devolution, transferencia
de competencias
dharma, dharma
diagram, diagrama
dialect, dialecto
dialectical materialism,
materialismo dialéctico
dialogue, diálogo
diamond trade,
comercio de diamantes
diaspora, diáspora
dictator, dictador
dictatorship, dictadura
Diem regime,
régimen de Diem
diesel machinery,
maquinaria de Diesel
differences, diferencias
different, diferentes
**diffusion of tobacco
smoking,** difusión de
humo del tabaco
dike, dique
dime, moneda de diez centavos
diminishing,
disminución

diocese, diócesis
diplomacy, diplomacia
diplomat, diplomático
diplomatic, diplomático
 diplomatic immu-nity, inmunidad diplomática
 diplomatic note, nota diplomática
 diplomatic rank, rango diplomático
 diplomatic recogni-tion, reconocimiento diplomático
direct, directo
 direct democracy, democracia directa
 direct election, elección directa
 direct election of Senators, elección directa de los senadores
 direct experience, experiencia directa
 direct popular rule, mandato popular directo
 direct primary, elección primaria directa
 direct tax, impuesto directo
 direct taxation, tributación directa
 direct trade, comercio directo
 direct trading, comercialización directa
direction, dirección
directional flow, flujo de dirección
disabled citizen, ciudadano inhabilitado
disagreement, desacuerdo
disarmament, desarme
disciple, discípulo
discount rate, tasa de descuento
discovery, descubrimiento
 discovery of dia-monds, descubrimiento de diamantes
 discovery of gold, descubrimiento de oro
discrimination, discriminación
 discrimination based on age, discriminación basada en la edad
 discrimination based on disability, discriminación basada en discapacidad
 discrimination based on ethnicity, discriminación basada en el origen étnico
 discrimination based on gender, discriminación basada en el género
 discrimination based on language, discriminación lingüística
 discrimination based on religious belief, discriminación basada en la religión o las creencias
discuss, discutir, debatir
discussion, discusión
disease, enfermedad
 disease microorgan-ism, microorganismo

patógeno
disease pandemic,
pandemia
diseases,
enfermedades
disenfranchised,
privado del derecho a
voto
disenfranchisement,
privación del derecho
a voto
disestablish, separar del
Estado (la Iglesia)
disincentive,
falta de incentivos
disparity, disparidad
**disparities in Ameri-
can ideals and re-
alities,** disparidades
entre los ideales
y la realidad esta-
dounidenses
dispersed, dispersado
dispersion, dispersión
displaced persons,
personas desplazadas,
expatriados
displacement,
desplazamiento
disposable income,
ingresos disponibles
dispute, disputa
dispute resolution,
resolución de litigios,
solución de conflictos
disseminate, diseminar
dissent, disensión
dissenter, disidente
dissenting opinion,
dictamen divergente
dissident, disidente
distance, distancia
distance decay,

descomposición a dis-
tancia
**distinctive characteris-
tics,** características
distintivas
distortion, distorsión
distribution, distribución
**distribution of eco-
systems,** distribución
de los ecosistemas
**distribution of goods
and services,**
distribución de bienes
y servicios
distribution of power,
distribución de poder
**distribution of re-
sources,** distribución
de recursos
distributive policies,
políticas distributivas
distributive system,
sistema distributivo
distributor, distribuidor
district, distrito
diverse, diverso, variado
diversification,
diversificación
diversify, diversificar
diversity, diversidad
**diversity in Ameri-
can life,** diversidad
en la cultura esta-
dounidense
**diversity of citizen-
ship suit,** caso de
diversidad de ciudada-
nía
divide, dividir
divide and rule,
dividir y vencerás
divided government,
gobierno dividido

divided loyalties,
conflicto de lealtades
dividend, dividendo
divine, divino
divine law, ley divina
divine right,
derecho divino
divine right of kings,
derecho divino de los
reyes
divinity, divinidad
division, división
**division (of Earth's
surface),** división (de
la superficie terrestre)
**division of Germany
and Berlin,** división
de Alemania y Berlín
division of labor,
división del trabajo
**division of the sub-
continent,** división
del subcontinente
divorce, divorcio
doctrinal, doctrinal
doctrine, doctrina
document, documento
documentary,
documental
documentation,
documentación
doge, dogo (dux)
doldrums, zona de calmas
ecuatoriales
dollar, dólar
dollar diplomacy,
diplomacia del dólar
domestic,
doméstico, nacional
domestic crop,
cultivo doméstico
domestic economy,
economía doméstica

domestic policy,
política interna
domestic program,
programa nacional
domestic tranquility,
tranquilidad domés-
tica
domesticated,
domesticado
domesticated animal,
animal domesticado
domestication,
domesticación
dominate, dominar
domination, dominación
Dominican Republic,
República Dominicana
dominion, dominio
**dominion of New
England,** Dominio de
Nueva Inglaterra
Domino Theory,
teoría del dominó
double jeopardy,
non bis in idem
double standard,
doble moral
doubling time,
tiempo de duplicación
**Dow Jones Industrial Av-
erage (DOW),**
índice Dow Jones
down, abajo
downstream, río abajo
downtown,
centro de la ciudad
**downtown business
area,** zona comercial
del centro de la ciudad
downwind, en la dirección
del viento
dowry, dote
draft, reclutamiento

draft evaders, evasores al reclutamiento
draft riot, motín en protesta del reclutamiento
drainage basin, cuenca hidrográfica
drama, drama
dramatization, dramatización
dramatize, dramatizar
drawing conclusions, sacar conclusiones
Dred Scott v. Sandford, Caso Dred Scott contra Sandford
dredge, dragar
dress code, codigo de vestimenta
drought, sequía
drug cartel, cartel de drogas
Drug Free Act, Ley de Escuelas Libres de Drogas
drug trafficking, narcotráfico
dry farming, agricultura seca
dual federalism, federalismo dual
dual society, sociedad dual
Duchy of Moscow, Principado de Moscú, Gran Ducado de Moscú
due process, debido proceso
due process clause, cláusula de debido proceso

dugout Phoenician ship, piragua
duke, duque
dune, duna
durable goods, bienes duraderos
Dust Bowl, Cuenca de Polvo
dust storm, tormenta de polvo
Dutch, neerlandés, holandés
Dutch colonies, colonias holandesas
Dutch colonization, colonización holandesa o neerlandesa
Dutch merchant class, clase comerciante holandesa
Dutch Republic, República Holandesa
Dutch West Indies, Antillas Neerlandesas o Indias Occidentales Holandesas
duty, deber, obligación, impuesto
dyke, dique
dynamic system, sistema dinámico
dynastic, dinástico
dynastic cycle, ciclo dinástico
dynastic politics, política dinástica
dynasty, dinastía

E Pluribus Unum,
E Pluribus Unum (de muchos, uno)
eagle, águila
eagle feather,
pluma de águila
early inhabitants,
primeros habitantes
Early Middle Ages,
Alta Edad Media
early modern society,
sociedad moderna temprana
earn, ganar
earned income,
ingresos salariales
earning, ganancia
earth-moving machinery,
maquinaria para excavaciones
earthquake, temblor, sismo, terremoto
earthquake zone,
zona sísmica
Earth-sun relation,
relación entre el Sol y la Tierra
east, este
East Africa,
África Oriental
East Asia,
Asia del Este
East Asian Co-Prosperity Sphere,
esfera de coprosperidad de Asia Oriental
East Coast, Costa Este (de los EE.UU.)

East Germany,
Alemania Oriental
East India Company,
Compañía Británica de las Indias Orientales
East Indies,
Indias Orientales
East Timor,
Timor Oriental
eastern, oriental
Eastern Australia,
Australia Oriental
Eastern Europe,
Europa del Este
Eastern Hemisphere,
Hemisferio Oriental
Eastern Mediterranean, Mediterráneo Oriental
Eastern Orthodox,
Iglesia Ortodoxa Oriental
Eastern Roman Empire, Imperio Romano de Oriente
eastern United States, Este de los Estados Unidos
Eastern woodlands,
Bosques orientales
ecological, ecológico
ecological system,
sistema ecológico
ecology, ecología
economic, económico
economic activity,
actividad económica
economic activity patterns, patrones de actividad económica
economic aid,
ayuda económica
economic alliance,

alianza económica
economic and political connections, conexiones políticas y económicas
economic base, base económica
economic bubble, burbuja económica
economic capital, capital económico
economic choice, elección económica
Economic Community of West African States (ECOWAS), Comunidad Económica de Estados de África Occidental
economic concepts, conceptos económicos
economic curve, curva económica
economic data, datos económicos
economic decisions, decisiones económicas
economic decision making, toma de decisiones económicas
economic dependency, dependencia económica
economic determinism, determinismo económico
economic development, desarrollo económico
economic differences, diferencias económicas
economic disparity,

disparidad económica
economic dispute, disputa económica
economic doctrine, doctrina económica
economic dominance, dominio económico
economic equilibrium, equilibrio económico
economic exchanges, intercambios económicos
economic factors, factores económicos
economic freedom, libertad económica
economic gain, ganancia económica
economic geography, geografía económica
economic goals, metas u objetivos económicos
economic goods, bienes económicos
economic growth, crecimiento económico
economic incentive, incentivo económico
economic indicator, indicador económico
economic institutions, instituciones económicas
economic interdependence, interdependencia económica
economic issues, cuestiones económicas
economic law, derecho económico

economic measurement, medida económica
economic model, modelo económico
economic nationalism, nacionalismo económico
economic plan, plan económico
economic power, poder económico
economic profit, beneficio económico
economic recovery, reactivación económica, recuperación económica
economic reforms, reformas económicas
economic region, región económica
economic rights, derechos económicos
economic risk, riesgo económico
economic sanctions, sanciones económicas
economic security, seguridad económica
economic specialization, especialización económica
economic stability, estabilidad económica
economic surplus, excedente económico
economic system, sistema económico
economic theory, teoría económica
economic trends, tendencias económicas

economic venture, emprendimiento económico
economically developing nation, nación en vías de desarrollo económico
economically interdependent, interdependiente económicamente
economics, economía
economist, economista
economy, economía
ecosystem, ecosistema
edge city, área urbana de periferia
edition, edición
editorial, editorial
education, educación
education system, sistema educativo
educational reform, reforma educativa
effect, efecto
efficacy, eficacia
egalitarian, igualitario
ego, el yo, el ego
Egypt, Egipto
Egyptian civilization, civilización egipcia
Egyptian time, época egipcia
Eisenhower Doctrine, Doctrina Eisenhower
elaborate, elaborar
elaboration, elaboración
elastic clause, cláusula flexible
elasticity, elasticidad
elder, mayor, anciano
elect[1], elegir
elect[2], electo
elected office,

cargo público
elected officials,
funcionarios electos
elected representative,
representante electo
election, elección
Election Day,
Día de las Elecciones
elector, elector
electoral, electoral
electoral college,
colegio electoral
electoral system,
sistema electoral
electorate, electorado
electric car,
vehículo eléctrico
electricity, electricidad
electronic city-state,
ciudad-estado elec-
trónica
elevation,
elevación, altura
elevation map,
mapa de altura
elevation profile,
perfil de elevación
elite, élite
elite status,
posición de élite
Elizabeth I, Isabel I
Ellis Island, Isla Ellis
emancipate, emancipar
emancipation,
emancipación
**Emancipation
Proclamation,**
Proclamación de
Emancipación
embalming,
embalsamamiento
embargo, embargo
Embargo Acts,

Leyes de Embargo
embedded values,
valores intrínsecos
**emerging capitalist
economy,** economía
capitalista emergente
emergence, emergencia
emigrant, emigrante
emigrate, emigrar
emigration, emigración
eminent domain,
expropiación
emirs, emires
empathy, empatía
emperor, emperador
Emperor Aurangzeb,
Emperador Aurangzeb
empire, imperio
empire-builder,
constructor de un
imperio
empirical, empírico
empirical approach,
enfoque empírico
empirical evidence,
evidencia empírica
empirical method,
método empírico
empiricism, empirismo
employee, empleado
employer, empleador
employment, empleo
**employment oppor-
tunity,** oportunidad
de empleo
empower, otorgar poderes
Ems telegram,
Telegrama de Ems
enabling act, ley orgánica
enact, promulgar
enact laws,
promulgar leyes
enclave, enclave

enclosure,
documento anexo
Enclosure Movement, Movimiento de
cercamiento
encomienda system,
sistema de encomienda
encounter, encuentro
encyclopedia,
enciclopedia
endangered species,
especies en peligro
ending date,
fecha de finalización
endow, dotar
endowed, dotado
endowment,
dotación, donación
enemies of the state,
enemigos del estado
energy, energía, energética
energy consumption,
consumo de energía
energy crisis,
crisis energética
energy industry,
industria energética
energy source,
fuente de energía
energy-poor region,
región pobre en energía
enforce laws,
hacer cumplir las leyes
enforced, forzoso, hecho
cumplir o respetar
enfranchise, conceder el
derecho al voto
enfranchised, exento
enfranchisement,
concesión del derecho
al voto

Engel v. Vitale,
caso Engel contra
Vitale
engineer, ingeniero
England, Inglaterra
English, inglés
**English Bill of
Rights,** Declaración
de derechos inglesa
English civil war,
Guerra Civil inglesa
English colony,
colonia inglesa
**English Common
Law,** Derecho anglosajón
English Parliament,
Parlamento inglés
English Revolution,
Revolución inglesa
English settlement,
asentamiento inglés
Enlightened Despot,
déspota ilustrado
Enlightenment,
Ilustración
enslaved, esclavizado
entertainment industry,
industria del entretenimiento
entitlement programs,
programas de ayuda
social
entitlements,
derechos económicos
entrepreneur, empresario
entrepreneurial,
emprendedor
**entrepreneurial
spirit,** espíritu emprendedor
entrepreneurship,
proceso emprendedor

enumerated powers,
poderes enumerados
enumerated rights,
derechos enumerados
enumeration,
enumeración
environment, ambiente,
medio ambiente
environmental, ambiental
**environmental
change,** cambio
ambiental
environmental conditions, condiciones
ambientales
environmental consequences, consecuencias ambientales
environmental degradation, degradación
ambiental
environmental determinism, determinismo
ambiental
Environmental Protection Act, Ley de
protección ambiental
environmental protection movement,
movimiento de protección ambiental
environmentalism,
ambientalismo
envoy, enviado
epic, epopeya, poema épico
Epic of Gilgamesh,
Epopeya de Gilgamesh
epidemic, epidemia
epidemic disease,
enfermedad epidémica
epistle, epístola
Equal Employment Opportunities Com-

mission (EEOC),
Comisión para la
Igualdad de Oportunidades de Empleo
equal justice for all,
justicia igualitaria
para todos
equal opportunity,
igualdad de oportunidades
equal pay for equal work,
a trabajo igual salario
igual
equal protection,
protección igualitaria
**equal protection
clause,** cláusula sobre
protección igualitaria
**equal protection of
the law,** protección
igualitaria de la ley
equal rights,
igualdad de derechos
Equal Rights Amendment, enmienda sobre
igualdad de derechos
**equal rights under
the law,** igualdad de
derechos bajo la ley
equality, igualdad
equality of condition,
igualdad de condiciones
equality of opportunity, igualdad de
oportunidades
equator, ecuador
equilibrium, equilibrio
equilibrium point,
punto de equilibrio
equilibrium price,
precio de equilibrio
equinox, equinoccio

equity, equidad
era, era, época
    Era of Good Feelings,
    Era de buenos sen-
    timientos
eradication, erradicación
Eric the Red, Eric el Rojo
Erie Canal, Canal de Erie
Erie Plain, l
    lanura de Erie
erode, erosionar
erosion, erosión
    erosion agent,
    agente de erosión
escalate, intensificar,
    aumentar
escalation, intensificación,
    subida o escalada
escaped slave,
    esclavo fugitivo
escapism,
    escapismo, evasión
escarpment, escarpa
espionage, espionaje
    Espionage Act,
    Ley de Espionaje
essay, ensayo
established, establecido,
    consolidado, arraigado
    established church,
    iglesia oficial
    established religion,
    religión oficial
establishment clause,
    cláusula de estable-
    cimiento del estado
    laico
estate tax,
    impuesto sobre
    la herencia
estate, estamento
Estates-General,
    Estados Generales

ethical belief,
    creencia ética
ethical considerations,
    consideraciones éticas
ethical dilemma,
    dilema ético
ethical standards,
    normas éticas
ethical systems,
    sistemas éticos
Ethiopia, Etiopía
Ethiopian art, arte etíope
Ethiopian rock churches,
    iglesias etíopes talla-
    das en piedra
ethnic, étnico
    ethnic art,
    arte étnico
    ethnic background,
    orígen étnico
    ethnic cleansing,
    limpieza étnica
    ethnic composition,
    composición étnica
    ethnic conflict,
    conflicto étnico
    ethnic diversity,
    diversidad étnica
    ethnic elitism,
    elitismo étnico
    ethnic enclave,
    enclave étnico
    ethnic group,
    grupo étnico
    ethnic heritage,
    herencia étnica
    ethnic identity,
    identidad étnica
    ethnic minority,
    minoría étnica
    ethnic neighborhood,
    vecindario étnico
    ethnic origin,

origen étnico
ethnic tension,
tensión étnica
ethnic tradition,
tradición étnica
ethnicity, etnicidad
ethnocentric,
etnocéntrico
ethnocentrism,
etnocentrismo
ethnographer, etnógrafo
ethnography, etnografía
eugenics, eugenesia
Eurasia, Eurasia
Eurasian empire,
Imperio euroasiático
Eurasian society,
sociedad euroasiática
Eurocentric, eurocéntrico
Eurodollar, dólar europea
Europe, Europa
European, europeo
**European colonial
rule,** régimen colonial
europeo
**European colonial-
ism,** colonialismo
europeo
**European coloniza-
tion,** colonización
europea
**European Commu-
nity,** Comunidad
Europea
European conquest,
conquista europea
European country,
país europeo
European Crusades,
Cruzadas europeas
**European Economic
Community,**
Comunidad Económi-

ca Europea
European encounter,
Encuentro europeo
**European Explora-
tion,** Exploración
europea
European explorer,
explorador europeo
**European imperial-
ism,** imperialismo
europeo
European Jew,
judío europeo
**European land hun-
ger,** avaricia de tierras
europeas
**European manorial
system,** sistema
señorial europeo
European monarchy,
monarquía europea
**European monetary
system,** Sistema
Monetario Europeo
**European opium
trade,** tráfico de opio
en Europa
**European Reforma-
tion,** Reforma en
Europa
**European Renais-
sance,** Renacimiento
en Europa
**European resistance
movement,**
movimiento de resist-
encia europeo
European settler,
colono europeo
European theater,
teatro europeo
European Union,
Unión Europea

eutrophication

eutrophication, eutrofización
evacuation route, ruta de evacuación
evaluate, evaluar
evaluation, evaluación
evangelical argument, argumento evangélico
evangelical movement, movimiento evangélico
evangelism, evangelismo
evangelize, evangelizar
evaporation, evaporación
event, suceso, acontecimiento
evidence, evidencia
evil empire, imperio del mal
evolution, evolución
evolutionary[1], evolucionista
evolutionary[2], evolucionario, evolutivo
evolutionary psychology, psicología evolucionista
evolve, evolucionar
ex post facto law, ley ex post facto (efecto retroactivo), ley retroactiva
excavate, excavar
excavations, excavaciones
exchange, intercambio
exchange of fauna, intercambio de fauna
exchange of flora, intercambio de flora
exchange of goods, intercambio de bienes
exchange of services, intercambio de servicios

exchange rate, tipo de cambio
exchange systems, sistemas de intercambio
exchange theory, teoría de intercambio social
exchange value, valor de cambio
excise tax, impuesto al consumo
exclusionary rule, regla de exclusión
excommunicate, excomulgar
excommunication, excomulgación
executive, ejecutivo
executive agreement, convenio o acuerdo ejecutivo
executive branch, poder ejecutivo
executive departments, departamentos del poder ejecutivo
executive order, orden ejecutiva
executive power, poder ejecutivo
executive privilege, privilegio del ejecutivo
exile, exilio
Existentialism, existencialismo
exodus, éxodo
expansion, expansión
expansionism, expansionismo
expansionist foreign policy, política exterior expansionista

expatriates, expatriados
expected rate of infla-tion, tasa prevista de inflación
Expediency Council, Consejo de Discernimiento
expedition, expedición
expenditure, gasto
expenses, gastos
experiment[1], experimento
experiment[2], experimentar
experimental, experimental
   experimental meth-od, método experimental
   experimental psy-chology, psicología experimental
explain, explicar
explanation, explicación
explicit, explícito
exploitation, explotación
exploration, exploración
   exploration route, ruta de exploración
explorer, explorador
exponential growth, crecimiento exponencial
export, exportar
exporters, exportadores
exporting firm, compañía de expor-tación
expressed, expresado
   expressed powers, poderes expresados
Expressionism, expresionismo
expropriate, expropiar
expropriation, expropiación
expulsion, expulsión

extended family, familia extensa
extensive farming, agricultura extensiva
exterminate, exterminar
extermination, exterminación
external taxes, impuestos externos
externalities, externalidades, efectos externos
extinct, extinto, desaparecido
extinction, extinción
extractive economies, economías de extracción
extractive mining, minas de extracción
extradite, extraditar
extradition, extradición
extraterritoriality, extraterritorialidad
eyewitness account, testimonio del testigo presencial

fable, fábula
facilities, instalaciones, dependencias, comodidades
facsimile transmission service, servicio de transmisión de fac-símil
fact, hecho
faction, facción

factors of production,
factores de producción
factory, fábrica
  factory girls,
  chicas de fábrica
  factory system,
  sistema de fábrica
fair¹, feria
fair², justo
  Fair Deal, Trato Justo
  fair distribution of
  wealth, distribución
  justa de la riqueza
  fair employment
  practice, prácticas de
  empleo justo
  Fair Labor Standards
  Act, Ley de Normas
  Laborales Justas
  fair notice of a
  hearing, notificación
  razonable de una au-
  diencia
  fair trade,
  comercio justo
  fair trial,
  juicio imparcial
faith, fe
fall line, línea de cascadas
  fall line of the
  Appalachians,
  línea de cascadas de
  los montes Apalaches
falsifiability,
  refutabilidad
family, familia
  family alliance,
  alianza de familias
  family assistance
  program, programa de
  asistencia familiar
  family farm,
  explotación agrícola de

  carácter familiar
  family history,
  historia familiar
  family life,
  vida familiar
  family role,
  rol familiar
  family tree,
  árbol genealógico
famine, hambruna
fanning, ventilación
far, lejos
Far West, Lejano oeste
farm, granja
  farm labor,
  trabajo agrícola
  farm labor move-
  ment, movimiento de
  trabajadores agrícolas
farmer, granjero
farming methods, métodos
  de explotación agrícola
farming techniques,
  técnicas de explo-
  tación agrícola
farmland,
  tierras de labranza
fasces,
  fasces o haz de lictores
fascism, fascismo
fascist, fascista
  fascist aggression,
  agresión fascista
  fascist government,
  gobierno fascista
  fascist regime,
  régimen fascista
fast-food restaurant,
  restaurante de comida
  rápida
Father Miguel Hidalgo,
  Cura Miguel Hidalgo
father of modern Egypt,

padre del Egipto moderno

father of our country, padre de la Patria

fault, culpa, error, falta

fault line, falla

fauna, fauna

featherbedding, mantenimiento de empleos no productivos

federal, federal

Federal Aviation Administration (FAA), Administración de Aviación Federal

Federal Bureau of Investigation (FBI), Oficina Federal de Investigaciones (FBI)

Federal Communications Commission (FCC), Comisión Federal de Comunicaciones

federal court, tribunal federal

federal court system, sistema de tribunales federales

federal deficit, déficit federal o deuda pública

Federal Deposit Insurance Corporation (FDIC), Corporación Federal de Seguro de Depósitos

federal district court, tribunal federal de distrito

Federal Farm Board, Junta Agrícola Federal

federal government, gobierno federal

Federal Housing Authorities, Autoridades federales de vivienda

federal income tax, contribuciones sobre ingresos federales

federal Indian policy, política gubernamental hacia los pueblos indios

federal judiciary, judicatura federal

federal republic, república federal

Federal Reserve, Reserva federal

Federal Reserve Board, Junta de la Reserva Federal

Federal Reserve System, Sistema de la Reserva Federal

federal spending, gasto federal

federal supremacy, supremacía federal

federal supremacy clause, cláusula de supremacía federal

federal system, sistema federal

federal tax, impuesto federal

federal tax revenue, ingresos por impuestos federales

Federal Trade Commission (FTC), Comisión Federal de Comercio

federal troops, tropas federales

federal union, unión federal

federalism, federalismo

Federalist, federalista

    Federalist Papers, artículos de El Federalista

    Federalist Party, Partido Federalista

federation, federación

fee, cuota

feedback loop, bucle de realimen-tación

feeding level, nivel de alimentación

fellahin, felah

felony, delito grave

female infanticide, infanticidio femenino, aborto selectivo de niñas

The Feminine Mystique, La mística de la feminidad

feminism, feminismo

feminist movement, movimiento feminista

feminist theory, teoría feminista

Ferdinand Magellan, Fernando de Magallanes

ferry, transbordador

fertile, fértil

    Fertile Crescent, Creciente Fértil

    fertile land, tierra fértil

    fertile soil, tierra fértil

    fertile valley, valle fértil

fertility rate, tasa o índice de fertilidad

fertilization, fertilización

fertilizer, fertilizante

festival, festival

feudal Japanese loyalty, sistema feudal japonés basado en la lealtad

feudal lord, señor feudal

feudal society, sociedad feudal

feudal system, sistema feudal

feudalism, feudalismo

fief, feudo

fiefdom, feudo

field inquiry, investigación de campo

field interviews, entrevistas de campo

filial piety, piedad filial

filibustering, filibusterismo u obstruccionismo

filibusters, filibusterismo u obstruccionismo

Filipino insurrection, insurrección en Filipinas

Final Solution, Solución final

finance, finanzas

financial, financiero

    financial gain, ganancia económica

    financial institution, institución financiera

    financial panic, pánico financiero

financing, financiamiento

finished product, producto terminado

Finland, Finlandia

Fire Eater, tragafuegos

fire station,

estación de bomberos
fire-cracked rock, piedra
termofracturada
firefighting, apagar incendios, extinción de
incendios
fireside chats,
charlas informales o
junto al fuego
firm, compañía, empresa
first aid, primeros auxilios
First Americans,
primeros habitantes
de América
First Congress,
Primer Congreso
**First Continental Con-
gress,** Primer Con-
greso Continental
first inhabitant,
primer habitante
First Lady, primera dama
first line of authorities,
autoridades de
primera línea
First New Deal,
Primer Nuevo Trato
first person,
primera persona
**first person point of
view,** punto de vista
de la primera persona
first-time offender,
infractor sin antece-
dentes penales
first-time offense,
primera infracción
fiscal, fiscal
fiscal crisis,
crisis fiscal
fiscal management,
administración fiscal
fiscal policy,

política fiscal
fiscal year, año fiscal
fishing, pesca
fishing community,
comunidad pesquera
Five Civilized Tribes,
Cinco Tribus Civiliza-
das
Five Nations,
Cinco Naciones o Con-
federación Iroquesa
Five Pillars of Islam,
Cinco pilares del islam
Five Relationships, Cinco
relaciones sociales
Five Year Plan,
Plan quinquenal
fixed expense, gasto fijo
fixed income, renta fija
fixed rate of interest,
tasa de interés fija
fjord, fiordo
flag, bandera
Flag Day,
Día de la Bandera
flash flood,
inundación repentina
flat board, tabla plana
flat tax, impuesto lineal
flatland, planicie, llanura
flat-map projection,
proyección cartográ-
fica
flawed peace,
paz defectuosa
flax, lino
flint, sílex, pedernal
flood, aluvión, inundación
flood-control project,
proyecto de control de
inundaciones
flooding pattern,
patrón de inundación

floodplain,
 terreno inundable
flora, flora
flow map, mapa de flujo
flow of energy,
 flujo de energía
flow pattern,
 patrón de flujo
flow resource,
 recurso de flujo
flowchart,
 diagrama de flujo
flower children,
 hijos de las flores,
 hippies
fluent, fluido, elocuente
focus group,
 grupo focal o de dis-
 cusión
folk society, sociedad rural
folklore, folklore
folktale, leyenda popular
food, alimento, comida
 **Food and Drug Ad-
 ministration,**
 Administración de
 Alimentos y Fármacos
 food chain, cadena
 alimenticia, cadena
 trófica
 **food plant domesti-
 cation,** domesticación
 de plantas alimenti-
 cias
 food processing,
 procesado de ali-
 mentos
 food production,
 producción de alimen-
 tos
 food storage,
 almacenamiento de
 alimentos

 food supply,
 abastecimiento de
 alimentos
 food web, red trófica,
 red alimentaria
foot binding,
 vendaje de pies
foothills, estribaciones
footnote,
 nota al pie de página
force, fuerza
forced collectivization,
 colectivización forzada
forced relocation,
 reubicación forzada
foreclosure,
 ejecución de hipoteca,
 embargo de bienes
 muebles
foreign, extranjero(a),
 foreign affairs,
 asuntos exteriores
 foreign aid,
 ayuda extranjera
 foreign capital,
 capital extranjero
 **foreign capital in-
 vestment,** inversión
 de capital extranjero
 foreign competition,
 competencia extran-
 jera
 foreign currency,
 divisa, moneda extran-
 jera
 foreign debt,
 deuda externa
 **foreign direct in-
 vestment,** inversión
 extranjera directa
 **foreign exchange
 market,** mercado de
 divisas

foreign market, mercado exterior

foreign policy, política exterior

foreign relations, relaciones exteriores

Foreign Service, Servicio Exterior de los Estados Unidos

foreign trade, comercio exterior

forensic anthropologist, antropólogo forense

forensic anthropology, antropología forense

forest, selva, bosque

forest cover, cubierta o cobertura forestal

forest fire, incendio forestal

forestry, silvicultura

form a more perfect union, formar una unión más perfecta

formal region, región formal

formations, formaciones

former, antiguo

former master, antiguo amo

former slave, antiguo esclavo

fort, fuerte

Fort Sumter, Fuerte Sumter

fortification, fortificación

fossil fuel, combustible fósil

Foundation of the Oppressed, Fundación de los Oprimidos

founders, fundadores

Founding Fathers, Padres fundadores

founding of Rome, fundación de Roma

Four Cardinal Principles, Cuatro principios cardinales

Four Freedoms speech, Discurso de las cuatro libertades

Four Modernizations, Cuatro modernizaciones

Four Noble Truths, Cuatro nobles verdades

Fourth of July, Día de la Independencia de los Estados Unidos

framers, Padres fundadores

France, Francia

franchise, derecho al voto, sufragio

Franco-Prussian War, Guerra Franco-Prusiana

franking privilege, privilegio postal

Frankish Empire, Imperio franco

fraternal organization, fraternidad, organización fraternal

fraternity, fraternidad

fratricide, fratricidio

fraud, fraude

Fredericksburg, Fredericksburgo

free enterprise,
libre empresa
free enterprise system, sistema de libre empresa
free exercise clause,
cláusula de libre ejercicio
free labor system,
sistema de trabajo libre
free market, mercado libre
free market economy, economía de mercado libre
free-market system,
sistema de libre mercado
free port,
puerto franco, zona franca
Free Soil Party,
Partido Tierra Libre
free state, estado libre
free trade, libre comercio
free trade zone,
zona de libre comercio
freedmen, libertos
Freedmen's Bureau,
Oficina de libertos
freedom, libertad
freedom from fear,
libertad del temor
freedom from want,
libertad de la necesidad
freedom of assembly,
derecho de reunión
freedom of association, libertad de asociación
freedom of choice,
libertad de elección

freedom of conscience, libertad de conciencia
freedom of expression, libertad de expresión
freedom of petition,
derecho de petición
freedom of press,
libertad de prensa
freedom of religion,
libertad religiosa
freedom of residence,
libertad de residencia
freedom of speech,
libertad de expresión
freedom ride,
marchas por la libertad
freedom riders,
pasajeros (jinetes) de la libertad
freedom to choose employment,
libertad de elegir trabajo
freedom to emigrate,
libertad de emigrar
freedom to enter into contracts,
libertad de contratación
freedom to marry whom one chooses,
libertad de contraer matrimonio con quien uno elija
freedom to travel freely,
libertad de viajar libremente
French, francés
French-Canadian,

francocanadiense
**French and In-
dian War,**
Guerra Franco-India
French colonization,
colonización francesa
**French colonization
of Indochina,**
colonización francesa
de Indochina
French colony,
colonia francesa
**French Declaration
of the Rights of Man,**
Declaración francesa
de los Derechos del
Hombre y del Ciuda-
dano
**French East India
company,** Compañía
Francesa de las Indias
Orientales
**French Estates-Gen-
eral,** Estados Gene-
rales franceses
**French invasion of
Egypt,** invasión fran-
cesa de Egipto
French Quebec,
Quebec francés
French Revolution,
Revolución francesa
French salon,
Salón francés
French settlement,
colonización francesa
French West Indies,
Antillas Francesas
Freudian psychology,
psicología freudiana
friar, fraile
friction, fricción
friction of distance,

fricción de la distancia
frictional employment,
empleo friccional
frictional unemployment,
desempleo friccional
friend, amigo
frigate, fragata
fringe benefit,
retribución en especie,
prestaciones extras
frontier, frontera
frontiersman, colonizador,
explorador
front-loading, distribución
anticipada
fuel, combustible
fugitive, fugitivo
Fugitive Slave Law,
Ley de Esclavos Fugiti-
vos
full dinner pail,
eslogan de prosperi-
dad del Partido Repub-
licano
full employment,
pleno empleo
**full faith and credit
clause,** cláusula de
entera fe y crédito
full-time employment,
trabajo de tiempo
completo
**functional distribution
of income,**
distribución funcional
del ingreso
functional region,
región funcional
functionalist explanation,
explicación funciona-
lista
fundamental,
fundamental

fundamental belief,
creencia fundamental
fundamental economic questions,
preguntas económicas fundamentales
Fundamental Orders of Connecticut,
Órdenes Fundamentales de Connecticut
fundamental principles of American democracy,
principios fundamentales de la democracia estadounidense
fundamental rights,
derechos fundamentales
fundamental value,
valor fundamental
fundamentalism,
fundamentalismo
fundamentalist,
fundamentalista
funding, financiación, financiamiento, fondos
funds, fondos
fungi, hongos
fur trade,
comercio de pieles
furrows, surcos
fusion of powers,
fusión de poderes
future, futuro
futurist, futurista

gag rule, ley mordaza

Galileo, Galileo
galleon, galeón
gambling,
juego con apuestas
Ganges River Valley,
valle del río Ganges
Gangetic states,
estados del Ganges
Garibaldi's nationalist redshirts, Camisas Rojas de Garibaldi
Garvey movement,
movimiento de Garvey
gasoline taxes, impuestos sobre gasolina
Gateway to the West,
Puerta a Occidente
gatherer, recolector
gauchos, gauchos
Gay Liberation Movement, Movimiento de Liberación Homosexual
gay rights, derechos de los homosexuales
gazetteer, índice geográfico
gender, género
gender bias,
prejuicio de género sexual
gender diversity,
diversidad de género
gender gap,
brecha de género
gender role,
rol de género
General Agreement on Tariffs and Trade (GATT), Acuerdo General de Aranceles y Comercio (GATT)
General Assembly,
Asamblea General

general election,
eleccción general
general warrant,
orden judicial
general welfare,
bienestar general
general welfare clause,
cláusula del bienestar
general
general will,
voluntad general
generation, generación
Generation X,
Generación X
generational conflict,
conflicto generacional
genetic engineering,
ingeniería genética
**genetically determined
behavior,**
comportamiento gené-
ticamente determinado
Geneva Accords,
Acuerdos de Ginebra
Genghis Khan, Gengis Kan
Genoa, Génova
genocide, genocidio
Gentleman's Agreement,
pacto verbal, pacto de
caballeros
gentrification,
aburguesamiento
gentry, alta burguesía,
pequeña nobleza
gentry elite,
élite burguesa
geocentric model,
modelo geocéntrico
geocode, código de zona
geográfica
geographer, geógrafo
geographic, geográfico
geographic areas,

áreas geográficas
**geographic aspects of
world events,**
aspectos geográficos
de los acontecimientos
mundiales
geographic border,
frontera geográfica
**geographic char-
acteristics,**
características
geográficas
geographic factor,
factor geográfico
geographic features,
características geográ-
ficas
geographic grid,
malla geográfica
geographic index,
índice geográfico
**geographic informa-
tion,** información
geográfica
**Geographic Informa-
tion Systems (GIS),**
Sistema de Infor-
mación Geográfica
(SIG)
geographic isolation,
alopatría, aislamiento
geográfico
geographic regions,
regiones geográficas
**geographic represen-
tation,** representación
geográfica
geographic skills,
habilidades geográfi-
cas
**geographic technolo-
gy,** tecnología geográ-
fica

geographic tools, herramientas geográficas

geography, geografía

geological processes, procesos geológicos

geologist, geólogo

geology, geología

geomorphology, geomorfología

geopolitical relationships, relaciones geopolíticas

geopolitics, geopolítica

geothermal energy, energía geotérmica

German, alemán

German concept of Kultur, concepto alemán de Kultur

German Empire, Imperio alemán

German Federal Republic, República Federal Alemana

Germanic peoples, pueblos germanos o germánicos

Germany, Alemania

Geronimo, Gerónimo

gerrymandering, maniobras para dividir un distrito a favor de un partido político

Gettysburg Address, Discurso de Gettysburg

geyser, géiser

Ghaznavid Empire, Imperio gaznávida

ghetto, ghetto

ghost town, pueblo fantasma

GI Bill, Carta de Derechos de los Veteranos

GI Bill on higher education, Carta de Derechos de los Veteranos respecto a la educación superior

Gibbons v. Ogden, caso Gibbons contra Ogden

gift tax, impuesto sobre do-naciones

gift taxation, tributación sobre do-naciones

Gilded Age, Época Dorada

GIS (Geographic Information Systems), SIG (Sistema de Información Geográfica)

glacier, glaciar

glasnost, glasnost

glass ceiling, techo de cristal

global, global

global civilization, civilización global

global communication, comunicación global

global community, comunidad global

global consequences, consecuencias globales

global economy, economía global

global grid, red global

global history, historia global

global impact, impacto global

global interdependence, interdependencia global

global market,

mercado global
global migration,
migración global
**global migration
pattern,** patrón de
migración global
Global North,
Norte global
Global South,
Sur global
global trade,
comercio global
global trade patterns,
patrones del comercio
global
global village,
villa global
global warming,
calentamiento global
globalism, globalismo
globalization, globalización
globalize, globalizar
globalizing trend, tendencia de la globalización
globe, globo
Glorious Revolution,
Revolución Gloriosa
goddesses, diosas
gods, dioses
Gold Coast, Costa de Oro
gold production,
producción de oro
gold rush, fiebre del oro
gold standard, patrón oro
Gold Standard Act,
Ley del patrón oro
Golden Age, Edad de Oro
Golden Door,
Puerta Dorada
Golden Gate Bridge,
Puente Golden Gate
Golden Horde,
Horda de Oro

good[1], bien
good character,
buen carácter
good law, buena ley
**Good Neighbor Poli-
cy,** Política del buen
vecino
good rule,
buena norma
good[2], artículo
**goods producing
economy,** economía
de producción de
bienes
GOP, Gran Viejo Partido
gospel, evangelio
gospel of wealth,
Evangelio de la riqueza
gothic, gótico
gothic art, arte gótico
Gothic cathedral,
catedral gótica
govern, gobernar
governance, gobernanza
governance systems,
sistemas de gober-
nanza
government, gobierno
government aid,
ayuda gubernamental
**government
directive,** directiva
de gobierno
**government em-
ployee,** funcionario
público
**government fostered
competition,** compe-
tencia promovida por
el gobierno
**government institu-
tions,** instituciones
gubernamentales

government policy, política gubernamental

government powers, poderes gubernamentales

government regulation, regulación gubernamental

government restriction, restricción gubernamental

government security, valores o títulos del Estado

government spending, gastos del Estado, gasto público

government subsidy, subsidio gubernamental

government system, sistema de gobierno

governmental functions, funciones gubernamentales

governmental interference, intervención gubernamental

governor, gobernador

Gracchi, Graco

gradation, gradación

graduated income tax, impuesto progresivo

graft, corrupción

grains, cereales, granos

grand, gran

Grand Alliance, Gran Alianza

grand jury, jurado de acusación, gran jurado

Grand Old Party

(GOP), Gran Viejo Partido (GOP)

grandfather clause, cláusula del abuelo

Grange Movement, Movimiento Grange

Granger laws, Leyes Granger

grant, otorgar, conceder

grant-in-aid programs, programas de subvención estatal

graph, gráfico

graphic data, información gráfica

grass roots campaign, campaña de la bases

grassland, pradera

great, gran

Great American Desert, Gran Desierto Americano

Great Awakening, Gran Despertar

Great Barrier Reef, Gran Barrera de Coral

Great Basin, Gran Cuenca o Great Basin

Great Britain, Gran Bretaña

Great Canal of China, Gran Canal de China

Great Chicago Fire, Gran incendio de Chicago

Great Compromise, Gran Compromiso

Great Depression, Gran Depresión

Great Khan Mongke, Gran Kan Möngke

Great Khan Ogodei,

Gran Kan Ogodei
Great Lakes,
Grandes Lagos
**Great Lakes ecosys-
tem,** ecosistema de los
Grandes Lagos
Great Lakes region,
región de los Grandes
Lagos
Great Leap Forward,
Gran Salto Adelante
Great Migration,
Gran migración
Great Plague,
Gran plaga
Great Plains,
Grandes Llanuras
**Great Plains Dust
Bowl,** efecto Dust
Bowl de las Grandes
Llanuras
**Great Powers in Eu-
rope,** grandes poten-
cias europeas
**Great Proletarian
Cultural Revolution,**
Gran Revolución Cul-
tural Proletaria
Great Purge,
Gran Purga
Great Reform Bill,
Ley de reforma
great seal,
gran sello
Great Society,
Gran Sociedad
Great War,
Gran Guerra
**Great Western
Schism,** Gran Cisma
de Occidente
**Greater East Asia Co-Pros-
perity Sphere,** Gran

esfera de coprosperi-
dad de Asia Oriental
Greco-Roman antiquity,
antigüedad grecolatina
Greece, Grecia
Greek, griego(a)
   Greek art, arte griego
   **Greek Christian
   civilization,**
   civilización grecocris-
   tiana
   Greek city-state,
   ciudad-estado griega
   Greek civilization,
   civilización griega
   Greek column,
   columna griega
   Greek comedy,
   comedia griega
   Greek democracy,
   democracia griega
   Greek drama,
   teatro griego
   Greek fire,
   fuego griego
   **Greek gods and
   goddesses,**
   divinidades griegas
   **Greek Orthodox
   Christianity,** cristian-
   ismo ortodoxo griego
   Greek philosopher,
   filósofo griego
   Greek rationalism,
   racionalismo griego
   Greek tragedy,
   tragedia griega
Green Mountain Boys,
   Muchachos de la Mon-
   taña Verde
Green Party, Partido Verde
Green Revolution,
   Revolución verde

greenbacks, billetes (verdes), billetes de banco

Greenback Labor Party, Partido Laboral Greenback

greenhouse effect, efecto invernadero

greenhouse gases, gases de efecto invernadero

Greenland, Groenlandia

greenway, vía verde, espacio verde

grid, cuadrícula, rejilla

grid system, plan hipodámico

gridiron pattern, trazado reticular

grievance, agravio, queja

Grimke sisters, hermanas Grimké

grinding stone, muela abrasiva

Gross Domestic Product (GDP), PIB (Producto Interno Bruto)

Gross National Product (GNP), PNB (Producto Nacional Bruto)

ground stone, piedra pulida

grounds, motivaciones, fundamentos

groundwater, agua subterránea

groundwater quality, calidad de las aguas subterráneas

groundwater reduction, reducción de las aguas subterráneas

group, grupo

group behavior, comportamiento de grupos

group entitlements, derechos de grupo

group expectations, expectativas de grupo

group identity, identidad de grupo

group membership, membresía de grupo

group overlap, coincidencia de grupos

growth, crecimiento

growth management, regulación del crecimiento

Guangzhou (Canton), Cantón o Guangzhou

guarantee, garantía

guarantee clause, cláusula de garantía

Guardian Council, Consejo de Guardianes

gubernatorial, (del/para) gobernador

guerilla soldier, guerrillero

guerilla warfare, guerra de guerrillas

guided discretion, criterio guiado

guild, gremio

gulf, golfo

Gulf of Mexico, Golfo de México

Gulf of Tonkin Resolution, resolución del Golfo de Tonkín

gulf stream, corriente del Golfo

gun control, control de armas

Gun Free School Act,

Ley de Escuelas Libres
de Armas
gunpowder, pólvora
Gupta Empire,
Imperio Gupta

habeas corpus,
hábeas corpus
habitat, hábitat
habitat destruction,
destrucción de hábitat
habitation, habitación
hacienda, hacienda
Hadith, hadiz
Hague, Haya
haiku, haiku
hailstorm, granizada
Haiti, Haití
Haitian Revolution,
Revolución haitiana
Hajj, peregrinación
Halfway Covenant,
Pacto del Medio
Camino
hammering campaign,
campaña crítica
Han dynasty, dinastía Han
Han Empire, Imperio Han
Hanging Gardens of
Babylon, Jardines
colgantes de Babilonia
Hapsburg Empire, Imperio
de los Habsburgo
harbor, puerto
hard money, moneda
fuerte, dinero me-

tálico
Harlem Renaissance,
Renacimiento de Har-
lem
harm reduction,
reducción del daño
harmattan, harmatán
harpoon, arpón
harvest, cosecha
harvest festival,
fiesta de la cosecha
hatchery, criadero
hate crime, crímenes
motivados por el odio
hate speech,
discurso de odio
Haudenosaunee (Iroquois),
Hodinonhsioni (pueblo
iroqués)
Hawaii, Hawai
Hawaiian culture,
cultura hawaiana
hay, heno
Haymarket Rebellion,
Revuelta de
Haymarket
hazardous waste han-
dling, manejo de
desechos peligrosos
Head Start, ventaja inicial
head water, aguas arriba
headright,
reparto de tierras por
cabeza
headright system,
sistema de reparto de
tierras por cabeza
health, salud
health care,
seguro de salud
health care facility,
clínica de asistencia
médica

health psychology,
psicología de la salud
health services,
servicios sanitarios
hearsay, prueba indirecta,
habladurías
heavy industry,
industria pesada
Hebrew, hebreo
hegemonic, hegemónico
hegemonic power,
poder hegemónico
hegemonic state,
estado hegemónico
hegemony, hegemonía
Hegira (Hijrah), hégira
Heian period,
período de Heian
heliocentric model,
modelo heliocéntrico
Hellenism, helenismo
Hellenist culture,
cultura helenística
Hellenistic, helenístico
Hellenistic art,
arte helenístico
Hellenistic period,
período helenístico
Helsinki Accord, Con-
ferencia de Helsinki,
Acuerdos de Helsinki
hemisphere, hemisferio
hemp, cáñamo
henchmen,
secuaces, esbirros
herder, pastor
herding societies,
pueblos de pastores
hereditary social system,
sistema social heredi-
tario
heredity, herencia
heresy, herejía

heretic, herético, hereje
heritability, heredabilidad
heritage, herencia,
patrimonio
**The Haritage Founda-
tion,** La Fundación de
la Herencia
Hermit Kingdom,
reino ermitaño
Hernando Cortes,
Hernán Cortés
hero, héroe
heroine, heroína
Herodotus, Heródoto
heroism, heroísmo
Hessians, soldados de
Hesse o hessianos
hezbollahs, hezbolá
hidden economy,
economía oculta,
economía subterránea
hierarchical, jerárquico
hierarchy, jerarquía
hieroglyph, jeroglífico
hieroglyphic, jeroglífico
High Court,
Tribunal Supremo
high crimes, delitos graves
**high culture entertain-
ment,** entretenimiento
cultural
High Middle Ages,
Plena Edad Media
high plains, altiplanicie
High Renaissance,
Alto Renacimiento
high tariffs,
aranceles altos
high veld, alto veld
higher court review,
revisión de la Corte
Suprema
higher law, ley suprema

highest law of the land,
Cláusula de suprem-
acía
highland, tierras altas
high-latitude place,
zona de latitud alta
**high-technology indus-
try,** industria de alta
tecnología
highway, carretera
hijacking, secuestro,
piratería aérea
hill, colina, cerro
Hinduism, hinduismo
Hindus, hindúes
hinterland,
tierra interior
hippies, hijos de las flores,
hippies
Hispanic American,
hispanoamericano
historian, historiador
historic preservation,
preservación histórica
historic site, sitio histórico
historical, histórico
historical account,
relato histórico
historical analogies,
analogías históricas
historical analysis,
análisis histórico
**historical biogra-
phies,** biografías
históricas
historical context,
contexto histórico
historical continuity,
continuidad histórica
**historical develop-
ments,**
eventos históricos
historical document,

documento histórico
historical eras,
épocas históricas
historical facts,
hechos históricos
historical fiction,
ficción histórica
historical figure,
figura histórica
**historical inevita-
bility,** inevitabilidad
histórica
**historical interpreta-
tions,** interpretaciones
históricas
historical map,
mapa histórico
**historical material-
ism,** materialismo
histórico
historical narrative,
narrativa histórica
historical origins,
orígenes históricos
**historical perspec-
tive,** perspectiva
histórica
historical route,
ruta histórica
**historical violations
of human dignity,**
violaciones históricas
de la dignidad huma-
na
history, historia
**history of oil dis-
covery,** historia del
descubrimiento del
petróleo
Hittite people, hititas
HIV, VIH
hoarding, acaparamiento
hogs, cerdos, puercos

holding company, sociedad de participación financiera
holiday, fiesta, día festivo
Holland, Holanda
Holocaust, Holocausto
holy city, ciudad santa
Holy Land, Tierra Santa
holy of holies, Sagrado de los sagrados, tabernáculo
Holy Trinity, Santísima Trinidad
home, hogar, asilo
    home country, país de origen
    home front, frente civil, frente interno, retaguardia
    home office, oficina central
    home rule, autogobierno local
homeless, sin techo, sin hogar
homestead, granja familiar
    Homestead Act, Ley Agraria
homesteader, hacendado
hominid, homínido
    hominid community, comunidad de homínidos
homogeneity, homogeneidad
homogenous, homogéneo
homophobia, homofobia
honest, honesto
honesty, honestidad
honor, honor
Hoovervilles, villas Hoover
hope, esperanza
horizontal consolidation, integración horizontal
horizontal integration, integración horizontal
hostage, rehén
hostility, hostilidad
House of Burgesses, Cámara de los Burgueses
House of Commons, Cámara de los Comunes
House of Lords, Cámara de los Lores
House of Representatives, Cámara de Representantes
House of Un-American Activities Committee (HUAC), Comité de Actividades Antiestadounidenses
house of worship, lugar de culto, casa de oración
House Rules Committee, Comité de Reglas de la Casa de Representantes
household, hogar
household appliance, aparato electrodoméstico
household responsibility system, sistema de responsabilidad doméstica
houses on stilts, palafitos
housing, vivienda
housing development, urbanización, desarrollo de vivienda
Huang He (Yellow River) civilization, civilización de Huang

He (Río Amarillo)
hub-and-spoke,
sistema de aporte y
dispersión
human, humano
human adaptation,
adaptación humana
human behavior,
comportamiento humano
human capital,
capital humano
human characteristics, características
humanas
human characteristics of a place,
características humanas de un lugar
human community,
comunidad humana
human connection to place, relación humana con un lugar
human control over nature,
control humano sobre
la naturaleza
human cost,
costo humano
human development,
desarrollo humano
human dignity,
dignidad humana
human entity,
entidad humana
human environment,
ambiente humano
human environment interaction, interacción entre los humanos y el medio ambiente

human feature,
rasgo humano
human geography,
geografía humana
human impact,
impacto humano
human intention,
intención humana
human interaction,
interacción humana
human migration,
migración humana
human modification,
modificación humana
human nature,
naturaleza humana
human needs,
necesidades humanas
human process,
proceso humano
human resource,
recurso humano
human rights,
derechos humanos
human rights violations, violaciones de
derechos humanos
human system,
sistema humano
human wants,
deseos humanos
human-built heritage,
patrimonio cultural
human-environment Interaction, interacción entre los humanos y el medio ambiente
human-induced change, cambio
inducido por los humanos

humanism, humanismo
humanists, humanistas
humanitarian,
humanitario
humanitarian aid,
ayuda humanitaria
humid continental climate, clima continental húmedo
humid tropical climate,
clima tropical húmedo
humidity, humedad
Hun invasions, invasiones de los hunos
Hundred Flowers Movement, Campaña de las cien flores
Hundred Years' War,
Guerra de los Cien Años
Hungarian revolt,
Revolución húngara
Hungary, Hungría
hunger, hambre
hunter, cazador
hunter-gatherer,
cazador-recolector
hurricane, huracán
hurricane shelter,
refugios de huracanes
hurricane tracks,
paso del huracán
Hutus, hutu
hybridization of crops,
hibridación de cultivos
hydroelectric power,
poder hidroeléctrico
hydrologic cycle,
ciclo hidrológico
hydrology, hidrología
hydrosphere, hidrósfera
hymn, himno
hypothesis, hipótesis

I

"I Have a Dream" speech,
Discurso "Yo tengo un sueño"
Iberian Empire,
Imperio ibérico
Ibn Battuta, Ibn Batuta
Ice Age, Edad de Hielo
ice shelf, barrera de hielo
iceberg, iceberg
icon, icono
iconic, icónico
idea, idea
ideal, ideal
idealism, idealismo
idealist, idealista
idealized realism,
realismo idealizado
identification,
identificación
identify, identificar
identity, identidad
identity politics,
política de identidad
identity theft,
usurpación de identidad
ideographic, ideográfico
ideographs, ideogramas
ideological conflict,
conflicto ideológico
ideological hegemony,
hegemonía ideológica
ideology, ideología
Iliad, Ilíada
illegal alien,
extranjero ilegal
illegal immigration,
inmigración ilegal

illegal search and seizure,
registro y confiscación
ilegal
imam, imán
immediate cause,
causa inmediata
immigrant, inmigrante
immigrate, inmigrar
immigration, inmigración
immigration acts,
Leyes de inmigración
**Immigration and
Naturalization
Services,** Servicios
de Inmigración y de
Naturalización
immigration laws,
Leyes de inmigración
immigration policy,
política migratoria
**immigration screen-
ing,** revisión de inmi-
gración
**Immigration Quota
Acts,** Leyes de Cuotas
de Inmigración
immunity, inmunidad
impact, impacto
impartial, imparcial
impartial tribunal,
tribunal imparcial
impartiality,
imparcialidad
impeach, acusar
impeachment, acusación
imperial, imperial
imperial absolutism,
absolutismo imperial
imperial conquest,
conquista imperial
imperial Mughal,
Imperio mogol
imperial policy,

política imperial
imperial power,
poder imperial
imperial presidency,
presidencia imperial
imperialism, imperialismo
imperialist, imperialista
implied powers,
poderes implícitos
import[1], importar,
import[2], artículo importado, importación
import duty,
impuesto de
importación
**import substitut-
ing industrialization
(ISI),** industrialización
por sustitución de
importaciones
important, importante
imported resource,
recurso importado
importers,
importadores
impress, requisar
Impressionism,
Impresionismo
Impressionist,
impresionista
impressment,
requisición, leva
imprisonment,
encarcelamiento
in vitro fertilization,
fertilización in vitro
inalienable, inalienable
inalienable rights,
derechos inalienables
inaugural address,
discurso de investidu-
ra, discurso de toma
de posesión

inaugurated confederation, confederación inaugurada
inauguration, investidura, toma de posesión
incarceration, encarcelamiento
incas, Incas
Incan civilization, civilización inca
Incan Empire, Imperio inca
Incan highway, camino del inca
incendiary, incendiario
incentive, incentivo
incest, incesto
income, ingreso, renta
    income distribution, distribución del ingreso
    income gap, brecha de los ingresos
    income tax, impuesto sobre la renta
incorporate, incorporar
incorporation, incorporación
    incorporation doctrine, doctrina de la incorporación
incremental dating, datación de los restos
indemnify, indemnizar
indentured servant, sirviente contratado, sirviente por contrato
indentured servitude, servidumbre por contrato
independence, independencia

Independence Day, Día de la Independencia
independence movement, movimiento de independencia
independent, independiente
    independent central bank, banco central independiente
    independent executive agencies, agencias ejecutivas independientes
    independent judiciary, independencia de los tribunales
    independent lord, señor independiente
    independent parties, partidos independientes
    independent regulatory agency, organismo de control independiente
    independent states, estados independientes
    Independent Treasury System, sistema de tesorería independiente
    independent variable, variable independiente
index, índice
India, India
Indian, indio
    Indian concept of ideal kingship, concepto indio de la monarquía ideal
    Indian culture,

cultura de la India
Indian Empires,
Imperios de la India
Indian laborer,
trabajador indio
Indian Nationalist Movement, Movimiento Nacionalista Indio
Indian Ocean,
Océano Índico
Indian removal,
remoción de los indios (nativos americanos)
Indian Removal Act,
Ley de Remoción de los Indios (nativos americanos)
Indian Reorganization Act,
Ley de Reorganización de los Indios (nativos americanos)
indian reservations,
reservas indias
Indian spice,
especia de la India
Indian time,
época de la India antigua
Indian uprising,
Rebelión de la India
Indian Wars,
Guerras Indígenas
indict, acusar
indictable, tipificado como delito, procesable
indictment, acusación
indigenous, indígena
indigenous cultures,
culturas indígenas
indigenous development, desarrollo indígena

indigenous groups,
grupos indígenas
indigenous people,
pueblos indígenas
indirect, indirecto
indirect democracy,
democracia indirecta
indirect election,
elección indirecta
indirect rule,
administración indirecta
indirect tax,
impuesto indirecto
indirect taxation,
tributación indirecta
individual[1], individual
individual choice,
elección individual
individual liberty,
libertad individual
individual responsibility, responsabilidad individual
individual[2], individuo
individual ownership,
soberanía del individuo, propiedad del individuo
individual respect,
respeto del individuo
individual rights,
derechos individuales
individual status,
condición de individuo
individualism,
individualismo
individualist,
individualista
individualistic,
individualista
Indo-Aryan people,
pueblo indoario

indoctrinate, adoctrinar
indoctrination,
adoctrinamiento
Indo-European language,
lengua indoeuropea
Indo-Gangetic plain,
llanura indogangética
Indonesia, Indonesia
**Indonesian archipel-
ago,** archipiélago de
Indonesia
inductive reasoning,
razonamiento
inductivo
indulgences, indulgencias
Indus Valley, valle del Indo
industrial, industrial
industrial age,
era industrial
industrial center,
centro industrial
**industrial develop-
ment,** desarrollo
industrial
industrial district,
distrito industrial
industrial economy,
economía industrial
industrial expansion,
expansión industrial
industrial growth,
crecimiento indurstrial
industrial North,
Norte industrial
industrial parity,
paridad industrial
industrial power,
potencia industrial
industrial products,
productos industriales
industrial relations,
relaciones industriales
Industrial Revolu-
tion, Revolución
Industrial
industrial society,
sociedad industrial
**Industrial Workers
of the World,**
Trabajadores Industri-
ales del Mundo
industrialization,
industrialización
industrialize,
industrializar
industrialized,
industrializado
industry, industria
inequality, desigualdad
**inequality of condi-
tion,** desigualdad de
condiciones
**inequality of oppor-
tunity,** desigualdad
de oportunidades
inequities, injusticia
inevitable discovery,
descubrimiento
inevitable
infant mortality rate,
tasa de mortalidad
infantil
infectious disease,
enfermedad infecciosa
infer, inferir, deducir
inference, inferencia
inferential statistics,
estadística inferencial
inferred information,
información inferida
inflammatory,
inflamatorio
inflate, inflar
inflation, inflación
inflation rate,
tasa de inflación

influence, influencia
influx, afluencia
informal economy,
    economía informal
informal government,
    gobierno informal
informal sector,
    sector informal
information,
    información
    Information Age,
    Era de la información
    information econom-
    ics, economía de la
    información
    information econo-
    my, economía de la
    información
    information quality,
    calidad de la infor-
    mación
    information
    superhighway,
    supercarretera de la
    información
informational text,
    texto de información
informed citizenry,
    ciudadanía informada
infrastructure,
    infraestructura
infringe, infringir
infringement, infracción
inhabitants, habitantes
inherent powers,
    poderes inherentes
inherent right to
    self-government,
    derecho inherente al
    autogobierno
inherit, heredar
inheritance law,
    ley de sucesión

initiative, iniciativa
injunction,
    requerimiento judicial
inland port,
    puerto fluvial
inlet, ensenada
innate ability,
    habilidad innata
Inner Asia, Asia Central
innovate, innovar
innovation, innovación
innovator, innovador
input,
    aportación, insumo
    input per hour,
    aportación por hora
    input per machine,
    aportación por máqui-
    na
    input per unit of
    land, aportación por
    unidad de tierra
    input per worker,
    aportación por traba-
    jador
Inquisition,
    Inquisición
inquisitorial method,
    método inquisitivo,
    método acusatorio
inquisitorial system,
    principio inquisitivo
inset map,
    mapa complementario
insider privatization,
    privatización desde
    dentro
installment buying,
    comprar a plazos
instinctive behavior,
    comportamiento in-
    stintivo
institution, institución

institutional,
institucional
institutional economics, economía
institucional
institutional slavery,
esclavitud institucional
institutionalization,
institucionalización
insurance, seguro
insure, asegurar
insurrection,
insurrección
integrate, integrar
integration, integración
integrity, integridad
intellectual life,
vida intelectual
intelligentsia,
la clase intelectual,
intelectualidad
intended results,
resultados previstos
intensive cultivation,
cultivo intensivo
intensive farming,
agricultura intensiva
interaction, interacción
interchangeable parts,
partes intercambiables, piezas uniformes
interdependence,
interdependencia
interdependent,
interdependiente
interest, interés
interest group,
grupo de interés
interest payment,
pago de intereses
interest rate,

tasa de interés
interior, interior
Interior lowlands,
tierras bajas del interior
interlocking directorate,
consejos de administración vinculados
intermediary,
intermediario
intermediate, intermedio
intermediate directions, puntos cardinales intermedios
intermediate goods,
bienes intermedios
internal improvements,
mejoras internas
Internal Revenue Service (IRS), Servicio de Impuestos Internos (IRS)
internal structure,
estructura interna
internal taxes,
impuestos internos
internal trade,
comercio interior
internal validity,
validez interna
internalization,
internalización
international,
internacional
International Conference on Population and Development,
Conferencia Internacional sobre la Población y el Desarrollo en El Cairo en 1994
international conflict, conflicto internacional

International Court of Justice, Corte Internacional de Justicia

International Date Line, línea internacional de cambio de fecha

international debt crisis, crisis de la deuda externa

international economic system, sistema económico internacional

international economy, economía internacional

international events, acontecimientos internacionales

international financial institutions (IFIs), instituciones financieras internacionales (IFI)

International Free-Trade Agreements, acuerdos internacionales de libre comercio

International Governmental Organizations, organizaciones gubernamentales internacionales

International Ladies Garment Workers Union, Unión Internacional de Costureras

international law, derecho internacional

international market, mercado internacional

International Mon- etary Fund (IMF), Fondo Monetario Internacional (FMI)

international organizations, organizaciones internacionales

International Red Cross, Cruz Roja Internacional

international relations, relaciones internacionales

international trade, comercio internacional

international trade routes, rutas comerciales internacionales

Internet, Internet

internment, internamiento

internment camps, campos de internación

internment of Japanese Americans, campos de concentración para japoneses en EE.UU.

interpret, interpretar

interpret law, interpretar la ley

interpretation, interpretación

interpretative theory, teoría interpretativa

interracial marriage, matrimonio interracial

interrelated, interrelacionado

interrelationships, interrelaciones

interrogation, interrogatorio

interstate,
    entre estados
interstate commerce,
    comercio interestatal
**Interstate Commerce
Act,** Ley de Comercio
Interestatal
**Interstate Com-
merce Commission,**
Comisión de Comercio
Interestatal
**Interstate Highway
Act,** Ley de Autopistas
Interestatales
**interstate highway
system,**
red de autopistas in-
terestatales
interstate highways,
autopistas
interestatales
interstate relations,
relaciones
interestatales
intervening opportunity,
oportunidad de
intervención
intervention,
intervención
interventionist,
intervencionista
intolerance, intolerancia
Intolerable Acts,
Leyes Intolerables
intrastate, interestatal
introduction of species,
introducción de
especies exóticas
Inuit, esquimal
invade, invadir
invasion, invasión
    invasion of privacy,
invasión a la

privacidad
inventing, invención
invention, invento
invest, invertir
investigate, investigar
investigation,
investigación
investigative technique,
técnica de
investigación
investment, inversión
investor, inversionista
inviolable rights,
derechos inviolables
**invisible aspects of
culture,** aspectos in-
visibles de la cultura
Invisible Hand,
mano invisible
involuntary migration,
migración forzada
Iran, Irán
    Iran-Contra affair,
escándalo Irán-Contra
Iranian hostage crisis,
Crisis de los rehenes
en Irán
Iraq invasion of Kuwait,
invasión iraquí de
Kuwait
Ireland, Irlanda
Irish, irlandés
    Irish immigrant,
inmigrante irlandés
    **Irish potato fam-
ine,** gran hambruna
irlandesa
    **Irish Republican
Army (IRA),**
Ejército Republicano
Irlandés
iron, hierro
    Iron Cage,

jaula de hierro
Iron Curtain,
Cortina de Hierro
**Iron Law of Oligar-
chy,** ley de hierro de la
oligarquía
iron metallurgy,
siderurgia
iron ore,
mineral de hierro
iron rice bowl,
tazón de arroz de
hierro
iron tools,
herramientas de hierro
Iron triangle,
triángulo de hierro
**iron triangle relation-
ships,** relaciones del
triángulo de hierro
iron weapons,
armas de hierro
Iroquois, iroqueses
**Iroquois Confed-
eracy,** Confederación
iroquesa
irrigate, irrigar
irrigation, irrigación
Isfahan, Isfahán o Ispahán
Islam, islam
Islamic, islámico(a)
Islamic beliefs,
creencias islámicas
**Islamic fundamental-
ism,** fundamentalismo
islámico
**Islamic fundamental-
ists,** fundamentalistas
islámicos
Islamic law,
ley islámica
Islamic republic,
república islámica

Islamic state,
estado islámico
Islamization,
islamización
island, isla
Ismail, Ismael
isolate, aislar
isolationism,
aislacionismo
isolationist, aislacionista
Israel, Israel
**Israeli-Palestinian
conflict,** conflicto
palestino-israelí
issue, cuestión, problema
isthmus, istmo
Italian, italiano
Italian humanism,
humanismo italiano
Italian Renaissance,
Renacimiento italiano
Italy, Italia

J

Jacksonian Democracy,
democracia jacksoni-
ana
Jacksonian era,
Era Jacksoniana
Jamaican sugar,
azúcar de Jamaica
Janissary Corps, jenízaros
Japan, Japón
Japanese, japonés(esa)
Japanese American,
japonés americano
**Japanese feudal so-
ciety,** sociedad feudal
japonesa

Japanese internment, campos de concentración para japoneses

Japanese modernization, modernización de Japón

Japanese occupation of Manchuria, ocupación japonesa de Manchuria

Japanese relocation, reubicación de japoneses

Japanese tea ceremony, ceremonia del té japonesa

jarls, condes, duques

Jataka tales, cuentos jataka

Jay Gardoqui Treaty, Tratado de Jay-Gardoqui

Jay's Treaty, Tratado de Jay

jazz, jazz

Jazz Age, era del jazz

Jean Jaures, Jean Jaurès

Jeffersonian democracy, democracia jeffersoniana

Jenne, Djenné

Jenne-jeno, Djenné-Djeno

Jerusalem, Jerusalén

Jesus Christ, Jesucristo

Jesus of Nazareth, Jesús de Nazaret

Jew, judío

Jewish, judío

Jewish civilization, civilización judía

Jewish diaspora, diáspora judía

Jewish monotheism, monoteísmo judío

Jewish refugee, refugiado judío

Jewish resistance movement, movimiento de resistencia judía

Jewish scapegoating, judíos como chivos expiatorios

Jewish time, época de los judíos

Jiang Jieshi, Chiang Kai-shek o Jiang Jieshi

jihad, yihad, jihad

Jim Crow Laws, Leyes de Jim Crow

jingoism, jingoísmo

Joan of Arc, Juana de Arco

job, trabajo

John F. Kennedy presidency, presidencia de John F. Kennedy

John of Piano Carpini, Juan de Piano Carpini

joint committee, comité mixto

joint stock company, sociedad anónima, sociedad por acciones

Jordan, Jordania

Joseph Francois Dupleix's theory of "divide and rule", teoría de "divide y vencerás" de Joseph François Dupleix

Joseph II, José II

Joseph Stalin, José Stalin

journal, periódico, diario

journey, viaje

joust, justa
Judaism, judaísmo
Judeo-Christian,
 judeocristiano
 **Judeo-Christian
 ethic,** ética judeocristiana
judicial, judicial
 judicial activism,
 activismo judicial
 judicial branch,
 poder judicial
 judicial court,
 tribunal judicial
 judicial power,
 poder judicial
 judicial realist,
 realista jurídico
 judicial restraint,
 restricción judicial
 judicial review,
 control judicial
Judiciary Act, Ley Judicial
Julius Caesar, Julio César
junta, junta
juris prudentes,
 jurisprudentes
jurisdiction, jurisdicción
jurisprudential thinking,
 razonamiento juris-
 prudencial
jurist, jurista, magistrado
 jurist's guardianship,
 tutela de los juristas
 islámicos
juristic person,
 persona jurídica
jury, jurado
 jury duty,
 llamamiento para
 formar parte de un
 jurado
just, justo

just compensation,
 compensación justa
justice, justicia
justification, justificación
Justinian, Justiniano
jute, yute
juvenile, menor de edad
 juvenile delinquency,
 delincuencia juvenil

Kaiser, káiser
Kalash church,
 iglesia kalash
Kamakura period,
 período de Kamakura
Kangxi emperor,
 emperador Kangxi
Kansas-Nebraska Act, Ley
 de Kansas-Nebraska
Kashmir, Cachemira
Kellogg-Briand Pact,
 pacto Briand-Kellogg
**Kennedy assassination
 ation,** asesinato de
 Kennedy
Kenya, Kenia
Kerensky, Kérenski
Kerosene, queroseno
key, clave
 key landforms,
 accidentes geográficos
 **key or pivotal deci-
 sions,** decisiones clave
 o cruciales
Keynesian economics,
 economía keynesiana
Keynesianism,
 keynesianismo

keystone state,
  estado clave
khans, kan
Khoisan group,
  grupo khoisánido
Khyber Pass,
  paso de Khyber
kibbutz, kibutz
kickbacks, sobornos
Kievan Russia,
  Rusia de Kiev
killer amendment,
  enmienda del asesino
kilometer, kilómetro
kindergarten,
  jardín de infantes
King Afonso I of Kongo,
  rey Alfonso I del Congo
King Alfred of England,
  rey Alfredo de Ingla-
  terra
King Cotton, rey Algodón
King James I, rey Jacobo I
King Joao II,
  Juan II de Portugal
King Phillip's War,
  Guerra del Rey Felipe
kingdom, reino
King's Mountain,
  King's Mountain
king's peace, paz del Rey
kinship, parentesco
  kinship group,
  grupo de parentesco
  kinship structure,
  estructura de
  parentesco
knight, caballero
knightly class,
  clase caballeresca
Knights of Labor,
  Caballeros del Trabajo
Know Nothing Party,

  partido Know Nothing
knowledge, conocimiento
Kootenai tribe,
  tribu kutenai
Koran, Corán
Korea, Corea
Korean, coreano(a)
  Korean culture,
  cultura coreana
  Korean War,
  Guerra de Corea
Ku Klux Klan (KKK),
  Ku Klux Klan (KKK)
Kurds, kurdos
Kush culture,
  cultura de Kush

L

labeling theory,
  teoría del etiquet-
  amiento
labor, trabajo
  labor conflicts,
  conflictos laborales
  Labor Day, Día del
  Trabajo en EE.UU.
  labor force, mano de
  obra, población activa
  **labor force immobil-
  ity,** inmovilidad de la
  mano de obra
  labor market,
  mercado laboral
  labor movement,
  movimiento laboral
  Labor Party,
  Partido Laborista
  labor relations,
  relaciones laborales

Labor Standards Act, Ley de Relaciones Del Trabajo

labor theory of value, teoría del valor-trabajo o teoría laboral del valor

labor-intensive cash crops, cultivos comerciales de trabajo intensivo

labyrinth, laberinto

lagoon, laguna

laissez-faire, liberalismo

lake, lago

lake desiccation, desecación de lagos

lake ecosystem, ecosistema de lago

Lake Erie, Lago Erie

Lalibela church, iglesia de Laibela

lame duck, presidente de salida

land, tierra

land bridge, istmo

land claim, reclamo de tierra

land clearing, limpieza de tierras

land degradation, degradación del suelo

land form, relieve

land grants, concesiones de tierras

land grant colleges, universidades agronómicas

Land Lease Act, Ley de Arrendamiento de Tierras

land masses, masas continentales

land policy, política agraria

land run, carrera por la tierra

land use, uso de suelo

land use regulation, regulación del uso de suelo

land value, valor de las tierras

landfill, tiradero, vertedero

landform, accidente geográfico

landform relief, relieve o accidente geográfico

landlocked, sin salida al mar

landlocked country, país sin salida al mar

landmark, monumento histórico

landmark case, caso que sienta precedente

landmark decision, decisión histórica

landmass, masa continental

landowner, terrateniente, hacendado

landscape, paisaje

landslide, victoria arrolladora

land-survey system, sistema de registro de la propiedad rural

land-use data, información sobre el uso del suelo

land-use pattern, modelo de uso del suelo

language, lenguaje, lengua

language region,
región lingüística
large firm, empresa grande
large-scale investment,
inversión a gran escala
Last Frontier,
Última Frontera
lateen sails, vela latina
Latin, latín
Latin America,
América Latina
**Latin American
revolution,**
revolución
latinoamericana
**Latin Catholic
church,**
Iglesia latina católica
Latino, hispanoamericano
latitude, latitud
lava, lava
law, ley, derecho
law and order,
ley y orden
law code,
código legal
law enforcement,
aplicación de las leyes
law enforcers,
agente del orden
law makers,
legisladores
law of demand,
ley de la demanda
**law of diminishing
marginal utility,**
ley de utilidad mar-
ginal decreciente
**law of diminishing
returns,** ley de los
rendimientos decre-
cientes
law of nature,

ley de la naturaleza
**law of retail gravi-
tation,** ley de gravi-
tación del comercio al
por menor
law of supply,
ley de la oferta
**law of supply and
demand,**
ley de la oferta y la
demanda
law-based state,
estado de derecho
lawmaker, legislador
lead, ejemplo, pista,
principal
leader, líder
leadership, liderazgo
league, liga, asociación,
confederación
League of Nations,
Sociedad de Naciones
**League of Nations
mandate,**
mandato de la Socie-
dad de Naciones
**League of Women
Voters,** Liga de mu-
jeres votantes
learn, aprender
learned behavior pattern,
patrón de compor-
tamiento aprendido
lease, alquiler
Lebanon, Líbano
Lee Iaccoca,
Lido Anthony "Lee"
Iacocca
leeward, sotavento
left realism,
realismo de izquierda
left wing, izquierda
Leftists, izquierdistas

legal, legal
   legal basis,
   base legal
   legal code,
   código legal
   legal recourse,
   recurso legal
   legal remedy,
   remedio legal
   legal right,
   derecho legal
   legal tender,
   moneda de curso legal
legend, signos convencionales
legion, legión
legionaries, legionarios
legislative, legislativo
   legislative branch,
   poder legislativo
   legislative district,
   distrito legislativo
   **legislative district-
   ing,** distrito legislativo
   legislative oversight,
   supervisión legislativa
   legislative power,
   poder legislativo
   legislative process,
   proceso legislativo
   **legislative suprema-
   cy,** supremacía legislativa
legislator, legislador
legislature, legislatura
legitimacy, legitimidad
legitimation crisis,
   crisis de legitimidad
Leisler's Rebellion,
   rebelión de Leisler
leisure activity,
   actividades recreativas
lend lease,

préstamo y alquiler
lending, préstamo, crédito
Lenin's ideology,
   ideología leninista
**Lenin's New Economic
   Policy,** Nueva Política
   Económica de Lenin
Leo Africanus,
   León el Africano
lesson of history,
   lección de historia
letter, carta, letras
   letter grid,
   cuadrícula de letras
   letter to the editor,
   carta al editor
levee, dique
level of measurement,
   niveles de medida
leveraged buy-outs,
   compras apalancadas
levy, impuesto, gravamen
liability,
   responsabilidad
   liability rules,
   normas de respons-
   abilidad
libel, difamación, calumnia
liberal, liberal
   liberal democracy,
   democracia liberal
   liberal feminism,
   feminismo liberal
liberalism, liberalismo
liberation theology,
   teología de la liber-
   ación
Libertarian, libertario
   Libertarian Party,
   Partido Libertario
libertarianism,
   libertarismo
liberty, libertad

Liberty Bell, Campana de la Libertad
Liberty Party, Partido de la Libertad
Liberty, Equality, Fraternity, Libertad, Igualdad y Fraternidad
library, biblioteca
Library of Congress, Biblioteca del Congreso
library resources, recursos bibliotecarios
Libya, Libia
licensing, acuerdo de licencia
Lieutenant Governor, vicegobernador, asistente del gobernador
life, vida
life cycle, ciclo de vida
life expectancy, esperanza de vida
life experience, experiencia de vida
life form, forma de vida
life, liberty, and the pursuit of happiness, Vida, libertad y búsqueda de la felicidad
lifestyle, estilo de vida
lifestyle theory, teoría del estilo de vida
light industry, industria ligera
like, gustar
limestone, piedra caliza
limitation, limitacion
limitation of powers, limitación de poderes
limit, límite
limited budget, presupuesto limitado
limited government, gobierno limitado
limited partnership, sociedad comanditaria simple
limited resources, recursos limitados
Lincoln-Douglas debate, debate Lincoln-Douglas
Lincoln's "House Divided" speech, discurso de Lincoln sobre "la casa dividida"
line, línea
line graph, gráfico lineal
lines of longitude, líneas de longitud
line item veto, veto selectivo
line-item veto, veto de partidas específicas
lineage, linaje
lingua franca, lengua franca o vehicular
linguistic diversity, diversidad lingüística
linkage, unión, enlace
liquidity, liquidez
literacy, alfabetismo, alfabetización
literacy rate, índice de alfabetización
literacy test, examen de alfabetismo, prueba de lectura
literary movement,

movimiento literario
literary narrative, narración literaria
literature, literatura
lithosphere, litósfera
litigant, litigante
litigate, litigar
litigation, litigación
Little Italy, Pequeña Italia
Little Rock Nine, Los Nueve de Little Rock
livestock, ganadería
loaded words, palabras con carga emocional
loan, préstamo, crédito
lobby¹, cabildear
lobby², grupo de presión
lobbying, cabildeo
lobbyist, cabildero
local, local
local community, comunidad local
local election, elección local
local government, gobierno local
local government officials, funcionarios del gobierno local
local government services, servicios del gobierno local
local history, historia local
local ordinance, ordenanza local
local region, región local
local resource, recurso local
local scale,

escala local
local water, agua local
local wind, viento local
location, ubicación
location principle, principio de ubicación
locator, localizador
lock, esclusa
lockout, cierre patronal
locomotive, locomotora
lodge, refugio, logia
logging, tala, industria maderera
logic, lógica
logical, lógico
logrolling, clientelismo, intercambio de favores
London, Londres
Lone Star Republic, República de la Estrella Solitaria
long ago, hace mucho tiempo
long-distance migration, migración de larga distancia
long-distance trade, comercio de larga distancia
longhouse, casa comunal
longitude, longitud
longitudinal studies, estudios longitudinales
loose construction of the Constitution, interpretación laxa de la Constitución
loose constructionist, interpretación liberal

Lord Dalhousie,
  Conde de Dalhousie
loss, pérdida
Lost Generation,
  Generación perdida
Louis XIV, Luis XIV
Louisiana, Luisiana
  Louisiana Purchase,
  compra de la Luisiana
lower court, tribunal de
  primera instancia
lower South colony,
  colonia del Sur
low-income area,
  zona de bajos ingresos
lowland, tierra baja, bajío
loyal opposition,
  oposición leal
Loyalist, partidarios del
  régimen
loyalty, lealtad
lumber, madera
lunar year, año lunar
luxuries, lujos
luxury goods,
  bienes de lujo
lynch, linchar
lynching, linchamiento
**Lyndon B. Johnson ad-
  ministration,**
  gobierno de Lyndon B.
  Johnson

macadam road, macadán
MacArthur Constitution,
  Constitución
  MacArthur
Machiavelli,

  Maquiavelo
machine, máquina
  machine politics,
  política de maqui-
  narias
macroeconomic policy,
  política
  macroeconómica
macroeconomics,
  macroeconomía
mafia, mafia
magistrate,
  magistrado, juez de
  primera instancia
magma, magma
Magna Carta,
  Carta Magna
magnetic compass,
  brújula
Magyar cavalry,
  caballería de Magyar
Mahdist state,
  Estado mahdista
main idea, idea principal
mainland, continente
mainstream America,
  cultura dominante de
  EE.UU.
maize, maíz
  maize cultivation,
  cultivo de maíz
majles, majlis
**major metropolitan cen-
  ter,** centro metropolitano importante
major parallel,
  paralelo principal
major world event,
  acontecimiento mun-
  dial importante
majority, mayoría
  majority leader,
  líder de la mayoría

majority rule, gobierno de la mayoría
majority whip, coordinador de la bancada mayoritaria
malaria, malaria
Malayo-Polynesia, malayo-polinesio
Malaysia, Malasia
Malaysian rain forest, selva de Malasia
maldistribution, mala distribución
male-dominated job, trabajo con predominancia masculina
Mali Empire, Imperio de Mali
malnutrition, desnutrición
Manchu Empire, Imperio manchú
mandate, mandato
Mandate of Heaven, Mandato del cielo
mandate system, protectorado
mandatory sentencing system, sistema de sentencia obligatoria
mangrove, manglar
Manhattan Project, Proyecto Manhattan
manifest destiny, destino manifiesto
manioc, mandioca
manor, feudo, heredad, señorío
manor system, sistema señorial
manorialism, régimen señorial
mantle, manto, sima
man-to-man combat, combate de hombre a hombre
manufacture, manufactura
manufactured goods, bienes manufacturados, artículos manufacturados
manufacturing, manufactura
manufacturing plant, planta de manufactura
manufacturing region, región manufacturera
Mao Zedong, Mao Tse-Tung
map, mapa
map elements, elementos de mapa
map grid, cuadriculado, cuadrícula de mapa
map key, signos convencionales del mapa
map projection, proyección cartográfica
map scale, escala de un mapa
map title, título del mapa
Mapp v. Ohio, caso Mapp contra Ohio
Marbury v. Madison, caso Marbury contra Madison
Marcus Aurelius, Marco Aurelio
marginal, marginal
marginal analysis, análisis marginal

marginal benefit, utilidad marginal
marginal cost, costo marginal
marine climate, clima oceánico
marine transportation, transporte marítimo
marine vegetation, vegetación marina
marital status, estado civil
maritime rights, derechos marítimos
maritime technology, tecnología marítima
maritime trade route, ruta comercial marítima
market, mercado
market clearing price, precio de equilibrio del mercado
market economic system, sistema económico de mercado
market economy, economía de mercado
market exchange, mercado de cambio
market price, precio de mercado
market reform, reforma del mercado
market revolution, revolución mercantil
market structure, estructura de mercado
market town, pueblo basado en el comercio
market-oriented agriculture, agricultura orientada al mercado
marketplace, mercado

Maroon society, sociedad cimarrona
marsh, marisma
Marshall Plan, Plan Marshall
martial law, ley marcial
Martin Luther King Jr. Day, Día de Martin Luther King Jr.
martyr, mártir
Marxism, marxismo
Marxism-Leninism, marxismo-leninismo
masculinization, masculinización
Mason-Dixon Line, Línea Mason-Dixon
mass, masa, misa
mass advertising, publicidad masiva
mass consumer economy, economía de consumo de masas
mass consumption, consumo de masas
mass culture, cultura de masas
mass media, medios de comunicación
mass production, producción en serie o en masa
mass society, sociedad de masas
mass starvation, hambre masivo, hambruna masiva
Massachusetts Body of Liberties, Cuerpo de libertades de Massachusetts
Massachusetts state constitution,

constitución del estado
de Massachusetts
massacre, masacre
materialism, materialismo
matriarch, matriarca
matriarchal, matriarcal
matriarchy, matriarcado
matrilineage, matrilinaje
matrilineal family,
familia matrilineal
matrilinear, matrilineal
Maurya empire,
Imperio maurya
Mauryan-Buddhist power,
poder budista-maurya
maximum employment,
pleno empleo
May Fourth movement,
Movimiento del Cuatro
de Mayo
Mayan, maya
**Mayan "Long Count"
calendar,** calendario
maya de cuenta larga
Mayan calendar,
calendario maya
Mayan city-state,
ciudad-estado maya
Mayan civilization,
civilización maya
Mayan pyramids,
pirámides mayas
Mayan religion,
religión maya
Mayas, Mayas
Mayflower Compact,
Pacto del Mayflower,
Convenio de Mayflower
mayor, alcalde, intendente
municipal
McCarthyism, macartismo
McCulloch v. Maryland,
caso McCulloch contra

Maryland
means, medio
**means of distribu-
tion,** medios de dis-
tribución
means of production,
medios de producción
means test, compro-
bación de ingresos
measure of crime,
medida de la delin-
cuencia
measurement, medida
Meat Inspection Act,
Ley de Inspección de
la Carne
meat packing, empaquetado de carne,
envase de carne
Mecca, Meca
mechanical reaper,
segadora mecánica
mechanical solidarity,
solidaridad mecánica
Medicaid, Medicaid
medical advance,
avance de la medicina
medical coverage,
cobertura médica
medical expenditure,
gastos médicos
medical provisions,
suministros medicos
Medicare, Medicare
medieval art, arte medieval
**medieval Christian soci-
ety,** sociedad cristiana
medieval
Medieval Europe,
Europa medieval
medieval theology,
teología medieval
meditate, meditar

Mediterranean Empire,
imperio mediterráneo
Mediterranean region,
región mediterránea
medium of exchange,
sistema monetario
megacity, megaciudad
megalithic monuments,
monumentos mega-
líticos
megalithic stone building,
construcción mega-
lítica
megalopolis,
megalópolis
Meiji Japan,
Japón de Meiji
Meiji Restoration,
Restauración Meiji
Mein Kampf, Mi lucha
melting pot,
crisol de culturas
memento, recuerdo
Memorial Day,
Día de los Caídos
Mennonites, menonitas
men's perceptions,
percepciones de los
hombres
mental map,
mapa mental
mental mapping,
mapa mental
mercantilism,
mercantilismo
mercator projection,
proyección de merca-
tor
mercenary, mercenario
merchandising,
comercialización
merchant, mercader, comerciante

Merchants of Death,
mercaderes de la
muerte
meridian, meridiano
**meridians of longi-
tude,** meridianos de
longitud
merit selection,
selección por méritos
meritocracy, meritocracia
Meroitic period,
período meroítico
mesa, mesa, meseta
Mesoamerica,
Mesoamérica
**Mesoamerican civiliza-
tions,** civilización
mesoamericana
Mesolithic, mesolítico
Mesopotamia civilization,
civilización mesopo-
támica
messiah, mesías
mestizo, mestizo
method, método
metropolis, metrópoli
metropolitan,
metropolitano(a)
metropolitan area,
área o zona metro-
politana
**metropolitan corri-
dor,** corredor metro-
politano
**metropolitan statisti-
cal area,** área estadís-
tica metropolitana
Mexican Cession,
Cesión Mexicana
Mexican Revolution,
Revolución mexicana
Mexican War,
Guerra México–Esta-

dos Unidos
Mexican-American War,
Guerra México–Estados Unidos
Mexico, México
microclimate, microclima
microeconomics,
microeconomía
Mid-Atlantic colony,
colonias del Atlántico central
middle, medio, centro
Middle Ages,
Edad Media
Middle Atlantic Region, región del Atlántico central
middle class,
clase media
Middle Colonies,
colonias centrales
Middle East,
Medio Oriente
Middle Kingdom,
Reino Medio
Middle Passage,
travesía intermedia
middle-class culture,
cultura de clase media
middlemen,
intermediarios
midlaltitude,
latitud media
midlaltitude forest,
bosque de latitud media
midnight judge,
juez de medianoche
midnight sun,
sol de medianoche
Midwest, Medio Oeste
migrant, trabajador extranjero

migrant community,
comunidad extranjera
migrant population,
población extranjera
migrant worker,
trabajador migratorio
migrate, migrar
migration, migración
migration counterstream, contracorriente migratoria
migration stream,
corriente migratoria
mile, milla
mileage table,
tabla de millaje
militant religious movement,
movimiento religioso militante
militarism, militarismo
militarist, militarista
militarist policy,
política militarista
military, militar
military aggression,
agresión militar
military campaign,
campaña militar
military court,
tribunal militar
military defense,
defensa militar
military draft,
servicio militar
military force,
fuerza militar
military industrial complex,
complejo industrial militar
military installation,
instalación militar

**military interven-
tion,**
intervención militar
military law,
derecho militar
**military mobiliza-
tion,** movilización
militar
military officer,
oficial militar
military power,
poder militar
**military prepared-
ness,** preparación
militar
military tactic,
táctica militar
military unit,
unidad militar
**military-industrial
complex,**
complejo industrial
militar
militia, milicia
mill, molino
millennialism,
milenarismo
**millennium (pl. millen-
nia),** milenio
mine, mina
mineral, mineral
mineral resource,
recurso mineral
miners, mineros
Ming Dynasty,
dinastía Ming
minimum wage,
salario mínimo
mining, minería
mining area,
zona minera
mining economy,
economía minera

mining town,
pueblo minero
minister, ministro
Minoan Crete,
Creta minoica
minority, minoría
minority group,
grupo minoritario
minority leader,
líder de la minoría
minority rights,
derechos de las mi-
norías
minority whip,
coordinador de la ban-
cada minoritaria
minstrel show, trovadores
minutemen,
civiles armados
Miranda v. Arizona,
caso Miranda contra
Arizona
Miranda rights,
derechos Miranda
Miranda rule,
advertencia Miranda
misdemeanor,
delito menor
misogyny, misoginia
mission, misión
missionary, misionero
Mississippi River,
río Misisipi
Mississippian culture,
cultura misisipiense
Missouri Compromise,
Compromiso de Misuri
Missouri River,
río Misuri
mixed constitution,
gobierno mixto
mixed economic system,
sistema económico

mixto
mixed economy,
economía mixta
mobile home, caravana
mobile society,
sociedad móvil
mobility, movilidad
mobilization, movilización
mobilize, movilizar
moccasin, mocasín
Moche civilization,
civilización moche o
mochica
mode of communication,
modo de comunicación
mode of discourse,
modo de discurso
mode of production,
modo de producción
model, modelo
Model Parliament,
parlamento modelo
model T, modelo T
modem, módem
moderate, moderado
moderate thinking,
pensamiento
moderado
modern, moderno
modern art,
arte moderno
modern China,
China moderna
**modern democratic
thought,** pensamiento
democrático moderno
**modern republican-
ism,** republicanismo
moderno
modern world,
mundo moderno
modernist,
modernista

modernity,
modernidad
modernization,
modernización
**modernizational
theory,** teoría de la
modernización
modify, modificar
Mohawk, mohawk
molybdenum, molibdeno
Monarch Mansa Musa,
rey Mansa Musa
monarchial system,
sistema monárquico
monarchy, monarquía
monastery, monasterio
monastic, monástico
monasticism, monacato
monetarism, monetarismo
monetary, monetario
monetary policy,
política monetaria
money, dinero
money supply,
oferta de dinero, masa
monetaria
Mongol, mogol
Mongol conquest,
conquista mongola
monk, monje
monocultural,
monocultural
monoculture, monocultivo
monogamy, monogamia
**monopolistic competi-
tion,** competencia
monopolística
monopoly, monopolio
monopolize, monopolizar
monotheism, monoteísmo
monotheist, monoteísta
Monroe Doctrine,
Doctrina Monroe

monsoon, monzón
  monsoon wind,
  viento monzón
Montgomery Bus Boycott,
  Boicot de los Autobus-
  es en Montgomery
month, mes
monument, monumento
moon race,
  carrera hacia la luna
moor, moro
moot, dudoso, debatible
moraine, morrena
moral, moral
  **moral development
  theory,** teoría del desarrollo moral
  moral economy,
  economía moral
  moral entrepreneurs,
  empresarios morales
  moral majority,
  mayoría moral
  moral obligation,
  obligación moral
  moral panic,
  pánico moral
  moral reasons,
  razones morales
  moral reform,
  reforma moral
  moral responsibility,
  responsabilidad moral
  moral rhetoric,
  retórica moral
  moral standard,
  norma moral
  moral values,
  valores morales
Mormon, mormón
Mormon, mormona
  Mormon church,
  Iglesia mormona

**Mormon migration to
  the West,**
  migración mormona
  hacia el oeste
**Moroccan resistance
  movement,** movi-
  miento de resistencia
  marroquí
Morocco, Marruecos
mortality rate,
  tasa de mortalidad
mortgage, hipoteca
mosaic, mosaico
Moslem, musulmán
mosque, mezquita
**Most Favored Nation
  Agreements,** cláusula
  de la nación más favo-
  recida
mother country,
  madre patria
**Mothers of the Plaza De
  Mayo,** Madres de la
  Plaza de Mayo
motive, motivo
motorized vehicle,
  vehículo motorizado
motto, lema, consigna
mound builder, constructor de montículos
mountain, montaña
  mountain men,
  montañeses
  mountain pass,
  puerto de montaña
  mountain peak,
  cima de montaña
  mountain range,
  cordillera
mouth of a river, desembocadura de un río
**moveable type printing
  machines,** sistema

de imprenta de tipos
móviles
movement, movimiento
Mt. Rushmore,
Monte Rushmore
muckraker, periodista sen-
sacionalista, expositor
de corrupción
mud slide, río de barro
Mudejar Muslim, mudéjar
mudslinging, vilipendio
Mughal Empire,
Imperio mogol
Muhammad, Mahoma
Muhammad Ali,
Mehmet Ali
mulatto, mulato
multicultural,
multicultural
multiculturalism,
multiculturalismo
multilateral,
multilateral
**multilateral agree-
ment,** acuerdo multi-
lateral
**multilateral aid orga-
nization,** organización
de ayuda multilateral
multilateralism,
multilateralismo
multilingual, multilingüe
multinational,
multinacional
**multinational corpo-
ration,** corporación
multilateral
**multinational organi-
zation,** organización
multilateral
multiple perspectives,
perspectivas multila-
terales

multiple-tier time line,
línea cronológica de
varios niveles
multivariate analysis,
análisis multivariado
mummification,
momificación
mummy, momia
Munich Agreemen,
Acuerdos de Múnich
municipal, municipal
municipal court,
tribunal municipal
municipal law,
ley municipal
municipality,
municipalidad
mural, mural
museum, museo
mushrooms, hongos
musket, mosquete
Muslim, musulmán
Muslim country,
país musulmán
Muslim Empire,
Imperio musulmán
Muslim League,
Liga musulmana
Muslim time,
época musulmana
**Muslim trading ves-
sel,** navío musulmán
de comercio
mutinous, amotinado
mutiny, motín
mutual aid societies,
sociedades de ayuda
mutua
mutual funds, fondos de
inversión mobiliaria
myself, yo mismo
myth, mito
mythology, mitología

N

Napoleon Bonaparte,
  Napoleón Bonaparte
Napoleonic code,
  código napoleónico
Napoleonic period,
  período napoleónico
Napoleon's invasions,
  Guerras Napoleónicas
nation, nación
  nation building,
  construcción de la
  nación
  nation-state,
  estado-nación
national, nacional
  **National Aeronautics
  and Space Admin-
  istration,** Adminis-
  tración Nacional de
  Aeronáutica y del
  Espacio (NASA)
  national anthem,
  himno nacional
  National Assembly,
  Asamblea Nacional
  **National Association
  for the Advancement
  of Colored People
  (NAACP),** Asocia-
  ción Nacional para el
  Avance de la Gente de
  Color (NAACP)
  **National Association
  of Security Dealers
  Automated Quota-
  tions (NASDAQ),**
  NASDAQ
  national autonomy,

autonomía nacional
  national bank,
  banco central
  national boundaries,
  fronteras nacionales
  national capital,
  capital nacional
  national convention,
  convención nacional
  national debt,
  deuda pública
  national defense,
  defensa nacional
  **national defense
  spending,** gasto en
  defensa nacional
  **National Demo-
  cratic Party,** Partido
  Democrático Nacional
  national economy,
  economía nacional
  **National Education
  Association,**
  Asociación Nacional de
  Educación
  national events,
  acontecimientos nacio-
  nales
  national flag,
  bandera nacional
  national forest,
  bosque nacional
  **national government
  spending,**
  gasto público
  national holiday,
  fiesta nacional
  national identity,
  identidad nacional
  **National Industrial
  Recovery Act,**
  Ley de Recuperación
  Industrial Nacional

national interest, interés nacional
national issues, asuntos nacionales
National Liberation Front (NLF), Frente Nacional de Liberación de Vietnam
national market, mercado interno
National Organization of Women (NOW), Organización Nacional de las Mujeres (ONM)
national origin, origen nacional
national park, parque nacional
National Park Service, Servicio de Parques Nacionales
national party, partido nacional
national policy, política nacional
National Recovery Administration, Administración para la recuperación nacional
National Republican Party, Partido Republicano Nacional
National Rifle Association (NRA), Asociación Nacional del Fusil
national security, seguridad nacional
National Security Acts, Leyes de Seguridad Nacional
National Security

Council, Consejo Nacional de Seguridad
national self-rule, autodeterminación nacional
national socialism, nacionalsocialismo
National Socialist German Workers Party (NSDAP), Partido Socialista Nacional de los Trabajadores Alemanes (NSDAP)
National Union Party, Partido Unión Nacional
National Woman Suffrage Association, Asociación Nacional por el Sufragio de la Mujer
National Women's Political Caucus, Comité Político Nacional de Mujeres
nationalism, nacionalismo
nationalist, nacionalista
nationalization, nacionalización
native, nativo
native American, Nativo americano
Native American ancestors, antepasados nativos americanos
Native American Indian, indio nativo americano
nativism, patriotismo, nativismo
nativist, patriota, nativista

natural, natural
    natural attitude,
    actitud natural
    natural barriers,
    barreras naturales
    natural boundaries,
    fronteras naturales
    natural disaster,
    desastre natural
    natural environment,
    ambiente natural
    natural hazard,
    riesgo natural
    natural history,
    historia natural
    natural law, derecho
    natural, ley natural
    natural monopoly,
    monopolio natural
    **natural population
    increase,** crecimiento
    de la población natu-
    ral
    natural resource,
    recurso natural
    **natural resource
    extraction,** extracción
    de recursos naturales
    natural rights,
    derechos naturales
    **natural rights phi-
    losophy,** filosofía de
    los derechos naturales
    natural sciences,
    ciencias naturales
    natural vegetation,
    vegetación natural
    natural wetlands,
    pantanos naturales
naturalization,
    naturalización
naturalized citizen,
    ciudadano natura-
    lizado
nature preserve,
    reserva natural
naval forces,
    fuerzas navales
naval supplies,
    suministros navales
naval warfare,
    guerra naval
navigable, navegable
    navigable river,
    río navegable
navigate, navegar
navigation, navegación
    Navigation Acts,
    Leyes de Navegación
    navigational tools,
    herramientas de nave-
    gación
Nazi, nazi
    Nazi genocide,
    genocidio nazi
    Nazi holocaust,
    holocausto nazi
    Nazi ideology,
    ideología nazi
    **Nazi war against the
    Jews,** guerra nazi con-
    tra los judíos
Nazism, nazismo
**Nazi-Soviet Non-Aggres-
    sion pact,** Pacto de
    no agresión germano-
    soviético
Neanderthal, Neandertal
near, cerca
**necessary and proper
    clause,** cláusula flex-
    ible o propia necesar-
    ia, cláusula necesaria
    y apropriada
necessary condition,
    condición necesaria

necessity, necesidad

need, necesidad

negative externality, externalidad negativa

negative incentive, incentivo negativo

negotiate, negociar

negotiation, negociación

neighbor, vecino

neighborhood, vecindad

neighborhood transportation, transporte vecinal

neocolonialism, neocolonialismo

neo-Confucianism, neoconfucianismo

neo-conservatism, neoconservadurismo

neo-liberalism, neoliberalismo

Neolithic, neolítico

Neolithic Agricultural Revolution, revolución agrícola neolítica

Neolithic agricultural society, sociedad agrícola neolítica

neopatrimonialism, neopatrimonialismo

nepotism, nepotismo

Nero, Nerón

net export, exportación neta

net widening, ampliación de las redes

Netherlands, los Países Bajos

network, red

neuropsychology, neuropsicología

neutral, neutral

neutral nation, país neutral

neutralist, neutralista

neutrality, neutralidad, neutralismo

New Amsterdam, Nueva Amsterdam

New Deal, Nuevo Trato

New Delhi, Nueva Delhi

New Economic policy, Nueva Política Económica

new economy entrepreneurs, empresarios de la nueva economía

New England, Nueva Inglaterra

New England colony, colonia de Nueva Inglaterra

New England mill town, ciudad textil en Nueva Inglaterra

New Federalism, Nuevo Federalismo

new freedom, Nueva Libertad

New Frontier, Nueva Frontera

New Granada, Nueva Granada

New Guinea, Nueva Guinea

new immigrants, nuevos inmigrantes

New Imperialism, Nuevo Imperialismo

new institutionalism, nuevo institucionalismo

New Jersey, Nueva Jersey

New Jersey Plan, plan de Nueva Jersey

New Jersey v. T.L.O.,
Nueva Jersey contra
T.L.O.
New Kingdom,
Imperio Nuevo
New Klan, nuevo Klan
New Left, Nueva Izquierda
New Mexico, Nuevo México
new nationalism,
nuevo nacionalismo
New Orleans,
Nueva Orleans
**new scientific rational-
ism,** nuevo racional-
ismo científico
New South, Nuevo Sur
New Testament,
Nuevo Testamento
New Urbanism,
nuevo urbanismo
New Woman, Nueva Mujer
New World, nuevo mundo
New Years Day, Año Nuevo
New York, Nueva York
New York City draft riots,
disturbios contra el
reclutamiento militar
en Nueva York
New York stock exchange,
bolsa de Nuevo York
New Zealand,
Nueva Zelanda
newcomer,
recién llegado, novato
Newfoundland, Terranova
**newly industrializing
countries (NICs),**
países recientemente
industrializados (NIC)
newspaper account,
noticia de periódico
newsprint,
papel de periódico

Nez Perce, Nez Percé
Nez Perce Tribe,
tribu Nez percé
Niger River, río Níger
Nile Delta, delta del Nilo
Nile Valley, valle del Nilo
**NIMBY (Not In My Back-
yard),** NIMBY (no en
mi patio trasero)
**nineteenth-century lit-
erature,** literatura del
siglo XIX
nirvana, nirvana
nitrogen cycle,
ciclo del nitrógeno
Nobel Peace Prize,
Premio Nobel de la Paz
nobility, nobleza
noble, noble
noble savage,
buen salvaje
Noh drama,
teatro noh japonés
Nok terra cotta figure,
figuras en terracota
de Nok
nomad[1], nómada
nomadic[2], nómada
**nominal Gross Domestic
Product,** Producto In-
terno Bruto nominal
nominal interest rate,
tasa de interés
nominal
nomination,
nombramiento
nonaggression pact,
pacto de no agresión
nonaligned, no alineado
nonalignment,
no alineación
nondurable goods,
bienes no durables

non-essential consumer goods, bienes de consumo no esenciales

nonexclusion, no exclusión

nonfiction, no ficción

nonhominid, no homínido

nonimportation agreement, acuerdo de no importación

nonmotorized vehicle, vehículo no motorizado

noninterference, no intervencionismo

nonpartisan, no-partidiario

nonprice competition, competencia no relacionada con los precios

nonprofit organization, organización no lucrativa

nonrenewable resource, recurso no renovable

non-renewable resources, recursos no renovables

nonrival product, producto que no es rival

nonunion worker, trabajador no sindicalizado

non-violence, no violencia

nonviolent direct action, acción directa no violenta

nonviolent resistance, resistencia no violenta

norm, norma

normal unemployment, desempleo normal

normalcy, normalidad

Normandy Invasion, Batalla de Normandía

Norse invasion, invasión nórdica

Norse long ship, embarcación nórdica

north, norte

North Africa, África del Norte

North America, Norteamérica, América del Norte

North American mound-building people, pueblos norteamericanos constructores de montículos

North American plains society, tribus de las llanuras de América del Norte

North Atlantic Free Trade Agreement (NAFTA), Tratado de Libre Comercio de América del Norte (TLCAN)

North Atlantic Treaty Organization (NATO), Organización del Tratado del Atlántico Norte) (OTAN)

North Korea, Corea del Norte

North Pole, Polo Norte

northeast, noreste, nordeste

northern, (del) norte

Northern Ireland, Irlanda del Norte

northern Italian city-state, ciudad-estado del norte de Italia

Northern states, estados del norte

northwest, noroesete

Northwest Ordinance, Ordenanza del Noroeste

Northwest Passage, Paso del Noroeste

Northwest posts, puestos del Noroeste

Northwest Territory, Territorio del Noroeste

Norway, Noruega

not-for-profit, asociación sin fines de lucro, no lucrativo

Nova Scotia, Nueva Escocia

now, ahora

nuclear, nuclear

   nuclear age, edad nuclear

   nuclear energy, energía nuclear

   nuclear family, familia nuclear

   nuclear politics, políticas nucleares

   nuclear power, energía nuclear

   nuclear technology, tecnología nuclear

   Nuclear Test Ban Treaty, Tratado de prohibición parcial de ensayos nucleares

   nuclear weapons, armas nucleares

   nuclear-waste storage, almacenamiento de residuos nucleares

   null and void, sin fuerza legal

   null hypothesis, hipótesis nula

nullification doctrine, doctrina de la anulación

Nullifier Party, Partido de la anulación

nullify, anular, invalidar, derogar

number grid, cuadrícula de números

Nuremberg Trials, Juicios de Núremberg

oasis, oasis

oath, juramento

   oath helpers, colaboradores de juramento

   oath of office, juramento de toma de posesión

oats, avena

objectification, deshumanización

objectify, deshumanizar

objective, objetivo

   objective good faith, buena fe objetiva

objectivity, objetividad

oblast, óblast

oblate spheroid, esferoide achatado

observation, observación, comentario

observe, observar, cumplir (ley)

observed information, información observada

obsidian, obsidiana

occupation, ocupación

occupational crime,
delito de cuello blanco
occupational distance,
distancia ocupacional
occupational specialization, especialización
ocupacional
ocean, océano
ocean circulation,
circulación oceánica
ocean current,
corriente marina
ocean ecosystem,
ecosistema marino
ocean pollution,
contaminación de los
océanos
Oceania, Oceanía
October Manifesto,
Manifiesto de octubre
Odyssey, Odisea
Office of Budget and Management,
Oficina de Presu-
puesto y Gestión
Office of Economic Opportunity, Oficina
de Oportunidades
Económicas
Office of Price Administration (OPA),
Oficina de Admin-
istración de Precios
(OPA)
official, funcionario, oficial
Ogallala Aquifer,
acuífero de Ogallala
Ohio River, río Ohio **oil,**
petróleo
oil crisis,
crisis petrolera
oil field,
yacimiento petrolífero,

campo petrolero
oil shale,
pizarra bituminosa
oil slick, marea negra
okrug, ókrug
Old Hickory, Viejo Nogal
old immigrants,
antiguos inmigrantes
Old Imperialism,
Viejo Imperialismo
Old Kingdom, Imperio
Antiguo de Egipto
Old Northwest, Territorio
del Noroeste
Old Regime France,
Antiguo régimen
francés
Old Testament,
Antiguo Testamento
old-growth forest, bosque
virgen, bosque prístino
oligarch, oligarca
oligarchical government,
gobierno oligárquico
oligarchy, oligarquía
oligopoly, oligopolio
Olive Branch Petition,
Petición de la Rama de
Olivo
Olmec civilization,
civilización olmeca
Omaha Platform,
plataforma de Omaha
ombudsman, ombuds-
man, defensor de los
derechos humanos
omen, presagio
omnibus bill,
proyecto de ley sobre
asuntos distintos
one child policy in China,
política de un solo hijo
en China

one class ideology,
ideología de una clase
one man one vote,
un hombre un voto
online commerce,
comercio electrónico
op-ed, opinión editorial
open door,
puertas abiertas
Open Door policy,
política de puertas
abiertas
open hearth process,
procedimiento
Siemens-Martin
open market purchase,
adquisición de mer-
cado abierto
open primary, elección
primaria abierta
open range, terreno abierto
open shop,
empresa con personal
sindicalizado y no
sindicalizado
open-mindedness,
criterio amplio
Opera House (Sydney,
Australia),
Ópera de Sídney
operant conditioning,
condicionamiento
operante
operationalization,
operacionalización
operationally defined,
definido operacional-
mente
Opium War,
Guerra del Opio
opportunity benefit,
beneficio de
oportunidad

opportunity cost,
costo de oportunidad
opportunity structure,
estructura de oportu-
nidades
oppose, oponerse
opposition, oposición
  opposition group,
  grupo de oposición
  Opposition Party,
  partido de oposición
oppression, opresión
oracle bone,
hueso oracular
oracles, oráculos
oral argument,
defensa verbal
oral history,
historia oral
oral language, lengua oral
oral tradition,
tradición oral
orator, orador
order, orden
  order of events,
  orden de los aconte-
  cimientos
  orders in council,
  decretos ministeriales
ordinal measures,
medidas ordinales
ordinance, ordenanza
ore, mineral, mena
Oregon, Oregón
  Oregon territory,
  territorio de Oregón
organic solidarity,
solidaridad orgánica
organization, organización
  Organization for
  European Economic
  Cooperation (OEEC),
  Organización para la

Cooperación Económica Europea

Organization of American States (OAS), Organización de Estados Americanos (OEA)

Organization of Petroleum Exporting Countries (OPEC), Organización de Países Exportadores del Petróleo (OPEP)

organizational studies, estudios organizacionales

organized crime, crimen organizado

organized labor, trabajo organizado, sindicato

Orient, Oriente

Oriental, oriental

orientation, orientación

origin, origen nacional

original jurisdiction, jurisdicción original

orographic precipitation, precipitación orográfica

Orosius, Orosio

Orthodox Christian Church, Iglesia Ortodoxa Cristiana

Orthodox Christianity, cristianismo ortodoxo

Ottoman Empire, Imperio otomano

out of many, one, de muchos, uno

outback, llanura desértica, llanura interior

outlaw[1], forajido, bandido

outlaw[2], prohibir

outline, resumen

output, rendimiento

output per hour, rendimiento por hora

output per machine, rendimiento por máquina

output per unit of land, rendimiento por unidad de tierra

output per worker, rendimiento por trabajador

outsource, subcontratar

outsourcing, subcontratación

outward migration, migración hacia el exterior

over simplify, sobresimplificar

overcutting of pine forest, tala excesiva de los bosques de pinos

overexpansion, expansión exagerada

overfishing, sobrepesca

over-generalization, sobregeneralización

overgraze, pastoreo excesivo

overland trade route, ruta comercial por tierra

overpopulation, sobrepoblación, superpoblación, exceso de población

overproduction, exceso de producción

overrepresentation, sobrerrepresentación

override, invalidar
   override a veto,
   invalidar un veto
overseas trade,
   comercio exterior
overseer, capataz,
   supervisor
oversimplification,
   sobresimplificación
overthrow, derrocamiento
ownership, propriedad
oxygen cycle,
   ciclo del oxígeno
ozone depletion,
   agujero de ozono
ozone layer, capa de ozono

Pacific, Pacífico
   Pacific Islands,
   Islas del Pacífico
   Pacific Northwest,
   Noroeste Pacífico
   Pacific Ocean,
   Océano Pacífico
   Pacific Railroad,
   empresa Pacific
   Railroad
   Pacific Rim,
   Cuenca del Pacífico
   **Pacific Rim econo-
   my,** economía de la
   Cuenca del Pacífico
   Pacific Theater,
   teatro de operaciones
   del Pacífico
pacifism, pacifismo
pacifist, pacifista
paddies, arrozales

Pakistan, Pakistán
Paleolithic, Paleolítico
   **Paleolithic cave
   painting,** pintura
   rupestre del Paleolítico
Paleolithic Era,
   Era Paleolítico
Palestine, Palestina
**Palestinian Liberation
   Organization (PLO),**
   Organización para la
   Liberación de Pales-
   tina (OLP)
Pallavas, Pallava
Pan-Africanism,
   panafricanismo
Panama, Panamá
   Panama Canal,
   Canal de Panamá
   Panama Revolution,
   Independencia de
   Panamá
Pan-Arabism, panarabismo
pancratium, pancracio
pandemic, pandémico
panel study,
   estudio de cohorte
Pan-Slavism, paneslavismo
pantheon, panteón
papacy, papado
papal state, estado papal
paper blockade,
   bloqueo en el papel
paper factory,
   fábrica de papel
paper money,
   papel moneda
papyrus, papiro
parables, parábolas
paragraph, párrafo
parallel, paralelo
   parallel timeline,
   línea de tiempo

paralela
parallels of latitude,
paralelos de latitud
paraphrase[1], parafrasear
paraphrase[2], paráfrasis
paraphrasing, paráfrasis
para-statals, paraestatales
parchment, pergamino
pardon, indulto
Paris, París
    Paris Peace Accords,
    Acuerdos de Paz de
    París
parish, parroquia
park, parque
parliament, parlamento
parliamentary,
    parlamentario(a)
    **parliamentary de-
    mocracy,** democracia
    parlamentaria
    **parliamentary gov-
    ernment,** gobierno
    parlamentario
    **parliamentary politi-
    cal system,** sistema
    político parlamentario
    **parliamentary
    sovereignty,**
    soberanía
    parlamentaria
    **parliamentary su-
    premacy,** supremacía
    parlamentaria
    **parliamentary sys-
    tem,** sistema
    parlamentario
parochial, parroquial
    parochial school,
    escuela parroquial
participate, participar
participatory government,
    gobierno participativo

**participatory manage-
    ment,** gestión partici-
    pativa
participatory research,
    investigación partici-
    pativa
participatory skills,
    habilidades para la
    participación
partition, reparto
    partition of Africa,
    reparto de África
partitioned, subdividido
partnership,
    sociedad, asociación
part-time employment,
    trabajo de medio
    tiempo
party, partido
    party dealignment,
    desalineación parti-
    dista
    party identification,
    identificación parti-
    daria
    party realignment,
    realineación partidista
    party system,
    sistema de partidos
pass a law,
    aprobar (una ley)
passage,
    viaje, travesía, pasaje
passive resistance,
    resistencia pasiva
passport, pasaporte
past, pasado
pastoral nomadic people,
    pueblo nómada dedi-
    cado al pastoreo
pasture, pastos, pastar
patent, patente
pathogen, patógeno

patriarchal society

patriarchal society,
sociedad patriarcal
patriarchs, patriarcas
patriarchy, patriarcado
patrician, patricio
patrilineal descent,
descendiente patri-
lineal
patrimonial state,
estado patrimonial
patrimonialism,
patrimonialismo
patrimony, patrimonio
patriot, patriota
patriotic, patriótico
patriotic symbols,
símbolos patrios
patriotism, patriotismo
patron, patrocinador
patronage,
mecenazgo, patrocinio
patron-client networks,
mecenazgo político,
mecenazgo
patron-client politics,
políticas patrón-cliente
patroon, propietario de
tierras, encomendero
holandés
pattern, patrón, modelo
pattern of change,
patrón de cambio
Paul the Apostle,
Pablo el Apóstol
Pax Romana, Paz Romana
Paxton Boys Massacre,
masacre de los Paxton
Boys
pay equity,
igualdad de salarios
payment, pago
payroll tax, impuesto sobre
los salarios, impuesto

sobre nómina
Peace Corps,
Cuerpo de paz
peace movement,
movimiento de paz
Peace of Paris,
Conferencia de Paz de
París
peace treaty,
tratrado de paz
peaceful coexistence,
coexistencia pacífica
peaceful demonstration,
manifestación pacífica
peacekeeper,
fuerzas encargadas de
mantener la paz
peacekeeping,
mantenimiento de la
paz
Pearl Harbor, Pearl Harbor
peasant, campesino
peasantry, campesinado
peat, turba
peculiar institution,
institución peculiar
pedestrian walkway,
paso peatonal
peer, par, igual, coetáneo
peer group,
grupo paritario
pen, pluma, bolígrafo
penal court, corte penal
penalty, pena, castigo
peninsula, península
Pennsylvania, Pensilvania
penny, penique
pension, pensión
Pentagon, Pentágono
People of the Book,
Pueblo del libro
people's communes,
comunas del pueblo

People's Republic of China, República Popular China
per capita GDP, PIB per cápita
per capita income, renta per cápita
perceptual region, región de percepción
perestroika, perestroika
period, período
   period of history, período histórico
periodizations, periodizaciones
periodize, periodizar
peripheral, periférico
perjury, perjurio
permafrost, permafrost
persecute, perseguir
persecution, persecución
Persian Empire, Imperio persa
Persian Gulf, Golfo Pérsico
   Persian Gulf Crisis, Crisis del Golfo Pérsico
   Persian Gulf War, Guerra del Golfo Pérsico
personal autonomy, autonomía personal
personal distribution of income, distribución personal del ingreso
personal history, historia personal
personal income, ingreso personal
personal letter, carta personal
personal liberty, libertad personal

personal life, vida privada
personal responsibility, responsabilidad personal
personal values, valores personales
personal virtue, virtud personal
personality, personalidad
perspective, perspectiva
Peru, Perú
pesticide, pesticida
pet bill, ley de mascotas
Peter the Great, Pedro el Grande
petite bourgeoisie, pequeña burguesía
petition, petición
   Petition of Right, Petición de derechos
petrochemical, petroquímico
petroleum, petróleo
   petroleum consumption, consumo de petróleo
phalanx, falange
Pharaoh, Faraón
Philadelphia, Filadelfia
   Philadelphia Convention, Convención de Filadelfia
philanthropist, filántropo
philanthropy, filantropía
Philippine annexation, anexión de Filipinas
Philippine archipelago, archipiélago de Filipinas
Philippines, Filipinas
philosopher, filósofo
philosophical, filosófico

**philosophical move-
ment,** movimiento
filosófico
philosophy, filosofía
Phoenicia, Fenicia
Phoenicians, fenicios
phosphate, fosfato
    phosphate reserves,
    reservas de fosfatos
photograph, fotografía
photography, fotografía
physical, físico(a)
    **physical anthropolo-
    gist,** antropólogo físico
    **physical anthropolo-
    gy,** antropología física
    physical capital,
    capital físico
    **physical character-
    istics,** características
    físicas
    **physical environ-
    ment,** ambiente físico
    physical feature,
    rasgo físico
    physical geography,
    geografía física
    physical map,
    mapa físico
    physical patterns,
    patrones físicos
    physical process,
    proceso físico
    physical regions,
    regiones físicas
    physical setting,
    escenario físico
    physical variation,
    variación física
physiographic,
    fisiográfico
physiography,
    fisiografía

**physiological population
    density,** densidad fisi-
    ológica de población
physiological psychology,
    psicología fisiológica
piazza, plaza
picket, piquete
pictograph, pictográfico
picture time line,
    línea cronológica en
    imágenes
pidgin language,
    pidgin, lengua de con-
    tacto
pie graph,
    gráfico de pastel
Piedmont, Piamonte
    Piedmont Region,
    región de Piamonte
pilgrim, peregrino
pilgrimage, peregrinación
pillars of faith,
    pilares de la fe
pioneer, pionero
    pioneer spirit,
    espíritu pionero
pipeline, oleoducto
Pizarro, Pizarro
place, sitio, lugar
    place of origin,
    lugar de origen
plague, peste
plain, llanura
    Plains States,
    Estados de la Llanura
plaintiff,
    demandante
planned city,
    ciudad planificada
planned community,
    comunidad planificada
plant community,
    comunidad vegetal

plant cultivation,
cultivo de plantas
plant population,
densidad vegetal
plant species,
especies vegetales
plantains, plátanos
plantation, plantación
plantation agriculture, agricultura de plantación
plantation colony, colonia de plantación
plantation system, sistema de plantación
plate, placa
plate tectonics, tectónica de placas
plateau, meseta
platform, plataforma
Plato, Platón
Plato's Republic, República de Platón
plaza, plaza
plea bargain, acuerdo entre la defensa y la parte acusadora
plebeian, plebeyo
plebiscite, plebiscito
pledge, compromiso
Pledge of Allegiance, Juramento de Lealtad
Plessy vs. Ferguson, caso Plessy contra Ferguson
plot, conjura, complot, argumento
pluralism, pluralismo
plutocracy, plutocracia
plutocratic, plutocrático
Plymouth colony, Colonia de Plymouth
pocket veto,

veto de bolsillo
poetry, poesía
poetry of Kabir, poesía de Kabir
poetry of Mirabai, poesía de Mirabai
pogroms, pogromos
point of view, punto de vista
Poland, Polonia
polarization, polarización
polarization of classes, polarización de clases
polarized, polarizado
polder, pólder
police authority, autoridad policial
police culture, cultura policial
police powers, poderes policiales
policy, política
policy implementation, implementación de políticas
policy issue, asunto de normativa
Polish rebellion, Revolución polaca
political, político
political accountability, responsabilidad política
political action, acción política
political action committee (PAC), comité de acción política
political affairs, asuntos políticos

political alliance,
alianza política
**political appoint-
ment,** nombramiento
político
political autonomy,
autonomía política
political behavior,
comportamiento
político
political border,
frontera política
political boundaries,
límites políticos
political candidate,
candidato político
political cartoon,
caricatura política,
cartón político
**political character-
istics,** características
políticas
political collapse,
colapso político
**political collapse
economy,** economía
de colapso político
political corruption,
corrupción política
political culture,
cultura política
**political develop-
ment,** desarrollo
político
**political economy
theory,** teoría de
economía política
political efficacy,
eficacia política
political entity,
entidad política
political freedom,
libertad política

political geography,
geografía política
political ideology,
ideología política
political institution,
institución política
political issues,
asuntos políticos
political life,
vida política
political machine,
clientelismo político
political map,
mapa político
political office,
cargo público
**political organiza-
tion,** organización
política
**political participa-
tion,** participación
política
political party,
partido político
political philosophy,
filosofía política
political platform,
plataforma política
political policing,
policía política
political psychology,
psicología política
political question,
cuestión política
political radical,
radical político
political region,
región política
**political relation-
ships,** relaciones
políticas
political rights,
derechos políticos

political scandals, escándalos políticos
political science, ciencias políticas
political scientist, politólogo
political socialization, socialización política
political sociology, sociología política
political spectrum, espectro político
political systems, sistemas políticos
political turmoil, confusión política
political unit, unidad política
politics, política
polity, sistema de gobierno
poll tax, impuesto de capitación
polling, votación
pollution, contaminación
polygamy, poligamia
Polynesia, Polinesia
polytheism, politeísmo
polytheist, politeísta
Pompeii, Pompeya
Pontiac's Rebellion, Rebelión de Pontiac
pony express, correo a caballo
pooled resources, recursos comunes
pooling, pool
pools, consorcios
poorly equipped, mal equipado
pop art, arte pop
Pope, Papa
Popul Vuh, Popol Vuh

popular consent, consenso popular
popular culture, cultura popular
popular figure, figura popular
popular psychology, psicología popular
popular sovereignty, soberanía popular
popular uprising, levantamiento popular
popular vote, voto popular
popular will, voluntad popular
population, población
population aging, envejecimiento de la población
population concentration, concentración de la población
population density, densidad de población
population distribution, distribución de la población
population diversity, diversidad de la población
population dynamics, dinámica de la población
population ecology, ecología de población
population explosion, explosión demográfica
population growth, crecimiento demográfico
population growth rate, tasa de crecimiento demográfico

population increase, aumento de la población

population move-ment, movimiento de población

population pyramid, pirámide de población

population region, región demográfica

population structure, estructura de la población

population trends, tendencias de población

populism, populismo

populist, populista

Populist Party, Partido Populista

Populist Movement, Movimiento Populista

pork-barrel, clientelismo, recompensas políticas

pork-barrel legisla-tion, legislación de "barril de tocino", legislación de recompensas políticas

port, portuario, puerto

port city, ciudad portuaria

port of entry, puerto de entrada

portage, transporte por tierra

Portugal, Portugal

Portuguese, portugués

Portuguese caravel, carabela portuguesa

position, posición, postura

positive externality, externalidad positiva

positive incentive, incentivo positivo

positive rights, derechos positivos

postal zone, zona postal

post-Civil War period, período posterior a la Guerra Civil

post-Cold War era, período posterior a la Guerra Fría

post-control theory, teoría de post-control

posterity, posteridad

post-industrial society, sociedad posindustrial

post-Mao China, China posterior a Mao

postmodern, posmoderno

postmodern art, arte posmoderno

post-modern era, época posmoderna

post-modernism, posmodernidad

post-modernist, posmoderno

post-reunification Germa-ny, Alemania posterior a la reunificación

postwar, posguerra

postwar inflation, inflación de la posguerra

postwar period, período de la posguerra

post-World War I, período posterior a la Primera Guerra Mundial

post-World War II, período posterior a la Segunda Guerra Mun-

dial
potash, potasa
pottery, cerámica, alfarería
Poughkeepsie Convention, Convención de Poughkeepsie
poverty, pobreza
poverty line, umbral de la pobreza
power, poder
   power bloc, bloque de poder
   power by the people, poder por el pueblo
   power loom, telar mecánico
   power of the purse, poder del bolsillo
   power to declare war, poder para declarar la guerra
   power to tax, poder para gravar
   power vertical, poder vertical
power-elite, élite del poder
   power-elite model, modelo de la élite del poder
powwow, asamblea, congreso
practical reasoning, razonamiento práctico
practice, práctica, costumbres, uso, hábito
   practices of government, prácticas gubernamentales
pragmatic, pragmático
pragmatism, pragmatismo
prairie, pradera
prayer in public schools, rezo en las escuelas

públicas
preamble, preámbulo
   preamble of the United States Constitution, preámbulo de la Constitución de EE.UU.
prebendalism, sistema de prebendas
precedence, precedencia, anterioridad
precedent, precedente
precinct, circunscripción
precious metal, metal precioso
precipitation, precipitación
pre-Columbian civilizations, Civilizaciones precolombinas
pre-Columbus, precolombino
predict, predecir
prediction, predicción
preemptive strike, ataque preventivo
pre-European life in Americas, civilización preeuropea en América
preferential treatment programs, programas de trato preferencial
prehistoric, prehistórico
prehistory, prehistoria
pre-industrial England, Inglaterra preindustrial
Preindustrial Age, Edad Preindustrial
prejudice, prejuicio
prepossession, prejuicio, idea preconcebida

present, presente
preservation, preservación, conservación
preserve the Union, preservación de la Unión
president, presidente
President Pro-tempore of the Senate, Presidente provisional del Senado
presidential, presidencial
1960 presidential campaign, campaña presidencial de 1960
presidential election, elección presidencial
presidential impeachment andtrial, acusación y juicio del presidente
presidential pardon, indulto presidencial
president's cabinet, gabinete presidencial
Presidents Day, Día del Presidente
presidio, presidio
press, prensa
presumption of innocence, presunción de inocencia
prevailing price, precio vigente
prevailing wind, viento dominante
preview, anticipo
previous condition of servitude, condición previa de servidumbre
price, precio
price ceiling, precio máximo, precio tope

price control, control de precios
price decrease, disminución de precios
price floor, precio mínimo
price increase, incremento de precios
price stability, estabilidad de precios
price war, guerra de precios
priest, sacerdote
priest-kings, reyes sacerdotes
primaries, elecciones primarias
primary, primario
primary city, ciudad principal
primary color, color primario
primary data, datos básicos
primary documents, documentos primarios
primary economic activity, actividad económica principal
primary election, elección primaria
primary group, grupo primario
primary labor market, mercado de trabajo primario
primary source, fuente primaria
primate, primado
prime meridian, primer meridiano
prime minister,

primer ministro
primeval, primigenio
primitive communism,
    comunismo primitivo
primitive economy,
    economía primitiva
primitive society,
    sociedad primitiva
primogeniture,
    primogenitura
principal line,
    línea principal
principal parallels,
    paralelos principales
principle, principio
    principles of
    democracy,
    principios democráti-
    cos
print, imprimir
printing press,
    prensa, imprenta
prior experience,
    experiencia previa
prior restraint,
    restricción previa
Priscus, Prisco
prison reform,
    reforma penitenciaria
prison subculture,
    subcultura carcelaria
privacy, privacidad
private, privado(a)
    private domain,
    ámbito privado
    private goods,
    bienes privados
    private investment
    spending, gasto de
    inversión privada
    private law,
    derecho privado
    private life,

vida privada
    private market,
    mercado privado
    private morality,
    moralidad privada
    private property,
    propiedad privada
    private sector,
    sector privado
    private sphere,
    esfera privada
    private white acade-
    my, academia privada
    de blancos
privateer, buque corsario
privatization,
    privatización
    privatization vouch-
    er, cupón o bono de
    privatización
privatize, privatizar
privilege, privilegio
privileges and immunities
    clause, cláusula de
    privilegios e inmuni-
    dades
pro bono, para el bien
    público
probability, probabilidad
    probability sample,
    muestra probabilística
probable cause,
    causa probable
probation,
    libertad condicional
problem, problema
    problem solving,
    resolución de proble-
    mas
procedural due process,
    proceso debido
procedural law,
    derecho procesal

process of Russification,
proceso de rusificación
processes, procesos
proclamation,
proclamación
produce, producir
producer, productor
product, producto
product standards,
normas de producto
production, producción
production cost,
costo de producción
production method,
método de producción
production output,
rendimiento de producción
production possibilities curve, curva de posibilidades de producción
production site,
lugar de producción
productive, productivo
productivity,
productividad
professional sector,
sector profesional
professional sport,
deporte profesional
profile, perfil
profit, beneficio, ganancia
profit incentive,
participación en beneficios
profit motive,
afán de lucro
profit opportunity,
oportunidad de beneficio
profitability, rentabilidad
profiteering, especulación

program, programa
progress, progreso
progressive, progresista
Progressive Era,
Era Progresista
progressive income tax, impuesto progresivo sobre la renta
Progressive movement, movimiento progresista
Progressive Party,
Partido Progresista
progressive tax,
impuesto progresivo
progressive taxation,
tributación progresiva
Progressivism,
progresismo
prohibited powers,
poderes prohibidos
Prohibition,
Prohibición, Ley Seca
Prohibition Party,
Partido de la Prohibición
projection, proyección
proletariat, proletariado
proliferation, proliferación
promissory note, pagaré, letra de cambio
propaganda, propaganda
propaganda campaign, campaña propagandística
propaganda techniques, técnicas propagandísticas
property, propiedad
property ownership, propiedad de los bienes
property rights,

derechos de propiedad
property tax,
impuesto sobre la
propiedad inmobil-
iaria, impuesto predial
property taxation,
tributación sobre la
propiedad inmobiliaria
prophet, profeta
**proportional representa-
tion,** representación
proporcional
proportional system,
sistema proporcional
proportional tax,
impuesto proporcional
proportional taxation,
tributación proporcio-
nal
proposal, propuesta
proposition, propuesta,
proposición, oferta
proprietary,
colonia propietaria
proprietary colony,
colonia propietaria
proprietor, propietario
proprietor's income,
ingresos del propietar-
io
prosperity, prosperidad
protectionism,
proteccionismo
protectionist,
proteccionista
protective tariff,
arancel proteccionista
protectorate, protectorado
protest, protesta
protest, protestar, marcha
Protestant, protestante
**Protestant Christi-
anity,** cristianismo

protestante
Protestant clergy,
clero protestante
**Protestant Reforma-
tion,** Reforma protes-
tante
**Protestant work
ethic,** ética protes-
tante del trabajo
Protestantism,
protestantismo
proverb, proverbio
province, provincia
provincial, provincial
provision, provisión, suministro; disposición
provisional government,
gobierno provisional
proviso, condición
psyche, psique
psychiatry, psiquiatría
psychoanalytic method,
método psicoanalítico
psycholinguistics,
psicolingüística
psychological, psicológico
**psychological reduc-
tionism,** reduccion-
ismo psicológico
psychologist, psicólogo
psychology, psicología
**psychology of reli-
gion,** psicología de la
religión
**psychology of tor-
ture,** psicología de la
tortura
psychopath, psicópata
psychotherapy,
psicoterapia
public, público
public agenda,
agenda pública

public benefit,
beneficio público
public debt,
deuda pública
public education,
educación pública
public forum,
foro público
public good,
bien público
public health,
salud pública
public health model,
modelo de salud
pública
Public Health Service, Servicio de Salud
Pública
public housing,
vivienda de interés
social
public image,
imagen pública
public land,
tierra de dominio
público
public law,
derecho público
public life,
vida pública
public meetings,
reuniones públicas
public morality,
orden moral
public office,
cargo público
public opinion,
opinión pública
public opinion poll,
sondeo de opinión
public policy,
política pública
public project,

proyecto público
public property,
propiedad pública
public safety,
seguridad pública
public servant,
funcionario público
public service,
servicio público
public service commission, comisión de
servicio público
public service utility,
empresa de servicio
público
public transit,
tránsito público
public transportation, transporte
público
public trial,
juicio público
public use,
uso público
public utilities,
utilidades públicas
public welfare,
bienestar público,
asistencia pública
public well-being,
bienestar público
public works,
obras públicas
Public Works Administration, Administración de Obras
Públicas
publicans, publicanos
publication, publicación
publisher, editor
publishing house, editorial
Pueblo Revolt,
rebelión de los indios

Pueblo
Puerto Rico, Puerto Rico
pull factors,
factores de atracción
pulp fiction, literatura
barata, literatura
basura
pump-priming, reactivar la
economía, inundar la
bomba
Punic Wars,
Guerras Púnicas
punishment,
castigo, pena
puppet government,
gobierno títere
purchasing power,
poder adquisitivo
pure competition,
competencia pura
Pure Food and Drug Act,
Ley de Alimentos y
Medicamentos Puros
Puritan, puritano
Puritan work ethic,
ética puritana del
trabajo
Puritan Revolution,
Revolución puritana
Puritan values,
valores puritanos
Puritanism, puritanismo
purpose of government,
función del gobierno
pursuit of happiness,
búsqueda de la felici-
dad
push factors,
factores de empuje
Put Out System,
industria a domicilio,
sistema doméstico
pyramid, pirámide

pyramid debt,
deuda piramidal

Qianlong emperor,
emperador Qianlong
Qing position on opium,
postura de Qing con
respecto al opio
**Qizilbash nomadic tribes-
men,** tribus nómadas
qizilbash
quadrant, cuadrante
Quaker, cuáquero
qualification, requisito,
capacidad
qualitative research,
investigación cualita-
tiva
quality control,
control de calidad
quality of life,
calidad de vida
quangos, autoridades
administrativas in-
dependientes, ente
semiautónomo
quantitative research,
investigación cuanti-
tativa
quarantine, cuarentena
quanity, cantidad
quarry, presa, cantera
quarter,
barrio, trimestre,
cuarta parte, moneda
de 25 centavos
Quartering Act, Ley de
acuartelamiento

quasi-experiment,
semiexperimento,
cuasi experimento
quaternary, cuaternario
queen, reina
Queen Hatshepsut,
reina Hatshepsut
question, pregunta,
cuestión, asunto
quipas, quipu
quorum, quórum
quota, cuota
quota laws,
leyes de cuotas
quota system,
sistema de cuotas
Qur'an, Corán

R

rabbi, rabino
Rabbinic Judaism,
judaísmo rabínico
race, raza, carrera
race relations,
relaciones de raza
race riots,
disturbios raciales
racial, racial
racial discrimination,
discriminación racial
racial diversity,
diversidad racial
racial group,
grupo racial
racial identity,
identidad racial
racial integration,
integración racial
racial minority,

minoría racial
racial realism,
realismo racial
racial role,
rol de raza
racial segregation,
segregación racial
racism, racismo
racist, racista
radical, radical
**Radical Reconstruc-
tion Congress,**
Congreso de Recon-
strucción Radical
Radical Republicans,
republicanos radicales
radicalism, radicalismo
radio, radio
rail transportation,
transporte ferroviario
railhead, cabeza de línea,
estación terminal
railroad, ferrocarril
**railroad construc-
tion,** construcción de
ferrocarriles
rain forest, selva tropical
rain shadow, sombra
pluviométrica
rainfall,
precipitación, lluvia
rally, concentración, mitin
Ramadan, ramadán
Ramses II, Ramsés II
ranch, rancho, hacienda
ranching, ganadería
rape, violación
rape shield laws,
leyes de protección en
casos de violación
rapid, rápido
**rapid industrializa-
tion,** industrialización

rápida
rapid transit,
sistema de transporte
rápido
Rasputin, Rasputín
rate, índice, tasa, tipo
**rate of natural
increase,**
tasa de crecimiento
natural
**rate of resource
consumption,** tasa de
consumo de recursos
ratification, ratificación
ratify, ratificar
ratifying convention,
convención de ratifi-
cación
ratio, razón
rational choice theory,
teoría de la elección
racional
**rational decision-making
process,** toma de deci-
siones racionales
rational self interest,
interés propio racional
rationalization,
racionalización
rationing, racionamiento
raw material,
materia prima
Raymond Poincare,
Raymond Poincaré
reactionary, reaccionario
reactionary thinking,
pensamiento reaccio-
nario
Reagan revolution,
revolución de Reagan
**Reagan-Gorbachev sum-
mit diplomacy,**
cumbre diplomática

entre Reagan y
Gorbachov
**Reagan's "Peace Through
Strength",** "paz por
fuerza" de Reagan
real cost, costo real
real GDP, PIB real
real interest rate,
tasa de interés real
real wages, salario real
Realism, realismo
reality, realidad
realpolitik, realpolitik,
realismo político
reapportion,
repartir de nuevo
reapportionment,
nueva repartición
reason¹, razón
reason², razonar
reasoned, razonado,
argumentado
reasoned judgment,
opinión argumentada
rebate, descuento,
reembolso
rebel, rebelde
recall, destitución
recall election,
elección de revocación
recant, retractarse
recent past,
pasado reciente
recession, recesión
reciprocity, reciprocidad
reclaim, recuperar,
reclamar, reivindicar
reclamation,
recuperación, reciclaje
reconcentration,
reconcentración
reconciliation,
reconciliación

reconquest of Spain,
reconquista de España
Reconstruction,
Reconstrucción
Reconstruction amendments,
enmiendas de la Reconstrucción
record, registro
recorded history, historia escrita
records from the past, registros del pasado
recover, recuperar, recobrar
recreation, recreo, esparcimiento
recreation area, área de recreo
recurrent pandemic, pandemia recurrente
recycle, reciclar
recycling, reciclaje
Red Army, Ejército Rojo
Red Guard, Guardia Roja
Red Russian, rusos rojos
Red Scare, Peligro Rojo
Red Sea, mar Rojo
Red Shirts, Camisas Rojas
redistribution of income, redistribución del ingreso
redistribution of wealth, redistribución de la riqueza
redistributive policies, políticas redistributivas
redistricting, redistribución de los distritos electorales
redress of grievances,
reparación de agravios
reduce, reducir
reduction, reduccion
reduction of species diversity, reducción de la diversidad de especies
reef, arrecife
reference, referencia
reference book, libro de referencia
referendum, referendo
reforestation, reforestación
reform, reforma
reform government, gobierno de reforma
reform legislation, leyes de reforma
reform movement, movimiento de reforma
Reformation,
Reforma protestante
reformer, reformador
refrigerated railroad car, vagón de tren refrigerado
refrigerated trucking, transporte refrigerado
refugee, refugiado
refugee population, población refugiada
refutability,
refutabilidad
Regents of the University of California v. Bakke, caso Universidad de California contra Bakke
regime, régimen
region, región
region of contact, región de contacto
regional boundary,

límite regional
regional change, cambio regional
regional folk hero, héroe popular regional
regional planning, planeación regional
regional planning district, distrito de planeación regional
regional song, canción regional
regionalism, regionalismo
regionalization, regionalización
regressive tax, impuesto regresivo
regressive taxation, tributación regresiva
regrowth, rebrote
regulate, regular
regulated family and community life, vida comunitaria y familia regulada, vida comunitaria y familiar reguladas
regulation, regulación, norma, regla, normativa
regulatory agency, organismo de control
regulatory commission, comisión reguladora
rehabilitative ideal, ideal de rehabilitación
reign[1], reinar
reign[2], reinado
Reign of Terror, Época de Terror
reincarnation, reencarnación
reindeer, reno

reinforcement, refuerzo
relationship, relación
relative[1], relativo
relative[2], pariente, familiar
relative autonomy, autonomía relativa
relative deprivation, privación relativa
relative humidity, humedad relativa
relative location, ubicación relativa
relative price, precio relativo
relevance, relevancia
reliability, fiabilidad
reliable, fiable, confiable
relics, reliquias
relief, ayuda social
relief map, mapa de relieve
religion, religión
religiosity, religiosidad
religious, religioso
religious holiday, fiesta religiosa
religious belief, creencia religiosa
religious discrimination, discriminación religiosa
religious dissenter, disidente religioso
religious evangelism, evangelismo religioso
religious facility, recinto religioso
religious freedom, libertad religiosa
religious fundamentalism, fundamentalismo religioso
religious group, grupo religioso

religious persecution, persecución religiosa
religious reformers, reformadores religiosos
religious revival, renacimiento religioso
religious right, derecho religioso
religious test, prueba religiosa
religious ties, vínculos religiosos
relocate, reubicar
relocation center, centro de reubicación
relocation strategy, estrategia de reubicación
remand, remitir a un tribunal inferior
remedial programs, programas de recuperación
remote sensing, teledetección
removal policy, política de remoción
removal power, poder de destitución
Renaissance, Renacimiento
Renaissance art, arte renacentista
Renaissance humanism, humanismo renacentista
renewable resource, recurso renovable
rent, alquiler, renta
rent control, control de alquileres
rental income, ingresos por percepción de alquileres
rentier state, estado rentista
rent-seeking, búsqueda de rentas
reparation, reparacion, indemnizacion
reparation payment, pago de indemnización
repeal, revocar
repeat offender, infractor reincidente
repertoire, repertorio
repossession, recuperación
representation, representación
representative[1], representativo
representative democracy, democracia representativa
representative government, gobierno representativo
representative leaders, líderes representativos
representative[2], representante
repression, represión
republic, república
republic of Texas, República de Texas
Republican, republicano
republican government, gobierno republicano
republican motherhood, maternidad republicana
Republican party, Partido Republicano

republicanism, republicanismo
18th century republicanism, republicanismo del siglo XVIII
requirement, requisito
repudiate, repudiar
reread, releer
rescue[1], rescate
rescue[2], rescatar
research[1], investigar
research[2], investigación
reservation, reservación, reserva
    reservation system, sistema de reservación
reserve army, ejército de reserva
reserve requirement, reservas mínimas
reserved powers, poderes reservados
reservoir, embalse
resettlement, reasentamiento
residency, residencia
resident, residente
residential pattern, modelo residencial
resignation, resignación
resistance, resistencia
    resistance movement, movimiento de resistencia
resocialization, resocialización
resolution, resolución
resolve, resolver
resource, recurso
    resource allocation, asignación de recursos
    resource base, base de recursos

    resource management, gestión de recursos
    resource scarcity, escasez de recursos
    resource use, uso de recursos
respect, respeto
    respect for law, respeto por la ley
    respect for others, respeto por los demás
    respect for the rights of others, respeto por los derechos de los demás, respeto por el derecho ajeno
responsibility, responsabilidad
restoration, restauración
restructuring, reestructuración
retaliation, represalia
retirement, jubilación, retiro
retreat[1], retirarse
retreat[2], retirada, repliegue
retribution, castigo
return on investment, rendimiento de la inversión
return to domesticity, regreso al ámbito doméstico
return to normalcy, regreso a la normalidad
reunification, reunificación
reusable, reutilizable
reuse, reutilizar
revenue, ingreso
    Revenue Act, Ley de ingresos

revenue sharing, distribución de los ingresos

revenue tariff, tarifa de ingresos

reverence, reverencia

reverse discrimination, discriminación inversa

revisionism, revisionismo

revival, renacimiento religioso

revolution, revolución

revolutionary government, gobierno revolucionario

Revolutionary War, Guerra Revolucionaria

reward, recompensa

Reynolds v. Sims, caso Reynolds contra Sims

rhetoric, retórica

rider, cláusula

ridge, cresta

ridge and valley region, región de cordillera y valle

ridge-and-valley pattern, modelo de la cordillera y el valle

right, derecho

right against self-incrimination, derecho contra la autoincriminación

right of appeal, derecho de apelación

right of extraterritoriality, derecho de extraterritorialidad

right to a fair trial, derecho a un juicio justo

right to acquire a property, derecho a adquirir una propiedad

right to choose one's work, derecho a elegir trabajo

right to copyright, derechos de autor

right to counsel, derecho a la asistencia de un abogado

right to criticize the government, derecho a criticar al gobierno

right to dispose of a property, derecho a disponer de una propiedad

right to due process of law, derecho a la jurisdicción

right to enter into a lawful contract, derecho a celebrar un contrato lícito

right to equal protection of the law, derecho a la protección igualitaria ante la ley

right to establish a business, derecho a establecer un negocio

right to hold office, derecho a ocupar un cargo público

right to hold public office, derecho a ocupar un cargo público

right to join a labor union, derecho a sindicalizarse

right to join a po-

litical party,
derecho a afiliarse a
un partido político
**right to join a profes-
sional association,**
derecho a afiliarse a
una asociación política
right to know,
derecho a la infor-
mación
right to life,
derecho a la vida
**right to life, liberty,
and the pursuit of
happiness,**
derecho a la vida, la
libertad y la búsqueda
de la felicidad
right to patent,
derecho a patentar
right to privacy,
derecho a la privaci-
dad
right to property,
derecho a la propiedad
**right to public educa-
tion,** derecho a la edu-
cación pública
right to vote,
derecho a votar
right to work,
derecho a trabajar
right to work state,
estado con legislación
relativa a libertad lab-
oral sin obligatoriedad
de afiliación sindical
right wing, derecha política
right-wing groups,
grupos derechistas
rights of the accused,
derechos de los acusa-
dos

**rights of English-
men,** derechos de los
ingleses
**rights of the dis-
abled,** derechos de las
personas con dis-
capacidad
rigid social class system,
sistema rígido de
clases sociales
Ring of Fire, Cinturón de
Fuego del Pacífico
Rio Grande River, río
Grande (río Bravo)
riot, disturbio, motín
risk, riesgo
risk management,
gestión de riesgos
risk reduction,
reducción de riesgos
rite of passage,
rito de iniciación
ritual, ritual
ritual sacrifice,
sacrificio ritual
river, río
river delta,
delta fluvial
river system,
sistema fluvial
river valley,
valle fluvial
**river valley civiliza-
tions,** civilizaciones de
los valles fluviales
Riyadh, Riad
road, sistema fluvial,
camino, carretera
road development,
desarrollo de carre-
teras
road map,
mapa de carreteras

road system,
red de carreteras
Roaring Twenties,
Felices años veinte,
Años Locos
Robert Owen's New Lanark System,
sistema de New Lanark de Robert Owen
rocketry, estudio y
experimentación con
cohetes
Rocky Mountains,
Montañas Rocallosas
Roe v. Wade, caso Roe
contra Wade
role, rol, papel
role convergence,
convergencia de roles
role of the government in the economy, papel del gobierno
en la economía
role playing,
juego de rol, psicodrama
Roman Catholic,
católico romano
**Roman Catholic
Church,**
Iglesia Católica
Romana
Roman civilization,
civilización romana
Roman Empire,
Imperio romano
**Roman occupation of
Britain,** ocupación
romana de Bretaña
Roman Republic,
República Romana
Roman system of roads,
red de carreteras ro-

manas
Romance languages,
lenguas romances
Romania, Rumania
Romanization of Europe,
romanización de Europa
Romanticism,
romanticismo
Rome, Roma
Roosevelt coalition,
coalición de Roosevelt
Roosevelt Corollary,
corolario Roosevelt
**Roosevelt's Treaty of
Portsmouth,** Tratado
de Portsmouth firmado
por Roosevelt
rose, rosa
Rosenburg trials,
juicios de los Rosenburg
roundhead,
cabezas redondas
royal absolutism,
absolutismo imperial
royal colony, colonia real
royal court,
corte real o noble
royal family, familia real
royal patronage,
mecenazgo real
royalty, realeza
rudder, timón
**Rudyard Kipling's "White
Man's Burden",**
La carga del hombre
blanco de Rudyard
Kipling
Rugged Individualism,
Individualismo tosco
Ruhr, río Ruhr
rule, regla, norma, gobierno

rule by the people, gobierno por el pueblo
rule of law, estado de derecho
rule of men, estado de hecho
ruling class, clase dirigente
runes, runas
running water, agua corriente
runoff, segunda vuelta
runoff primary, segundas elecciones primarias
rural, rural
rural area, área rural
Rural Electrification Administration, Administración de Electrificación Rural
rural exodus, éxodo rural
rural migration, migración rural
rural region, región rural
rural-to-urban migration, migración del campo a la ciudad, éxodo rural
Russia, Rusia
Russian absolutism, absolutismo ruso
Russian Chronicle, crónica rusa
Russian peasantry, campesinado ruso
Russian Revolution, Revolución rusa
Rust Belt, cinturón industrial
rutile sand, arena de rutilo

Rwanda, Ruanda
Rwanda salinization, salinización de Ruanda

sabbath, sabbat, sábado (judíos), domingo (cristianos)
Sacco and Vanzetti trial, juicio de Sacco y Vanzetti
Sachem, sachem
sacraments, sacramentos
sacred, sagrado
Safavid Empire, Imperio safávida
safety, seguridad
saga, saga
Sahara desert, desierto del Sahara
saint, santo
salary, salario
sale, venta
Salem witch trials, juicios de las brujas de Salem
sales tax, impuesto sobre las ventas
salt accumulation, acumulación de sal
SALT I Treaty, Tratado SALT I
Salt March, Marcha de la sal
salutary neglect, indiferencia saludable
Samarkand, Samarcanda
same, igual
Samori Ture, Samori Turé
sample, muestra

sampling, muestreo
  sampling error, error
  de muestreo, error
  muestral
  sampling frame,
  marco de muestreo
samurai, samurái
  Samurai class,
  clase de los samuráis
sanction, sanción
sanctioned country,
  país sancionado
sand dunes,
  dunas de arena
sand movement,
  movimiento de arena
Sandinistas, Sandinistas
sanitation,
  servicios sanitarios
Sargon, Sargón
Sassanid Empire,
  Imperio sasánida
satellite, satélite
  satellite city,
  ciudad satélite
  satellite image,
  imagen satelital o de
  satélite
  satellite imagery,
  imágenes de satélite
  satellite nation,
  país satélite
  satellite state,
  Estado satélite
  satellite system,
  sistema de satélites
  satellite town,
  ciudad satélite
  **satellite-based com-
  munications system,**
  sistema de comuni-
  cación por satélite
  satellite-produced

  images, imágenes producidas por satélites
Saudi Arabia,
  Arabia Saudita
savanna, sabana
save, ahorrar
savings, ahorros
  savings account,
  cuenta de ahorros
Saxon peoples,
  pueblos sajones
scabs, esquirol
scalawags, granujas
scale, escala
scandal, escándalo
Scandinavia, Escandinavia
scarce, escaso
  scarce resource,
  recurso escaso
scarcity, escasez
scenic area, región
  panorámica
Schenck v. United States,
  caso Schenck contra
  los Estados Unidos
Schlieffen Plan,
  Plan Schlieffen
scholar, erudito
school, escuela
  school attendance,
  asistencia escolar
  **school attendance
  zone,** zona de asistencia escolar
  school board,
  consejo escolar
  school district,
  distrito escolar
  school prayer,
  rezo en las escuelas
  school voucher,
  bono escolar
scientific, científico

scientific break-through, descubrimiento científico
scientific management, administración científica
scientific method, método científico
scientific racism, racismo científico
scientific revolution, revolución científica
Scipio Africanus, Publio Cornelio Escipión el Africano
scope, alcances
Scopes trial, juicio de Scopes
scorched-earth policy, táctica de tierra quemada
Scotch, escocés
Scotland, Escocia
Scots-Irish, escocés de Ulster
Scramble for Africa, disputa por África, reparto de África
scribe, escriba
scripture, escritura
sculptor, escultor
sculpture, escultura
Scythian society, pueblo escita
sea, mar
sea level, nivel del mar
sea wall, dique de mar, rompeolas
seaway, ruta marítimas
search and seizure, allanamiento de morada, registro e incau-tación
search warrant, orden de registro
season, estación, temporada
seasonal pattern of life, ciclo estacional de vida
seasonal unemployment, desempleo estacional
sec ede, separarse
secession, secesión
Second Continental Congress, Segundo Congreso Continental
second front, segundo frente
Second Great Awakening, segundo Gran Despertar
second industrial revolution, segunda revolución industrial
Second New Deal, segundo Nuevo Trato
secondary, secundario
secondary color, color secundario
secondary economic activity, actividad económica secundaria
secondary education, educación secundaria
secondary group, grupo secundario
secondary labor market, mercado de trabajo secundario
secret ballot, voto secreto
sect, secta
section, sección
sectional, seccional
Sectionalism, regionalismo
sectionalist, regionalista

sector model, modelo de
sector, modelo de Hoyt
secular, secular
   secular government,
   gobierno secular
   secular ideology,
   ideología secular
   secular ruler,
   gobernante secular
   secular state,
   estado secular
secularism, secularismo
secularization,
   secularización
securities, valores,
   valores bursátiles
   **Securities and Ex-
   change Commission
   (SEC),** Comisión de
   Valores y Cambios
security, seguridad, título
sedentary agriculture,
   agricultura sedentaria
sediment, sedimento
sedition, sedición
   Sedition Act,
   Ley de sedición
 seditious, sedicioso
   seditious libel,
   difamación sediciosa
seed drill, sembradora
segregation, segregación
Seine, Sena
seismic activity,
   actividad sísmica
seizure of Constantinople,
   toma de Constan-
   tinopla
select committee,
   comité especial
selective incorporation,
   incorporación selectiva
selective service,

servicio selectivo
self, el yo
   self government,
   autogobierno
   self-determination,
   autodeterminación
   self-discipline,
   autodisciplina
   self-employment,
   autoempleo
   self-evident truths,
   verdades manifiestas
   self-governance,
   autonomía
   self-government,
   autogobierno, au-
   tonomía
   self-interest,
   interés personal
   self-protection,
   autoprotección
   self-report studies,
   estudios autoinforma-
   dos
   self-rule, autonomía,
   autogobierno
   self-sufficiency,
   autosuficiencia
Seljuk Empire,
   Imperio selyúcida
sell, vender
seller, vendedor
semiarid area,
   zona semiárida
semilunar calendar,
   calendario semilunar
Seminole removal,
   remoción de los
   semínolas
Senate, Senado
senator, senador
senatorial courtesy,
   cortesía senatorial

Seneca, Séneca
    Seneca Falls Convention, Convención de Seneca Falls
seneschal, senescal
senior citizen home, asilo de ancianos
separate but equal, separados pero iguales
separation, separación
    separation of church and state, separación de la Iglesia y el Estado
    separation of powers, división de poderes
Separatist, grupo separatista
    separatist movement, movimiento separatista
Sepoy Mutiny, Motín de los Cipayos
sequence, secuencia
    sequence occupance, ocupación secuencial
serf, siervo
serfdom, servidumbre
service, servicio
    service charge, importe del servicio
    service economy, economía de servicios
    service group, grupo de servicio
    service industry, industria de servicios
settle, asentarse, establecerse
settlement, colonización, asentamiento, poblado
    Settlement House, casa de ayuda, hogar de asentamiento transitorio
    settlement impact, impacto del asentamiento
    settlement pattern, patrón de asentamiento
settler, colono, colonizador, poblador
Seven Years' War, Guerra de los Siete Años
sex, sexo
sexism, sexismo
sexual assault, violencia sexual
sexual division of labor, división sexual del trabajo
sexual harassment, acoso sexual
shadoof, cigoñal
shaman, chamán
Shang Dynasty, dinastía Shang
share the wealth, compartir la riqueza
sharecropper, aparcero
sharecropping, aparcería
shared consumption, consumo compartido
shared power, poder compartido
    shared powers political system, sistema político de poderes compartidos
shareholder, accionista
Shay's Rebellion, Rebelión de Shays
Shaysites, seguidores de Shays

Sheba, reino de Saba
sheikh, jeque
shelter, refugio, albergue
Sherman Anti-Trust Act,
    Ley Sherman Antitrust
shield law,
    ley de protección
shift, cambio, turno
    **shift in demand
    curve,** cambio en la
    curva de demanda
    shift in supply curve,
    cambio en la curva de
    oferta
shifting agriculture,
    agricultura itinerante
shifting civilization,
    civilización cambiante
Shi'ism, chiismo
Shi'ite, chiita
Shiloh, Silo
Shintoism, sintoísmo
ship, barco
    ship design,
    diseño naval
 shires, condados
shock therapy,
    terapia de choque
shogun, sogún, shogun
shopping center,
    centro comercial
shortage,
    escasez, carestía
**short-term and long-term
consequences,**
    consecuencias a corto
    y largo plazo
Shoshone-Bannock tribe,
    tribus shoshones y
    bannock
Shoshone-Paiute tribe,
    tribus shoshones y
    paiutes

**shot heard round the
    world,** disparo que
    se escuchó en todo el
    mundo
shrines, santuarios
shuttle, transbordador
Shuttle Diplomacy,
    diplomacia de lanzade-
    ra, diplomacia itiner-
    ante
Siberia, Siberia
Sicily, Sicilia
side effect, efecto secun-
    dario, efecto colateral
siege, sitio
    siege of Troy,
    sitio de Troya
Sierra Nevada,
    Sierra Nevada
signature, firma
significant event,
    acontecimiento
    significativo
Sikh, sij
silent barter,
    trueque silencioso
Silent Majority,
    mayoría silenciosa
silk, seda
    Silk Road,
    ruta de la seda
silt, cieno
silting, encenagamiento
silver production,
    producción de plata
similarities, semejanzas
Singapore, Singapur
single household,
    familia monoparental
single member plurality,
    escrutinio nominal
    mayoritario
single-industry city,

ciudad monoindustrial
**single-member plurality
electoral system,**
sistema electoral de
escrutinio nominal
mayoritario
Sinocentric, sinocéntrico
Sino-Japanese War,
Guerra Sino-Japonesa
Sioux, siux
sirocco, siroco
sisal, henequén, agave
sit-down strikes,
huelga de brazos
caídos
site, sitio
sit-in, sentada
situation, situación
**situational crime preven-
tion,** prevención del
delito situacional
Six Day War,
Guerra de los Seis
Días
skerry, arrecife, islote
sketch maps, croquis
skilled worker,
trabajador cualificado
skills, habilidades
skyscraper, rascacielos
slander,
difamación, calumnia
slash-and-burn farming,
agricultura de tala y
quema
slate, lista de candidatos
Slaughterhouse Cases,
casos de los matade-
ros
slave, esclavo
slave codes,
códigos de esclavitud
slave holder,

amo de esclavos
slave narrative,
narrativa esclavista
slave rebellion,
rebelión de esclavos
slave state,
estado esclavista
slave trade,
trata, comercio de es-
clavos
slave uprisings,
levantamientos de
esclavos
slavery, esclavitud
Slavic world,
mundo eslavo
slogan, eslogan, lema
slum, barrio bajo, barriada
slumlord, casero negligente
smallpox, viruela
smelting, fundición
smog, niebla tóxica, esmog
smokehouse,
cámara de ahumado
smuggling,
contrabando
social, social
social actions,
acciones sociales
social agency,
asistencia social
social anthropology,
antropología social
social attitudes,
actitudes sociales
social behavior,
conducta social
social bond,
vínculo social
social change,
cambio social
social class,
clase social

social commentary, comentario social

social construction of reality, construcción social de la realidad

social constructionism, construccionismo social

social contract, contrato social

social contract theory, teoría del contrato social

social control theory, teoría del control social

social convention, convención social

Social Darwinism, darwinismo social

social democracy, democracia social

social democratization, democratización social

social equity, equidad social

social ethics, ética social

social fact, hecho social

social factor, factor social

social formation, formación social

social gospel, evangelio social

social gospel movement, movimiento del evangelio social

social group, grupo o círculo social

social identity, identidad social

social impact, impacto social

social inequality, desigualdad social

social influence, influencia social

social institutions, instituciones sociales

social integration, integración social

social intervention programs, programas de intervención social

social issue, problema social

social justice, justicia social

social mobility, movilidad social

social movement, movimiento social

social network, red social

social norms, normas sociales

social order, orden social

social philosophy, filosofía social

social position, posición social

social psychology, psicología social

social reform, reforma social

social reformer, reformador social

social relationship, relación social

social rights, derechos sociales

sole proprietorship

Social Security, seguridad social

Social Security Act, Ley de seguridad social

Social Security Administration, Administración de Seguridad Social

Social Security number, número de seguridad social

Social Security tax, impuesto de seguridad social

social security withholding, retención de la seguridad social

social services, servicios sociales

social status, condición social, estatus social

social structure, estructura social

social welfare, bienestar social

socialism, socialismo

socialist, socialista

socialist democracy, democracia socialista

socialist market economy, economía de mercado socialista

Socialist Party, Partido Socialista

Socialist Realism, realismo socialista

socialist worker, trabajador socialista

socialization, socialización

society, sociedad, asociación

socioeconomic, socioeconómico

socioeconomic group, grupo socioeconómico

socioeconomic status, condición socioeconómica

sociologist, sociólogo

sociology, sociología

Socrates, Sócrates

Socratic method, método socrático

sod, tepe, tierra, suelo

sodium nitrate, nitrato de sodio

soft money, moneda débil

soil, suelo

soil acidification, acidificación de suelo

soil conservation, protección del suelo

soil creep, corrimiento de tierras

soil erosion, erosión del suelo

soil fertility, fertilidad del suelo

soil region, región de suelos

soil salinization, salinización del suelo

solar energy, energía solar

solar power, energía solar

solar radiation, radiación solar

solar system, sistema solar

solar year, año solar

soldier, soldado

sole proprietorship, empresa individual

solicitor general,
  procurador general
solidarity, solidaridad
Solomon, Salomón
Solon, Solón
solution, solución
Song Dynasty,
  dinastía Song
Songhai Empire,
  Imperio Songay
Sons of Liberty,
  Hijos de la Libertad
soothsayers, adivinos
sophisticated, sofisticado
sorghum, sorgo
soul, alma
sound money,
  moneda sólida, mone-
  da estable
soup kitchen, comedor
  de beneficencia
source, origen, fuente
source of a river,
  nacimiento de un río
south, sur
  South Africa,
  Sudáfrica
  **South African
  (Anglo-Boer) War,**
  Guerra Anglo-Bóer
  en Sudáfrica
  South America,
  Sudamérica
  South Asia,
  Asia Meridional
  South Carolina,
  Carolina del Sur
  South India,
  sur de la India
  South Korea,
  Corea del Sur
  South Pacific,
  Pacífico Sur

  South Pole,
  Polo Sur
Southeast Asia,
  Sureste asiático
southern, (del) Sur
  Southern Africa,
  África del Sur
  **Southern Christian
  Leadership Confer-
  ence,** Conferencia de
  Líderes Cristianos
  del Sur
  Southern Europe,
  Europa del Sur
  Southern Iberia, sur
  de la Península Ibérica
  Southern Ocean,
  océano Antártico
  Southern states,
  estados sureños
Southwest, sudoeste
Southwest Asia,
  Sudoeste asiático
sovereign, soberano(a)
  sovereign nation,
  nación soberana
  sovereign powers,
  poderes soberanos
  sovereign state,
  estado soberano
sovereignty, soberanía
Soviet, soviético(a)
  Soviet bloc,
  bloque soviético
  Soviet domination,
  dominación soviética
  Soviet espionage,
  espionaje soviético
  **Soviet invasion of
  Afghanistan,** invasión
  soviética de Afganistán
  **Soviet invasion of
  Czechoslovakia,**

invasión soviética de
Checoslovaquia
**Soviet non-aggres-
sion pact,** pacto de no
agresión soviético
Soviet Union (USSR),
Unión Soviética
(URSS)
space exploration,
exploración espacial
space race,
carrera espacial
space shuttle,
transbordador espacial
Spain, España
Spanish Armada,
Armada Invencible
Spanish Civil War,
Guerra Civil española
Spanish colony,
colonia española
Spanish Muslim society,
comunidad musulma-
na española
Spanish settlement,
asentamiento español
Spanish-American War,
Guerra Hispano-Esta-
dounidense
spatial, espacial
spatial arrangement,
arreglo espacial
spatial distribution,
distribución espacial
spatial organization,
organización espacial
spatial patterns,
patrones espaciales
spatial perception,
percepción espacial
spatial scale,
escala espacial
speakeasies,

bar clandestino
Speaker of the House,
presidente del Con-
greso
special economic zone,
zona económica espe-
cial
special interest group,
grupo de interés espe-
cial
special interests,
intereses especiales
Special Olympics,
Olimpiadas Especiales
special purpose map,
mapa especial
special relationship,
relación especial
special rights,
derechos especiales
specialization,
especialización
**specialization of
labor,** especialización
del trabajo
specialize, especializarse
**specialized economic in-
stitution,** institución
económica especia-
lizada
specie, monedas
speciesism, especismo
spectator sport,
deporte de espectáculo
speculation, especulación
speech, discurso
speedy trial,
juicio sumario
spender, despilfarrador
spending, gastos
sphere, esfera
sphere of influence,
esfera de influencia

spice trade, comercio de
   las especias
spinning jenny, hiladora
   con usos múltiples
spinning wheel, rueca
spirit of capitalism,
   espíritu del capita-
   lismo
spirit of individualism,
   espíritu del individu-
   alismo
spirits, licores, bebidas
   alcohólicas
spiritual beliefs,
   creencias espirituales
split-ticket rating,
   voto dividido
spoils, prebendas
   spoils system,
      sistema de prebendas
spontaneous privatiza-
   tion, privatización
   espontánea
sports stadium,
   estadio deportivo
spread of disease,
   propagación de una
   enfermedad
Square Deal, Trato Justo
squash,
   agolpamiento de gente
squatter, ocupante ilegal,
   paracaidista
squire, escudero, señor
St. Augustine,
   San Agustín
stable government,
   gobierno estable
stage of life, etapa de vida
stagecoach, diligencia
stagflation, estanflación
   stagnation of wages,
      estancamiento de los

salarios
stalemate, punto muerto,
   estancamiento
Stalinism, estalinismo
Stalinist totalitarianism,
   totalitarismo estalini-
   sta
Stalin's purge,
   purgas de Stalin
stalwart, incondicional
Stamp Act, Ley del Timbre
Stamp Act Congress,
   Congreso sobre la Ley
   de Estampillas
standard, norma, estándar
   standard currency,
      divisa estándar
   standard measures,
      medidas estándar
   standard of behavior,
      modelo de compor-
      tamiento
   standard of living,
      nivel de vida
   Standard Oil Compa-
      ny, compañía Stan-
      dard Oil
   standard weights,
      pesos estándar
standing committee,
   comité permanente
staple crop,
   alimento básico
staple crop production,
   producción de alimen-
   tos básicos
Star-Spangled Banner,
   Bandera Llena de
   Estrellas
Star Wars,
   Defensa "Star Wars"
stars and stripes,
   franjas y estrellas

starvation,
inanición, hambre
Starving Time,
época del hambre
state, estado
state action,
acción estatal
state bill of rights,
carta de derechos del
estado
state boundaries,
fronteras estatales
state bureaucracy,
burocracia estatal
state capitalism,
capitalismo de estado
state capitol,
capitolio estatal
state constitution,
constitución estatal
state corporatism,
corporativismo estatal
state court,
tribunal estatal
state debt,
deuda estatal
state election,
elección estatal
state government,
gobierno estatal
state legislature,
legislatura estatal
state of nature,
estado de la
naturaleza
state of seige,
estado de sitio
state revenue,
ingresos estatales
state sales tax,
impuestos estatales
sobre la venta
state senator,

senador estatal
state sovereignty,
soberanía estatal
state suicide theory,
teoría del suicidio del
estado
state symbols,
símbolos del estado
state tax,
impuesto estatal
states powers,
poderes de los estados
states' rights,
derechos de los
estados
statehood,
condición de estado
statement, declaración
station, estación,
statistical, estadístico
statistical abstract,
resumen estadístico,
compendio estadístico
statistically significant,
estadísticamente
significativo
Statue of Justice,
Estatua de la Justicia
Statue of Liberty,
Estatua de la Libertad
status,
estatus, condición,
posición
status quo, statu quo
statute, ley, estatuto
statute law,
derecho escrito
statutory law,
derecho escrito
statutory requirement,
requisito por estatuto
steam engine,
máquina de vapor

steam locomotive,
locomotora de vapor
steamboat, barco de vapor
steamship, barco de vapor
steel, acero
steel construction,
construcción de acero
steel-tipped plow,
reja de arado de acero
steppe, estepa
stereotype, estereotipo
stewardship theory,
teoría de custodia
stigma, estigma
stimuli, estímulo
stocks, acciones, valores
stock breeding,
cría de ganado
stock dividends,
dividendo en acciones
stock exchange,
bolsa de valores
stock market,
mercado bursátil,
mercado de valores
stock market crash,
colapso de la bolsa
stockholder, accionista
stockyard, corral
Stono Rebellion,
Rebelión de Stono
storage, almacenamiento
stories from the past,
historias del pasado
storing money,
ahorrar dinero
storm, tormenta
story, historia
strait, estrecho
Strait of Malacca,
estrecho de Malaca
strategic, estratégico
strategy, estrategia

stratification,
estratificación
straw man, falacia del
hombre de paja
stream, corriente
street gang,
pandilla callejera
streetcar suburbs,
suburbios de tranvía
**strict construction of the
Constitution,** inter-
pretación estricta de la
Constitución
strict constructionism,
construccionismo
estricto
strike, huelga
strip mining, explotación a
cielo abierto
**structural adjustment
program (SAP),**
programa de ajuste
estructural
structural explanation,
explicación estructural
structural functionalism,
funcionalismo estruc-
tural
structural unemployment,
desempleo estructural
structuralist approach,
enfoque estructur-
alista
**structures and func-
tions of the Supreme
Court,** estructuras y
funciones de la Corte
Suprema
**Student Nonviolent Coor-
dinating Committee
(SNCC),** Comité No
Violento Coordinador
de Estudiantes

student placement laws,
leyes sobre colocación
de estudiantes
student rights,
derechos estudiantiles
style of homes,
estilos de los hogares
sub-Arctic environment,
clima subártico
subcontinent,
subcontinente
subculture, subcultura
subculture transmission, transmisión
subcultural
subject, súbditos
subjective, subjetivo
subjectivism, subjetivismo
subjectivity, subjetividad
submarine, submarino
sub-Saharan Africa,
África Subsahariana
subservient,
servil, supeditado
subsidy, subsidio
subsistence agriculture,
agricultura de subsistencia
subsistence economy,
economía de subsistencia
subsistence farm,
granja de subsistencia
subsistence farming,
agricultura de subsistencia
subsistence method,
método de subsistencia
substantive due process,
debido proceso sustantivo
substitute goods,

bienes sustitutivos,
bienes sustitutos
substitute product,
producto sustituto
suburb, suburbio
suburban, suburbano
suburban area,
área suburbana
suburbanization,
suburbanización
subversion, subversión
subversive, subversivo
subway, metro
Sudan, Sudán
Suecia, Suecia
Suez Canal, Canal de Suez
sufficient condition,
condición suficiente
suffrage, sufragio
suffrage movement,
movimiento sufragista
Sufism, sufismo
sugar cane, caña de azúcar
Sui dynasty, dinastía Sui
Switzerland, Suiza
Suleiman the Magnificent, Suleimán el
Magnífico
summarize, resumir
summer solstice,
solsticio de verano
Sunbelt, Cinturón del Sol
Sunni, sunita
Sunnism, sunismo
super majority,
mayoría cualificada
superdelegates,
superdelegados
superiority,
superioridad
superpower rivalry,
rivalidad de las superpotencias

superpowers,
superpotencias
superstition, superstición
supplier, proveedor,
abastecedor
supply, oferta
   supply and demand,
   oferta y demanda
   supply curve,
   curva de la oferta
   supply route,
   ruta de suministro
   **supply-side econom-
   ics,** economía de
   oferta
support, apoyo
supporting details,
   detalles de apoyo
supremacy clause,
   Cláusula de supre-
   macía
Supreme Being,
   Ser Supremo
Supreme Court,
   Corte Suprema
surcharge, sobrecarga
surplus, excedente,
   superávit
   surplus food,
   alimentos excedentes
Surrealism, surrealismo
Surrealist, surrealista
surrender, rendirse
survey, encuesta, sondeo
surveyor, agrimensor,
   topógrafo
survivor syndrome,
   síndrome del sobrevi-
   viente
   survivor's guilt,
   culpa del sobreviviente
sustainable, sustentable,
   sostenible

**sustainable develop-
ment,** desarrollo sus-
tentable o sostenible
**sustainable environ-
ment,** ambiente sus-
tentable
Swahili, suajili, swahili,
   kiswahili
swamp, pantano, ciénaga
   swamp lands,
   terrenos pantanosos
sweat lodge, cabaña de
   sudación, temazcal
sweatshop, maquila,
   fábrica opresora
Swedish, sueco
Sykes-Picot Agreement,
   Tratado Sykes-Picot
symbiotic, simbiótico
symbol, símbolo
symbolic speech,
   discurso simbólico
symbolism, simbolismo
synagogue, sinagoga
synergy, sinergia
synthesize, sintetizar
Syria, Siria
system, sistema
   system of alliances,
   sistema de alianzas
   **system of checks
   and balances,** sistema
   de controles y con-
   trapesos
   **system of weights
   and measures,**
   sistema de pesos y
   medidas
systemic, sistémico
   systemic approach,
   enfoque sistémico
systems of roads,
   redes de carreteras

T

table of contents, tabla de contenido
taboo, tabú
tacit social contract, contrato social tácito
Tacoma Strait, estrecho de Tacoma
tactic, táctica
taiga, taiga
tail water, nivel de aguas abajo
Taiping Rebellion, rebelión Taiping
Taiwan, Taiwán
take turns, turnarse
tall tale, cuento increíble
Tammany Hall, Tammany Hall
Tang China, China de Tang
Tang Empire, Imperio Tang
tannin, tanino
Taoism, taoísmo
target suitability, idoneidad del objetivo
tariff, arancel, tarifa
tax, impuesto
tax deduction, deducción de impuestos
tax division, división de impuestos
tax exemption, exención de impuestos
tax reduction, reducción de impuestos

tax revenue, ingresos fiscales
tax structure, estructura tributaria
taxation, gravamen, tributación
taxation without representation, impuestos sin representación
Tea Act, Ley del Té
tea company, compañía de té
teacher, maestro, profesor
team member, miembro del equipo
Teapot Dome Scandal, Escádalo del Teapot Dome
technocrats, tecnócratas
technological, tecnológico
technological hazard, riesgo tecnológico
technological innovations, innovaciones tecnológicas
technological unemployment, desempleo tecnológico
technology, tecnología
tectonic plate, placa tectónica
telecommunication, telecomunicación
telecommuting, teletrabajo, trabajo a distancia
teledemocracy, teledemocracia
telegraph, telégrafo
telephone area code, prefijo telefónico
telescope, telescopio

temperance, templanza, moderación
    temperance movement, movimiento de la templanza
temperature, temperatura
    temperature fluctuation, fluctuación de temperatura
temple, templo
    temple of Madurai, templo de Madurai
    temporary dominance, dominación temporal
Ten Commandments, Diez mandamientos
tenant, inquilino, arrendatario
    tenant farmer, granjero arrendatario
tenement, vecindad
    tenement housing, vivienda multifamiliar
Tennessee Valley Authority Act, Autoridad del Valle del Tennessee
Tenochtitlan, Tenochtitlán
tension, tensión
Tenure of Office Act, Ley de Permanencia en el Cargo
Teotihuacan civilization, civilización teotihuacana
tepee, tipi
term limitation, limitación del mandato
terrace, terraza
    terrace farming, agricultura de terrazas
terraced rice fields, arrozales en terrazas

terrain, terreno
territorial acquisition, adquisición territorial
territorial expansion, expansión territorial
territory, territorio
terrorism, terrorismo
tertiary, terciario
    tertiary economic activity, actividad económica terciaria
Tet Offensive, ofensiva de Tet
Texas, Texas
    Texas Revolution, Revolución de Texas
    Texas War for Independence, Guerra de Independencia de Texas
textile, textil
    textile industry, industria textil
textual analysis, análisis textual
textual evidence, evidencia textual
Thailand, Tailandia
Thanksgiving, Acción de gracias
theater of conflict, escenario del conflicto
thematic graph, gráfico temático
thematic map, mapa temático
theme, tema
then, entonces
theocracy, teocracia
theocratic, teocrático
    theocratic government, gobierno teocrático

theology, teología
theory, teoría
    theory of comparative advantage, teoría de la ventaja comparada
    theory of relativity, teoría de la relatividad
thermal, termal
thesis, tesis
    thesis statement, argumento de la tesis
third party, tercera persona, tercero
Third World, tercer mundo
    Third World countries, países del tercer mundo, países tercermundistas
third-person point of view, punto de vista de la tercera persona
thirteen colonies, trece colonias
thirteen virtues, trece virtudes
Thirty Years' War, Guerra de los Treinta Años
three branches of government, tres poderes del gobierno
three piece iron, arado de hierro en tres piezas
Three-Fifths Compromise, Compromiso de los tres quintos
threshold, umbral
    threshold population, umbral de población
Thutmose III, Tutmosis III
Tiahuanaco society, cultura Tiahuanaco

Tiananmen Square protest, protesta de la Plaza de Tiananmen
Tiberius Gracchus, Tiberio Graco
tidal process, proceso de mareas
tight-rail system, sistema de trenes ligeros
Tigris-Euphrates Valley, valle del Tigris y el Éufrates
timber, madera
    timber cutting, tala de árboles
    timber extraction, extracción de madera
timberline, límite del arbolado
Timbuktu, Tombuctú
time, hora, horario, tiempo
    time line, línea cronológica
    time zone, zona horaria, husos horarios
    time period, período de tiempo
    time, place, manner restrictions, restricciones de tiempo, lugar y manera
timeframe, límite del tiempo
Timur the Lame (Tamerlane), Tamerlán
Tinker v. Des Moines, caso Tinker contra el Distrito escolar independiente de Des Moines
tithe, diezmo

title, título
    Title VII, Título IV
tobacco, tabaco
today, hoy
token integration, falsa
    política de integración
    de minorías
Tokugawa shogunate,
    shogunato Tokugawa
Tokyo, Tokio
tolerance, tolerancia
tolerant, tolerante
tolerate, tolerar
Toleration Party, Partido
    de la Tolerancia
toll road, peaje, cuota,
    carretera de peaje,
    carretera de cuota
Toltecs, toltecas
tomorrow, mañana
tools, herramientas
topography,
    topografía
Torah, Torá
tornado, tornado
tort, agravio
total benefit,
    beneficio total
total cost, costo total
    total institution,
    institución total
    total market value,
    valor total de mercado
    total war,
    guerra total
totalitarian, totalitario
    totalitarian regime,
    régimen totalitario
    totalitarian state,
    estado totalitario
    totalitarian system,
    sistema totalitario
    totalitarianism,

    totalitarismo
totem pole, tótem
tourist center,
    centro turístico
towpath, camino de sirga
town, ciudad, pueblo, po-
    blado
    town meeting,
    reunión municipal
Townshend Acts,
    Leyes de Townshend
Townshend Plan,
    Plan de Townshend
township,
    municipio, municipali-
    dad, ayuntamiento
    township and village
    enterprises (TVEs),
    empresas municipales
    y comunales
toxic dumping,
    vertedero tóxico
toxic waste handling,
    manejo de desechos
    tóxicos
trade, comercio
    trade advantage,
    ventaja comercial
    trade agreement,
    acuerdo comercial
    trade balance,
    balanza comercial
    trade barrier,
    barrera arancelaria
    trade deficit,
    déficit comercial
    Trade Expansion Act,
    Ley de Expansión
    Comercial
    trade fair,
    feria comercial,
    feria de muestras
    trade imbalance,

déficit comercial

trade market, mercado comercial

trade pact, pacto comercial

trade route, ruta comercial

trade surplus, superávit comercial, excedente comercial

trade union, sindicato, gremio

trade wind, vientos alisios

trade-off, contrapartida

trading post, establecimiento comercial en una colonia

trading triangle, triángulo de comercio

tradition, tradición

traditional American family, familia estadounidense tradicional

traditional cultural identity, identidad cultural tradicional

traditional economic system, sistema económico tradicional

traditional economy, economía tradicional

traditional village, aldea tradicional

traditionalism, tradicionalismo

traditionalist, tradicionalista

traffic lights, semáforos

tragedy, tragedia

trail, sendero

Trail of Tears, Sendero de lágrimas

training, entrenamiento, instrucción, capacitación

traitor, traidor

transaction cost, costo de transacción

trans-Atlantic slave trade, comercio trasatlántico de esclavos

transcendentalism, trascendentalismo

transcendentalists, trascendentalistas

transcontinental, transcontinental

transcontinental railroad, ferrocarril transcontinental

transfer payment, pago de transferencia

transformation, transformación

transmission of beliefs, transmisión de creencias

transmission of culture, transmisión de la cultura

trans-Mississippi region, Trans-Misisipi

transmit, transmitir

transnational corporation, corporación transnacional

transport, transportar

transport system, sistema de transporte

transportation, transportación, transporte

transportation arteries, arterias de transporte

transportation corridor, corredor de transporte

transportation cost, costo de transporte

transportation hub, nodo de transportes

transportation network, red de transporte

transportation revolution, revolución de los transportes

transportation route, ruta de transporte

transportation system, sistema de transporte

transregional alliance, alianza interregional

Trans-Siberian railroad, Transiberiano

travel, viajar

travel effort, esfuerzo del viaje

travois, rastra

trawl, red de arrastre

treason, traición

treatise, tratado

treaty, tratado

Treaty of Guadalupe Hidalgo, Tratado de Guadalupe Hidalgo

Treaty of Nanking, Tratado de Nanking

Treaty of Paris, Tratado de París

Treaty of Shimonoseki, Tratado de Shimonoseki

Treaty of Versailles, Tratado de Versalles

treaty ratification, ratificación de un tratado

trench warfare, guerra de trincheras

trenches, trincheras

trend, tendencia

triad, tríada

trial, juicio

trial by jury, juicio por jurado

trial of Galileo, juicio de Galileo

Triangle trade, comercio triangular

triangular trade route, ruta del comercio triangular

tribal council, consejo tribal

tribal government, gobierno tribal

tribal identity, identidad tribal

tribal lands, tierras tribales

tribal membership, pertenencia tribal

tribal system, sistema tribal

tribalism, tribalismo

tribe, tribu

tribunal, tribunal

tribune, tribuna

tributary, tributario, afluente

tribute, tributo, homenaje

trickle down economics, economía de goteo

Triple Alliance, Triple Alianza

Triple Entente, Triple Entente

triremes, trirremes
triumvirate, triunvirato
Trojan war,
    Guerra de Troya
Tropic of Cancer,
    trópico de Cáncer
Tropic of Capricorn,
    trópico de Capricornio
tropical rain forest,
    selva tropical
tropical soil degradation,
    degradación de los
    suelos tropicales
tropics, trópicos
troubadours, trovadores
truce, tregua
truck farms, huertas
truck-farming commu-
    nity, comunidad de
    huertas
Truman Doctrine,
    Doctrina Truman
trust¹, confianza
trust², monopolio
trust³, trust
    trust responsibil-
    ity, responsabilidad
    del Estado hacia los
    nativos americanos
    trust territory,
    territorio en
    fideicomiso
trustbuster,
    cazador de monopolios
trustee, fiduciario
trusteeship,
    servicios fiduciarios
truth, verdad
tsetse fly, mosca tsé-tsé
tsunami, tsunami
tuberculosis, tuberculosis
tucupi, tucupí
tundra, tundra

tungsten, tungsteno
Turkestan, Turquestán o
    Turkestán
Turkey, Turquía
Turkic Empire,
    Imperio turco
Turkic migration,
    migración turca
turning point,
    punto crítico,
    momento decisivo
turning point in human
    history, momento
    decisivo en la historia
    de la humanidad
turnpike, autopista de
    peaje, autopista de
    cuota
turquoise, turquesa
turret, torrecilla
Tweed Ring,
    organización
    Tweed Ring
Twelve Tables,
    Doce Tablas
twentieth century,
    siglo veinte
twin cities,
    ciudades gemelas
Two Treatises on Govern-
    ment, Dos tratados
    sobre el gobierno civil
two-party system,
    sistema bipartidista,
    bipartidismo
Type 1 error,
    error de tipo I
Type 2 error,
    error de tipo II
typhoon, tifón
typology, tipología
tyranny, tiranía

U

U.S. Communist Party,
Partido Comunista de
los Estados Unidos

U.S. Constitution,
Constitución de
EE.UU.

**U.S. domestic energy
policy,** política ener-
gética interna de los
Estados Unidos

U.S. domestic policy,
política interna de
EE.UU.

U.S. foreign policy,
política exterior de
EE.UU.

**U.S. Free Enterprise
System,** sistema de
libre empresa esta-
dounidense

U.S. isolationist policy,
política aislacionista
de los Estados Unidos

**U.S. Smoot-Hawley Tar-
iff,** Ley de aranceles
Smoot-Hawley

U.S. Supreme Court,
Corte Suprema de los
Estados Unidos

U.S. territory, territorio de
los Estados Unidos

U.S. vs. Nixon, caso
Estados Unidos contra
Nixon

U.S.S.R ., U.R.S.S.

Ukraine, Ucrania

Umayyad Dynasty,
dinastía Omeya

UN resolution,
resolución de la ONU

**unanimous consent de-
cree,** decreto de con-
sentimiento unánime

unavoidable conflict,
conflicto inevitable

Uncle Sam, Tío Sam

Uncle Tom's Cabin,
La Cabaña del Tío Tom

unconditional surrender,
rendición incondicio-
nal

unconstitutional,
anticonstitucional

underclass,
clase marginada

underconsumption,
subconsumo

underground economy,
economía subterránea

Underground Railroad,
ferrocarril subterráneo

underpopulation, despoblación, infrapoblación

underrepresented group,
grupo infrarrepresen-
tado

understanding,
comprensión

Underwood Tariff,
Tarifa Underwood

undocumented worker,
trabajador indocumen-
tado

unemployment, desempleo
unemployment rate,
tasa de desempleo

unenumerated rights,
derechos fundamen-
tales

unequal, desigual
unequal treaty,

tratado desigual
unfinished state,
Estado inacabado o
inconcluso
unfunded liability, responsabilidad o deuda sin
fundamentos
unfunded mandates,
mandatos sin financi-
amiento
unguided discretion,
criterio no guiado
unicameral, unicameral
**UNICEF (United Nations
Children's Fund),**
UNICEF (Fondo de las
Naciones Unidas para
la Infancia)
unification, unificación
**unification of Ger-
many,** unificación de
Alemania
unification of Italy,
unificación de Italia
unified India, India unida
unify, unificar
unintended results,
resultados no
previstos
union, unión
Union Army,
Ejército de la Unión
union movement,
movimiento sindical
union republic,
república de la unión
unionize, sindicar
unique, único
unit of analysis,
unidad de análisis
unitary, unitario
unitary government,
Estado unitario

unitary state,
estado unitario
unitary system,
sistema unitario
unite, unificar
United Arab Emirates,
Emiratos Árabes Uni-
dos
United Nations,
Naciones Unidas
**United Nations
Charter,** Carta de las
Naciones Unidas
**United Nations Chil-
dren's Fund (UNI-
CEF),** Fondo de las
Naciones Unidas para
la Infancia (UNICEF)
United States,
Estados Unidos
United States citizenship,
ciudadanía esta-
dounidense
**United States Constitu-
tion,** Constitución de
los Estados Unidos
**United States domestic
policy,** política interna
de los Estados Unidos
**United States foreign
policy,** política
exterior de los
Estados Unidos
**United States interven-
tion,** intervención de
los Estados Unidos
United States of America,
Estados Unidos de
América
**United States Steel
Corporation,**
empresa U.S. Steel
unity, unidad

**Universal Declaration
of Human Rights,**
Declaración Universal
de Derechos Humanos
universal language,
lenguaje universal
**universal white male
suffrage,** sufragio
universal para los
hombres blancos
universality,
universalidad
university,
universidad
unlimited government,
gobierno ilimitado
unlimited needs,
necesidades ilimitadas
unlimited wants,
deseos ilimitados
**unrestricted submarine
warfare,** guerra sub-
marina ilimitada
unskilled worker, trabajador no cualificado
Untouchables,
Intocables
unwritten constitution,
constitución no escrita
up, arriba
Upanishad, Upanisad
uprising, motín
upstream, río arriba
Upton Sinclair,
Upton Sinclair
upward mobility,
movilidad ascendente
urban, urbano
urban area,
zona urbana
urban bourgeoisie,
burguesía urbana
urban center,

centro urbano
urban community,
comunidad urbana
urban commuting,
tráfico urbano
urban decay,
degradación de zonas
urbanas
urban design,
diseño urbano
urban development,
desarrollo urbano
urban ecology,
ecología urbana
urban growth,
crecimiento urbano
urban heat island,
isla de calor
Urban League,
Liga Urbana
urban morphology,
morfología urbana
urban planning,
planeación urbana
urban riot,
disturbio urbano
urban sprawl,
explosión urbana
urbanism, urbanismo
urbanization, urbanización
urbanize, urbanizar
USA Patriot Act,
Ley Patriótica de los
Estados Unidos
use, uso
use of explosives,
uso de explosivos
usurpation, usurpación
utilitarianism, utilitarismo
utility, utilidad
utilization, utilización
utopia, utopía
utopian community,

comunidad utópica
utopian reform,
reforma utópica

vaccine, vacuna
validity, validez
valley, valle
value, valor
vanguard party,
partido de vanguardia
variable, variable
variable expenses,
gastos variables
vassal, vasallo
Vatican, Vaticano
vedas, vedas
Vedic gods, dioses védicos
vegetation, vegetación
vegetation region,
región de vegetación
Venice, Venecia
vernacular, vernáculo
Versailles, Versalles
Versailles Treaty,
Tratado de Versalles
vertical consolidation,
integración vertical
vertical integration,
integración vertical
vertical merger,
consolidacion vertical,
fusión vertical
veteran, veteranos
Veterans Day,
Día de los Veteranos
veterans' memorial,
monumento a los veteranos

veto[1], vetar
veto[2], veto
veto override,
contrarrestar, anular
el veto
veto power,
poder de veto
vice president,
vicepresidente
viceroy, virrey
victimless crime,
crimen sin víctimas
Victorian values,
valores victorianos
victorious, victorioso,
vencedor, victor,
vencedor
victory, victoria
Vietnam War,
Guerra de Vietnam
Vietnamese, vietnamita
**Vietnamese boat
people,** refugiados del
mar vietnamitas
Vietnamization,
vietnamización
viewpoint, punto de vista
vigilantism,
grupos paramilitares
Viking longboat,
nave vikinga
Vikings, vikingos
village, pueblo, aldea
Vincennes, Vincennes
violence, violencia
Virgin Islands,
Islas Vírgenes
**Virginia Declaration of
Rights,** Declaración de
Derechos de Virginia
Virginia House of Burgesses, Cámara de los
Burgueses de Virginia

Virginia Plan,
Plan de Virginia
virtual company,
empresa virtual
virtual representation,
representación virtual
visa, visa
vizier, visir
Vladimir of Kiev,
Vladimiro de Kiev
vocation, vocación
volcanism, vulcanismo
volcano, volcán
Volstead Act,
Ley de Volstead
volume, volumen
voluntary exchange,
intercambio voluntario
voluntary migration,
migración voluntaria
volunteer, voluntario
volunteer force,
fuerza de voluntarios
volunteerism, voluntariado
vote[1], votar
vote[2], voto
**vote of no confi-
dence,** voto de censu-
ra, moción de censura
voter registration,
padrón electoral, regis-
tro de electores
voting, votación
voting rights,
derechos de voto
Voting Rights Act,
Ley del derecho al voto
voting ward, distrito
electoral
voyage, viaje, travesía
voyages of discovery,
viajes de descubrim-
iento

voyageur, viajero

wadi, uadi
wage, sueldo, salario
wage controls,
control de los salarios
wage rate,
escala de salarios
wages, remuneración
Wagner Act, Ley Wagner
wagon train,
tren de vagones
Wales, Gales
Wall Street, Wall Street
wants, deseos
war, guerra
war bond,
bono de guerra
war crime,
crimen de guerra
war debts,
deudas de guerra
War Hawks,
halcones de guerra
War Labor Board,
Junta Laboral de
Guerra
War of 1812,
Guerra de 1812
war of attrition,
guerra de desgaste
War on Poverty,
Guerra contra la
pobreza
War Powers Act,
Ley de Poderes
de Guerra
War Production

Board, Junta de Pro-
ducción de Guerra
war strategy,
estrategia de guerra
ward, distrito
warlord, caudillo
warrant, orden judicial
warrant chiefs,
intermediarios
warranty, garantía
Warren Court,
Corte de Warren
warrior culture,
cultura guerrera
Warsaw Pact,
Pacto de Varsovia
wartime diplomacy,
diplomacia en tiempos
de guerra
wartime inflation,
inflación de guerra
wartime manpower losses,
pérdida de mano de
obra en tiempos de
guerra
Washington, Washington
**Washington's Fare-
well Address,**
Discurso de despedida
de Washington
water, agua
water availability,
disponibilidad de agua
water basin,
cuenca de agua
water crossing,
paso elevado
water cycle,
ciclo del agua
water masses,
masas de agua
water pollution,
contaminación del

agua
water rights,
derechos de aguas
water spring,
manantial
water supply,
abastecimiento de
agua
water vapor,
vapor de agua
waterfall, cascada
Watergate, Watergate
Watergate Scandal,
escándalo de Water-
gate
watershed,
línea divisoria
de aguas
waterway, canal navegable
We the People ...,
Nosotros el pueblo ...
weaknesses, debilidades,
flaquezas
wealth, riqueza
Wealth of Nations,
Riqueza de las
naciones
weapon, arma
weaponry, armamento
weather, tiempo
weather phenomena,
fenómenos meteo-
rológicos
weathering, desgaste
weaving, tejido
week, semana
Weimar Republic,
República de Weimar
welfare, bienestar,
asistencia social
welfare capitalism,
capitalismo de bienes-
tar

welfare reform,
reforma de bienestar
welfare state,
estado de bienestar
west, oeste
    West Africa,
    África Occidental
    West Asia,
    Asia Occidental
    West Coast,
    Costa oeste
    West Germany,
    Alemania Occidental
    West Indian colony,
    colonia india occidental
western, occidental
    Western and Eastern European societies,
    sociedades europeas occidental y oriental
    Western art and literature, literatura y arte occidental
    Western culture,
    cultura occidental
    Western Europe,
    Europa Occidental
    western expansion,
    expansión de Occidente
    Western hegemony,
    hegemonía de Occidente
    Western Hemisphere,
    Hemisferio Occidental
    Western political thought, pensamiento político occidental
    Western Roman Empire, Imperio Romano de Occidente
    Western values,
    valores occidentales
westernization,
occidentalización
Westminster model,
sistema de Westminster
westward expansion,
expansión hacia el oeste
westward migration,
migración hacia el oeste
westward movement,
Movimiento hacia el Oeste
wetlands,
tierras de pantanos
wheat, trigo
wheel, rueda
    Wheel of Life,
    rueda de la vida
Whig Party, Partido Whig
Whiskey Rebellion,
Rebelión del whiskey
white backlash,
reacción blanca
White Citizens Councils,
Consejo de Ciudadanos Blancos
white-collar, cuello blanco
    white-collar crime,
    delito de cuello blanco
    white-collar sector,
    sector de cuello blanco
    white-collar worker,
    oficinista
White House, Casa Blanca
White Man's Burden,
carga del hombre blanco, la responsabilidad del hombre blanco
White Paper Reports

on Palestine, Libro blanco sobre Palestina
white primaries, elecciones primaras para los blancos
White Russian, ruso blanco
White Sea, Mar Blanco
white supremacy, supre-macía blanca
wigwam, wigwam
wildcat bank, banca riesgosa
wildcat strike, huelga salvaje
wilderness area, zona selvática, zona virgen
wildlife, fauna silvestre
    wildlife refuge, refugio de vida silvestre
William the Conqueror, Guillermo el Conquistador
Wilmot Proviso, condición Wilmot
Wilson's Fourteen Points, Catorce puntos de Wilson
wind storm, tormenta de viento
windward, barlovento
winner-take-all system, sistema electoral donde el ganador se lleva todo
winter solstice, solsticio de invierno
witch hunt, cacería de brujas
woman suffrage, sufragio femenino
women in the clergy, mujeres en el clero

Women's Liberation Movement, Movimiento de liberación femenina
women's movement, movimiento feminista
women's perceptions, percepciones de las mujeres
women's rights, derechos de las mujeres
woodland, bosque
Woodland Natives, nativos americanos de los bosques
wool, lana
work1, trabajar
work2, trabajo
    work animal, animal de trabajo
    work experience, experiencia laboral
    work ethic, ética laboral
    work rule, norma de trabajo, norma laboral
worker, trabajador
    worker safety, seguridad de los trabajadores
workers' compensation, indemnización a los trabajadores
workforce, mano de obra
working conditions, condiciones de trabajo
working-class, clase trabajadora
workplace, lugar de trabajo
Works Progress Administration, Administración para el Progreso del Empleo
world, mundo

world atmospheric circulation, circulación atmosférica mundial

World Bank, Banco Mundial

World Bank Group, Grupo del Banco Mundial

World Council of Churches, Consejo Mundial de Iglesias

World Court, Corte Internacional

world economy, economía mundial

world empire, imperio mundial

world events, acontecimientos mundiales

world geopolitics, geopolítica mundial

World Health Organization (WHO), Organización Mundial de la Salud (OMS)

world history, historia mundial

world influenza pandemic, pandemia mundial de influenza

world leader, líder mundial

World Patterns of Economic Activity, patrones mundiales de la actividad económica

world population, población mundial

world population growth, crecimiento de la población mundial

world power, potencia mundial

world processes, procesos mundiales

world regions, regiones del mundo

world religions, religiones del mundo

world resources, recursos mundiales

world temperature increase, incremento de la temperatura mundial

worldview, punto de vista mundial

world war, guerra mundial

World War I, Primera Guerra Mundial

World War II, Segunda Guerra Mundial

Wounded Knee, Wounded Knee

WPA project, proyecto de la Administración para el Progreso del Empleo

writ, orden, mandato

writ of certiorari, auto de avocación

writ of habeas corpus, mandato de hábeas corpus

writ of mandamus, auto de ejecución

writing system, sistema de escritura

writings, obras escritas

writs of assistance, orden de asistencia

written code, código escrito

written language, lenguaje escrito

written record, registro escrito

xenophobia, xenofobia

Xiongnu society, pueblo xiongnu

Yalta Conference, Conferencia de Yalta

yard size, superficie

year, año

yellow dog contract, contrato con promesa de no afiliarse a ningún sindicato

yellow journalism, periodismo amarillista

Yellow Peril, Peligro Amarillo

yellow press, prensa amarillista

yeoman farmer, pequeño propietario rural

yesterday, ayer

yield[1], producir, rendir

yield[2], rendimiento

Young Italy, Joven Italia

Young Turk movement, movimiento de los Jóvenes Turcos

Yuan Dynasty, dinastía Yuan

Yucatan Peninsula, Península de Yucatán

yurt, yurta

Zagwe Dynasty, dinastía Zagüe

zaibatsu, zaibatsu

zakah, azaque

zealot, fanático

zen, zen

the Zenger case, Caso Zenger

Zheng He maritime expeditions, expediciones marítimas de Zheng He

Zhou Dynasty, dinastía Zhou

ziggurat, zigurat

Zionism, sionismo

Zionist Movement, movimiento sionista

zone of subduction, zona de subducción

zoned use of land, zonificación de uso del suelo

zoning, zonificación

zoning regulation, regulación de zonas

zoology, zoología

Zoroastrianism, zoroastrismo

Zulu empire, Imperio zulú

Zuni, zuñi

Velázquez Press

For over 150 years, Velázquez Spanish and English Dictionary has been recognized throughout the world as the preeminent authority in Spanish and English dictionaries. Velázquez Press is committed to developing new bilingual dictionaries for children, students, and adults based on the tradition of Velázquez Spanish and English Dictionary.

We invite you to go to www.AskVelazquez.com to access online services such as our free translator, irregular verb conjugator, and member forum. We also invite you to add on to the Dictionary. If you know of a K-12 science term that is not included, please let us know at info@academiclearningcompany.com for future editions.

Por más de 150 años, Velázquez Spanish and English Dictionary ha sido reconocido como la máxima autoridad en diccionarios de español e inglés en todo mundo. Velázquez Press está comprometido a eleborar diccionarios bilingües para niños, estudiantes y adultos en la tradición del Velázquez Spanish and English Dictionary.

Lo invitamos a visitar www.AskVelazquez.com para acceder a los servicios en línea como nuestro traductor automático, información sobre ortografia de verbos irregulares en español y el foro. Si sabe de algún término de ciencia de los grados escolares kinder a 12 que no está incluido, por favor, mande un correo electrónico a info@academiclearningcompany.com para ediciones futuras.

Other Velázquez Dictionaries

Velázquez Spanish and English Dictionary

- More than 250,000 entries with accessible pronunciation guides for BOTH Spanish and English
- Revised for the 21st century
- Thumb-indexed to help user find words faster
- Covers regional variations of US, Latin American and European Spanish
- For teachers and students, notes on grammar integrated into the main body
- Entries include examples of usage for better understanding of connotations and usage

BOOK INFORMATION
- ISBN 13: 978-1-5949-5000-1 • Pub Date: August 2007
- Format: Hardcover, 2,008 pages • Size: 7.5 in. x 9.5 in.
- Price: $29.95 USD

Velázquez Large Print Spanish and English Dictionary

- Carries the Seal of Approval of NAVH
- Over 38,000 easy-to-read bold entries with guide phrases
- Great for mature and visually impaired readers and students
- Includes pronunciation keys in BOTH the Spanish and English sections
- Easy-to-use format and up-to-date
- User's Guide included
- Durable hardcover binding for long-lasting use

BOOK INFORMATION
- ISBN 13: 978-1-5949-5002-5 • Pub Date: January 2006
- Format: Hardcover, 1,006 pages • Size: 8.25 in. x 9.5 in.
- Price: $22.95 USD

Velázquez World Wide Spanish and English Dictionary

- Word-to-word translation for state standardized testing
- Contains no offensive words. Adopted by many states for classroom use
- Over 85,000 colored entries for easy-to-find reference
- BOTH Spanish and English pronunciation keys and explanation of sounds

BOOK INFORMATION
- ISBN 13: 978-1-5949-5001-8 • Pub Date: March 2007
- Format: Paperback, 691 pages • Size: 5.25 in. x 6.8 in.
- Price: $12.95 USD

Velázquez Spanish and English Dictionary, Pocket Edition

- Over 75,000 entries and 110,000 translations in a convenient pocket size
- Includes BOTH Spanish and English pronunciation keys, and explanation of sounds
- Spanish and English grammar synopses to better understand words in context
- Great for students, office, or day-to-day use

BOOK INFORMATION
- ISBN 13: 978-1-5949-5003-2 • Pub Date: May 2006
- Format: Paperback, 640 pages • Size: 4.25 in. x 7 in.
- Price: $5.98 USD

Velázquez Spanish and English Glossary for Mathematic classroom

- Over 10,000 mathematical translations with more than 4,000 new entries updated in 2010
- Word to word translations format to meet state standardized tests
- Translations of multiple-word terms
- Coverage of mathematic terms in arithmetic, logic, algebra, geometry, trigonometry, statistics, and calculus
- Includes common vocabulary for the mathematics classroom

BOOK INFORMATION
- ISBN 13: 978-1-59495-017-9 • Pub. Date: June 2010
- Format: Paperback • Size: 5 in x 8 in
- Price: $12.95 USD

Velázquez Spanish and English Glossary for Science classroom

- Over 8,000 scientific translations
- Word to word translations format to meet standards of state standardized tests
- Translations of multiple-word terms
- Extensive coverage of science terms in the areas of biology, chemistry, physics, earth science and life science
- Covers words that apply to the mathematic and scientific method
- Includes common vocabulary for the science classroom
- Great tool for Spanish speaking parents to help with students' science homework

BOOK INFORMATION
- ISBN 13: 978-1-59495-010-0 • Pub Date: April 2009
- Format: Paperback, 160 pages • Size: 5 in. x 8 in.

  - Price: $12.95 USD